BUDGETING, PLANNING, AND FORECASTING IN UNCERTAIN TIMES

Michael Coveney and Gary Cokins

CGMA
Chartered Global Management Accountant®

Powered by
AICPA | CIMA

13948-359

Notice to Readers

Budgeting, Planning, and Forecasting in Uncertain Times does not represent an official position of the American Institute of Certified Public Accountants, and it is distributed with the understanding that the author and the publisher are not rendering legal, accounting, or other professional services in this publication. If legal advice or other expert assistance is required, the services of a competent professional should be sought.

1 2 3 4 5 6 7 8 9 0 PIP 1 9 8 7 6 5 4

ISBN: 978-1-94023-531-8

Publisher: Linda Prentice Cohen
Acquisitions Editor: Robert Fox
Project Manager: Charlotte Ingles

ACKNOWLEDGEMENTS

As you would expect from a book of this type, we have had considerable support from a range of people. In particular we would like to thank Dean Sorensen, a US based thought leader in planning who speaks and writes frequently about the need for greater integration between the strategic, financial and operational aspects of how organizations plan and manage their business. Also Anthony Parker, a clear thinking financial professional living in London with considerable experience in building planning models for some of the UK's largest companies.

We would also like to thank Robert Fox of the AICPA and his editors for their encouragement and support in the writing of this book.

CONTENTS

INTRODUCTION 1

SECTION 1: BACKGROUND TO THE PLANNING FRAMEWORK 5

1 PLANNING FUNDAMENTALS 7

What is Planning? 7

Components of Planning 8

Planning in Today's Business Environment 10

The Increasing Speed of Business and Globalisation 10

The Increasing Complexity of Business 11

The Decreasing Planning Time Horizon 11

Planning Challenges 12

Dissatisfaction With the Planning Process 12

Issues With the Planning Culture 13

Need for a Holistic Approach 13

Need for Better Planning Technologies 13

Planning Principles 13

Principle 1: Planning Connects Inputs and Outputs and is Therefore Directly Related to Organisational Activities 14

Principle 2: Planning is About Maintaining a Shared Understanding of the Economics of a Business 14

Principle 3: Planning is About Shifting Focus From the Past and Onto the Future 15

Principle 4: Planning is About Aligning Budgets With Strategy to Achieve Corporate Objectives 16

Principle 5: Planning is a Continuous Process 16

Principle 6: Planning is a Learning Process 17

Objectives of the Planning Framework 17

2 PLANNING METHODS AND METHODOLOGIES 21

Planning: Who, What, When, and How 21

Planning Within a Sole Trader 21

Planning as a Small Manufacturer 22

Planning as a Listed Company 23

Planning as an International Group 23

The Rise of Management Frameworks and Methodologies 24

Popular Management Methodologies 25

Budgetary Control 25

Quality Management Movement 26

Lean Management 27

Balanced Scorecard 28

Beyond Budgeting 29

Planning and Success 30

Planning Process Maturity 31

Planning Objectives 31

Planning and Forecasting Maturity Levels 33

Basic Planning 33

Financial Integration 34

Partial Integration 35

Matrix Planning 35

Dynamic Planning 36

3 PLANNING TECHNOLOGIES 39

Supporting the Decision-Making Process 39

Planning Technologies: The Spread Sheet 40

Two or Three Dimensional 41

Cell Meaning 41

Limited Business View 42

Single User 42

Lack of Workflow Capabilities 43

Planning Technologies: Multi-Dimensional Databases 43

Multi-Dimensional 44

Business Hierarchies	45
Name-Based Rules	45
Multi-User, Role-Based Security	46
Unlimited Size	46
Financial Intelligence	46
Spread Sheet Access	47
Multi-Dimensional System Issues	47
Comprehension	47
Complexity	48
Data Uniformity	48
Effort and Price	49
Modelling Tools	49
SECTION 2: BUSINESS PLANNING FRAMEWORK	53
4 BUSINESS PLANNING FRAMEWORK	55
Logical Overview of the Framework	55
Framework Components	56
Operating Activity Model (OAM)	56
Cash Funding Model (CFM)	59
Detailed History Models (DHM)	59
Target Setting Model (TSM)	61
Detailed Forecasting Model (DFM)	61
Optimise Resources Model (ORM)	61
Performance Measures Model (PMM)	62
Strategy Improvement Model (SIM)	62
Management Processes	64
Knowledge	65
Reporting From the Planning Framework	66
Case Study Overview	66
About the Case Study Organisation	66

	Company Structure	67
	Company Strategy	68
	Versions and Other Information	68
5	**OPERATIONAL ACTIVITY MODEL**	**69**
	Overview	69
	Model Structure	69
	Measurement Types and Relationships	70
	Step 1: Define High-Level Objectives	71
	Step 2: Define Core Business Processes and Assumptions	72
	Step 3: Identify Core Business Process Activities	73
	Step 4: Identify Support Activity Measures	79
	Step 5: Define Profit and Loss and Other Financial Measures	80
	Putting the Model Together	85
	Measures and Attributes	85
	Model Dimensions	86
	Model Rules	86
	Reporting From the OAM	87
	Departmental Outcomes, Activity, and Resources	87
	Outcome Versus Activity	89
	Outcome Versus Assumptions and Resources	90
6	**CASH FUNDING MODEL**	**91**
	Model Purpose	91
	Defining the Model	92
	Model Content	92
	Additional Data Requirements Within the OAM	93
	Identifying Cash Payment Profiles Within the OAM	93
	Defining Payment Profiles Within the CFM	94
	Other Cash Measures and Rules	95

Reporting From the CFM   97

   Displaying Cash Requirements by Department   97

   Evaluating Sources of Cash   99

   Scenario Analysis   100

7 DETAILED HISTORY AND PERFORMANCE MEASURES MODELS   101

Reporting Past and Future Performance   101

   Relevance   101

   Context   102

   Data Issues   103

Reporting Performance From the Planning Framework   104

Identifying DHMs   105

Case Study—DHMs   106

   Sales Analysis   106

   HR   107

   General Expenses   108

Defining the PMM   109

   PMM Content   109

   PMM Business Dimensions   110

   Case Study Measures for XYZ, Inc.   110

   Reporting From the PMM   112

8 PREDICT AND OPTIMISE PLANNING MODELS   113

Predicting the Future   113

Target Setting Model (TSM)   115

   Driver-Based Modelling   115

   TSM Content for XYZ, Inc.   116

   Using the TSM   120

Detailed Forecast Model (DFM)   121

   Overview   121

	Developing the DFM	121
	Linking the DFM to the OAM	123
Optimise Resources Model (ORM)		123
	Overview	123
	Case Study Example	124
9	STRATEGY IMPROVEMENT MODEL	127
	Responding to Change	127
	Model Focus	128
	Link to the OAM and CFM	129
	Defining SIM Content	130
	Linking SIM Content to Management Methodologies	131
	Planning Capabilities	132
	Communicate Goals	132
	Propose and Validate Projects	133
	Select and Approve Projects	133
	Monitor and Forecast Projects	133
	Assess Alternatives	134
10	THE PLANNING AND MONITORING PROCESS	135
	Defining Processes	135
	Components of a Process	135
	Performance Management Processes and Tasks	137
	Strategic Planning	138
	Purpose	138
	Tasks: Inputs, Outputs, and Sequence	138
	People and Planning Models	139
	Tactical Planning	140
	Purpose	140
	Tasks: Inputs, Outputs, and Sequence	141
	People and Planning Models	141

Financial Planning 142

    Purpose 142

    Tasks: Inputs, Outputs, and Sequence 142

Forecasting 143

    Purpose 143

    Tasks: Inputs, Outputs, and Sequence 144

Management Reporting 145

    Purpose 145

    Tasks: Inputs, Outputs, and Sequence 145

Moving Toward Continuous Planning 145

SECTION 3: IMPLEMENTING A PLANNING FRAMEWORK 147

11 LATEST DEVELOPMENTS IN PLANNING AND ANALYTICS
TECHNOLOGIES 149

Corporate Performance Management (CPM) Applications 149

The Rise of Business Analytics 150

    The Next Competitive Edge 150

    BI Versus Analytics Versus Decisions 151

    Business Analytics, Big Data, and Decision Management 151

    Predictive Business Analytics: The Next New Wave 152

    Game-Changer Wave: Automated Decision-Based Management 153

Application Integration 153

Cloud-Based Applications 154

In-Memory Chip Technology 155

12 IMPLEMENTING THE PLANNING FRAMEWORK 157

Planning and the Role of the Chief Executive 157

    Entrenched Beliefs Concerning Performance 157

    Organisational Culture 158

    The Unwritten Rules of Budgeting 158

Rewarding Bad Behaviour   159

Failure to Execute   159

Implementing Change   159

Agree on the Role of Planning   160

Model Existing Processes   160

Establish Improvement Themes   161

Plan- and Resource-Specific Change Programmes   161

Monitor Implementation   161

Use Technology to Support Change   162

Continually Develop the Planning Models Within the Framework   162

APPENDIX I: CGMA BUDGET AND PLANNING SURVEY RESULTS   165

APPENDIX II: REQUIREMENTS OF A PLANNING SYSTEM   213

INTRODUCTION

Planning is something we all do, whether that is to go on holiday, prepare for retirement, or to simply buy a car. Without planning it is all too easy to get lost or waste resources that in hindsight would have been better placed elsewhere. The same is true for business and public sector governments. Planning is a critical management task because its outcome determines decisions and actions that not only affect future success, but it can also threaten an organisation's very survival.

It does not matter which type of management philosophy you follow or the business guru you seek to emulate—all will emphasise that planning plays a key role in gaining success. The author and successful entrepreneur Jim Rohn once said, Either you run the day or the day runs you. He also said that if you don't plan, chances are you'll fall into someone else's plan. And guess what they have planned for you? Not much.

However, the problem is that the world in which we operate today is very different from what it was ten years ago. More significant is that the business environment, especially its increased volatility, is vastly different from when the major business planning methodologies and practices now in use today were developed.

Practices such as 'Budgetary Control' that seek to devolve decision making to departments was established back in the 1920s and written up in the book of the same name by James McKinsey, who later became the founder of the McKinsey consulting firm. Organisations are taught that a key exercise is to set annual budgets to allocate resources and then track performance against them. This was fine in the 1920s (and throughout most of the 20th century) as the physical barrier of location, allied with the available communication technologies, made it difficult for organisational performance to be influenced by competitors and other events in a time frame of under a year. However, as the *New York Times* journalist Thomas Friedman wrote in his book, *The World is Flat*, the digital age is removing these boundaries.

Today's business landscape has reduced the ability to forecast with any degree of accuracy to months. Most of this uncertainty over the future has its roots in advances in information technology and, in particular, the development of the Internet. In the past ten years the Internet has removed geographic boundaries, has provided consumers with a 24/7 buying experience that allows them to easily interact with a large range of suppliers, and has allowed both real and virtual companies to get established and effectively communicate with potential customers across the world in a fraction of times past.

The Internet has also made it possible for intermediaries to tailor products for individual needs rather than the mass marketing of generic products found in the last century, all of which has put additional pressure on manufacturers and providers.

As if this wasn't enough, social networks and communities such as Facebook, Twitter, Tumblr, and LinkedIn are able to exert significant influence over customer purchasing habits based on a range of non-product factors, such as social responsibility and fast changing fashion.

This increasing speed and complexity of business has caused a rapid decrease in the planning time horizon. As a consequence, the traditional planning processes of strategic planning, annual budgeting, quarterly forecasting, and monthly reporting have become unsuitable for most organisations' needs. In light of this, senior management struggles in determining what planning techniques they should adopt as a replacement.

In recent years, organisations have recognised that managing performance is more than just controlling costs; it is more about aligning resources to the corporate strategy. This has given rise to a number of strategic management methodologies such as the balanced scorecard. However, interestingly this modern management technique, first introduced in an article for the *Harvard Business Review* in 1992 by authors David Norton and Robert Kaplan, is often seen as a reporting tool and rarely thought of as a planning or budgeting system.

Planning is about managing uncertainty, and today's more complex business environment has only increased the need for better planning. To be effective planning systems should allow organisations to link strategy with resources and to simulate various business scenarios before embarking on a course of action. It is something that needs to occur on a continuous basis to ensure that scarce resources are always invested for maximum effect.

Planning systems should also recognise that although different organisational departments are assigned responsibilities to deliver specific outcomes, they ultimately must all collectively serve a common purpose. Getting an organisation to create plans that truly support mission-related corporate objectives is something that is easy to imagine and yet very difficult to do. This is because most planning systems have their focus on departments and not necessarily on how they affect the organisation as a whole.

In the British Museum in London there are a series of exhibits dedicated to the development of clocks and watches. Anyone who has taken the back of an old windup watch can't help but be amazed at the intricate nature of the mechanism. To work at all, the precision required is beyond most anyone's comprehension no matter what experience they have in working metal. But to function with any degree of accuracy, the skills necessary are extraordinary. Yet, back in the 1500–1600s those skills were found in clockmakers of that time. Or were they?

In the museum is a plaque entitled, 'Who made watches?' The inscription on it reads as follows:

> Watches were not made by one craftsman working alone. Even in the 1500s, spring makers, gilders and engravers worked alongside the watchmaker. By the 1700s, the making of watch mechanisms was becoming a specialist industry. Unfinished mechanisms were supplied to watch finishers. Dials and cases were then added ready for retail. The 1819 publication *Ree's Cyclopedia* lists 34 separate trades involved in making a standard English watch.

The key to successful watch making is to carefully co-ordinate the skill and expertise of different people who work on different components, but who are collectively working to a common goal.

The same is true for business planning. Although there may be a few exceptional business leaders who can single-handedly direct a company, for most organisations it requires the co-ordination of managers with different skills who work on different activities in order to achieve organisational objectives.

Coping with the speed and complexity found in today's business environment requires a reliance on technology. Therefore, planning systems must enable the different functions to work together in a continuous approach to assess, direct, monitor, and optimise corporate performance. But where do you start? How can you integrate the various parts of an organisation when they are involved in such a wide range of activities?

Well, that is the subject of this book—how to develop enterprise-wide planning processes, backed up by a network of planning models and enabling technology solutions, that will help organisations embrace change as an every day event.

This book is not another management methodology book, and it does not advise organisations to turn their backs on the latest in management practices. The purpose of this book is to help managers to take a long, hard look at the way they plan, the types of planning models they use, and to adopt an approach that makes sense in today's turbulent business environment.

It does not matter whether you are in charge of a multi-billion dollar commercial concern, a senior executive of a government or not-for-profit organisation, the owner of small business, or just someone working in a department—the ideas outlined here will challenge the way your organisation plans and will help you to better manage performance in your area of responsibility.

To help achieve this aim we have divided the book into the following sections.

Section 1 provides a background to the planning framework and contains chapters on the following:

1. *Planning fundamentals.* This looks at the things an organisation can actually manage and the planning challenges they face.

2. *Planning methods and methodologies.* This chapter provides an overview of the rise of management methodologies that shape planning and the levels of planning maturity adopted by organisations.

3. *The role of technology.* The final chapter in this section examines the state of planning technologies, in particular the contrast between spread sheet-based approaches and those that use multi-dimensional databases.

Section 2 describes the planning framework in detail with chapters on the following:

4. *Business planning framework.* This chapter provides an overview of the framework and how it enables the development of joined-up plans.

5. *Operational activity model.* This model is central to the planning framework and provides a way to connect resources with workload and the outcomes required to achieve long-term objectives.

6. *Cash funding model.* Cash is vital to the operation of any organisation. This model enables management to view cash requirements and to evaluate its source.

7. *Detailed history models.* These models provide backup to actual results, where those responsible for performance can analyse what happened in more detail.

8. *Predict and optimise models.* The models described in this chapter allow the setting of realistic targets and the prediction of future performance. From this operational activity can be optimised to make the best use of scarce resources.

9. *Strategy improvement model.* Strategy is primarily concerned with improving the outcomes of business processes. This model looks at how improvements can be captured, approved, and monitored.

10. *The planning and monitoring processes.* This chapter looks at how to create a continuous management process for planning and managing performance that utilises the models described in this section.

Section 3 describes the practical implementation of the planning framework:

11. *Latest developments in planning technologies.* This takes a look at the role of technology and the latest developments in software that will shape planning systems of the future.

12. *Implementing the framework*. This last chapter takes a pragmatic approach at how organisations can change the way they plan and monitor performance.

The final section contains the appendices that provide additional information that may be of interest:

13. *Results from the planning survey*. The American Institute of Certified Public Accountants in the US and the Chartered Institute of Management Accountants in the UK conducted a survey on the state of planning specifically for this book. In Appendix I you can find more details of the responses we received.

14. *Requirements of a technology solution*. Appendix II contains an overview of the capabilities that the reader may want to use when choosing a technology system for planning.

As you work your way through the book, hopefully you will see that it is full of practical advice based on the authors' day-to-day experiences in helping organisations to better plan and manage performance. However, the book does not provide an all-encompassing solution to planning, and it is not possible to include all the materials we have gathered during our research. Therefore, we have created a complimentary website where you can download templates, surveys, and our latest materials as we continue to press forward in making planning a common-sense activity. You can find the website at www.BusinessPlanningFramework.com.

We wish you well in all your planning efforts,

Michael Coveney
Gary Cokins

February, 2014

Section 1

BACKGROUND TO THE PLANNING FRAMEWORK

PLANNING FUNDAMENTALS

Planning in today's volatile business environment is very different from what it was ten years ago. Creating effective plans requires organisations to understand the things they can control, acknowledge the things they cannot control, and create a planning process that makes sense.

WHAT IS PLANNING?

Bloodhound SSC (www.bloodhoundssc.com) is a project that makes most boys' (as well as men and some girls) hearts race. Their mission is 'to confront and overcome the impossible using science, technology, engineering, and mathematics'. This statement may not be that interesting, but the way they plan to achieve their goal is: to create a car that will travel at over 1,000 miles per hour.

1,000 mph cars are not easy to build. At that speed the drag on the car is over 20 tons, the force on the wheel rims is greater than 50,000g. Everything is conspiring to destroy the car or make it take off like a rocket, both of which are undesirable. To achieve that vision the team is using a Rolls Royce EJ200 jet engine coupled with a Falcon rocket engine, which together produces over 135,000 HP, which is 25,000 HP more than the Queen Elizabeth 2 ship liner.

So how does the small team based in England go about this seemingly impossible task? Well it is down to managing three factors, each of which are controllable. First are the business processes that bring different members of the team together to plan and create the car. Second are the outcomes generated by those business processes, such as the car with incredible amounts of thrust. Third are the resources that the business processes will consume to deliver those outcomes. Those resources include money, talent, and a lot of fuel.

These three factors—processes, outcomes and resources—have to work together if they are to have any chance of achieving the mission. However, although these factors are under the control of management, the team operates in an environment that is both uncontrollable and sometimes unknowable. For example, the surface on which the car will run has to be perfect, but that is subject to the uncontrollable vagaries of the weather. Similarly, permission has to be granted by the federal government of the country where the car will run, and they must ensure local population support or they could take action to prevent the record attempt. Although contracts and agreements can be made to control these areas, the reality is that they are outside of the team's control. As such they are more like assumptions that carry a certain level of risk.

The role of planning for the Bloodhound project is to consider all facets of the mission to ensure its success. This involves a whole range of activities from building the car to raising funds. It also includes assessing those things that are not predictable or knowable and ensuring that the risk they pose are either eliminated or minimised.

And so it is with business planning.

Every organisation has a purpose for its existence. For commercial companies this is typically to make a financial return for its owners; for not-for-profit organisations this is to benefit the chosen subject that may be people, objects, or ideals; and for governments this is to provide a safe environment where citizens can prosper.

The way this purpose is achieved is through a series of interconnected business processes that typically consume resources to produce directly related outcomes. For example, a commercial manufacturer will produce goods it can sell for a profit by taking raw materials and adding value by shaping, combining, and transforming them into things customers are willing to buy. For a service company the business processes could include training people in skills and techniques that enable them to pass on knowledge for a profit to clients.

Business processes are key to an organisation's success. They are generally under the control of management, such as the workload that is applied within each activity, how resources are allocated, and the quality of any outputs. But these business processes are also conducted within a business environment where some elements that impact workload, resources and outcomes are both uncontrollable and unknowable by management. Uncontrollable elements include market trends, inflation, and the supply of finance, but other elements are unknowable until it is too late (such as competitor actions and natural disasters). Each of these areas has an impact on the purpose of the organisation. It is the role of management to adjust what can be controlled, to suit the uncontrollable and unknowable aspects of the business environment, in order to deliver business goals.

Planning allows managers to assess the future for a range of scenarios that reflect an ever-changing business environment. Planning is also a continuous process by which past trends are analysed, assumptions are made about the future, and predictions are made based on a range of inputs and changes to business processes. This is not an annual event as the business environment in which we operate is continually changing. Therefore, plans have to continually adapt if an organisation is to survive and thrive.

Planning is not a science and is unlikely to produce extremely accurate forecasts. Its value is in providing managers with a way to communicate what drives success, to evaluate the risks an organisation faces, and to guide the best way to allocate resources to achieve desired outcomes, given an anticipated business environment and the limitations in which the organisation operates.

Figure 1-1: Six Ways of Viewing Business Processes, Resources, and Outcomes

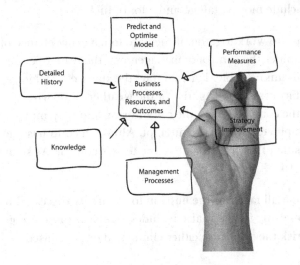

COMPONENTS OF PLANNING

Given that planning is about managing business processes within an anticipated yet uncontrollable business environment, there are six ways of looking at them, as depicted in figure 1-1.

Detailed history. This view looks at past processes and related outcomes. It is focused on what happened and can be analysed in minute detail as to the resources that were applied, the outcomes that were generated, the structure of the organisation, and a whole host of other information. For a commercial organisation this could include data on customers, products and channels. For a not-for-profit this could be by project or funding source.

The value of this view is in assessing whether the inputs and the outputs generated were worth it, given the business environment that existed.

Predict and optimise. This looks at the mathematical relationships between the organisation's business processes from which future performance can be predicted. Its focus is on the future and can be used to set targets, allocate resources, assess different management structures, and evaluate the different sources of funds.

Performance measures. This view of business processes looks at the economics of individual activities, processes, and the enterprise as a whole. It recognises that organisations do not operate in a vacuum and are in continual competition for resources and customers. Performance measures consist of key performance indicators (KPIs) that relate inputs with outputs. For example, seeing how assets are being utilised compared to the industry 'norm', or the quality and accessibility of services compared to peer organisations. This provides the basis for an explicit dialogue about resources required to achieve objectives, and about any assumptions being made concerning service level and quality targets the organisation seeks to achieve.

Strategy improvement. In looking at how performance can be improved or how to meet the challenge of a change in the business environment, management may consider a range of strategic initiatives. These may include changes to existing business processes, the creation of new ones, or the terminating of others. The strategy improvement view looks at how selected initiatives could impact existing business processes, along with the cost implications, and how initiatives can be combined for optimum effect.

Management processes. These are the established management activities through which business processes are reviewed, resources allocated, and adjustments are made. They typically encompass the six traditional processes of strategic, tactical, and financial planning; forecasting; management reporting; and risk management. They are often seen as discreet processes that are driven by a date on the calendar. However, increasingly organisations are seeking to perform these as a single continuous and fully integrated activity.

Knowledge. This last view looks at the business processes through the eyes of experience and intuition. It recognises that measures do not tell the whole story and that stored up within management's 'know-how', as well as from external sources, there is much anecdotal information through which performance can be justified.

It is important to note that these six views cannot be treated in isolation. By this we mean that no one view can ever provide all of the relevant information in the context of the business processes. For example, knowing that an organisation was 10 per cent over budget on using resources does not tell you whether that was actually a bad performance. To gauge this you would need to look at past and future trends of the activity to which the resource was assigned, what output was generated, and how other organisations were performing the same task.

None of these views can be left out or management could easily jump to a wrong conclusion. The aim of planning is to take decisions on the things that can be controlled, by reviewing all relevant information, as this gives any organisation the best chance of achieving its purpose.

In chapter 4, 'Business Planning Framework', we will show at a summary level how these different views can be translated into a series of planning models, while chapters 5 to 10 will drill down into each area with examples.

PLANNING IN TODAY'S BUSINESS ENVIRONMENT

In case you have not noticed, we live in an unpredictable world where the future is increasingly uncertain. When using the word 'unpredictable' or 'volatile', what we are saying is that the mechanism used for predicting the future has inaccuracies. Things happened that were not foreseen or that impacted the plan differently from what was expected. As mentioned earlier, some of these things are external and beyond an organisation's control. For example, a competitor changing their prices, a company introducing a disruptive technology, the impact of natural events such as the weather, a change in government policy, a significant change in the local economy, or a combination of any of these.

Despite these factors, senior executives are still expected to navigate their organisations through all of these challenges to ensure that limited resources are allocated to the right products and services for maximum return. For them planning is about providing a reasoned explanation as to when, where, and how the organisation expects to achieve its long-term strategic goals. However, today's business environment is problematic and has a number of significant challenges to overcome.

The Increasing Speed of Business and Globalisation

Perhaps the biggest challenge is the speed of business. In the 1980s it was difficult for an organisation to enter a market, introduce a new product or service, or to make a major change to its business model. The problem was primarily one of communication.

To reach potential customers, there must be a reliable method to contact them, to explain how the product or service can help them, and for them to be able to respond and ask questions. Before the era of the Internet these methods (for example, direct mail, television, or newspaper advertising) were slow, and difficult to target ideal customers. It also required a local presence to handle any responses, which is expensive in time, effort, and the resources required to recruit and train sales staff.

As mentioned in the introduction to this book, the Internet and the advent of e-commerce has totally changed this. To start with, geographic boundaries are removed, and the technology allows both real and virtual companies to be established and effectively communicate to customers in a fraction of the time of previous years. Not only can the medium use a combination of text, sound, pictures, and video, but it can also be interactive and made to automatically respond to specific customer enquiries.

Today, the reach of the Internet is far more advanced than previous marketing channels and is more adaptable, targeted, and substantially cheaper. Organisations no longer need to have a local presence, product promotion is global 24/7, and social media sites mean that others can promote products at no involvement or cost to the supplier.

This capability has transformed the speed at which new entrants can come to market, from years to months and even weeks. To combat this threat, existing suppliers have responded by changing their business model. Again, Internet-based technologies have allowed them to do this at unprecedented speed. Organisations like Dell can introduce changes to product specifications and pricing scenarios in minutes in response to a competitor, where in previous times, months of planning were required together with the expense of reprinting product literature and re-training staff.

The Internet has totally changed the business environment by making it inordinately faster than in times past. To survive organisations must now plan and adapt at the speed of the Internet.

The Increasing Complexity of Business

The second challenge facing organisations is the complexity of business that has been caused by technology. Twenty years ago organisations were typically aligned with defined markets where they offered mass-produced products and services. There was little scope for collecting feedback other than by conducting manually intensive surveys. With better communication, organisations today can gain competitive advantage by marketing specific products directly to individuals. Similarly, better and faster information has allowed more agile production techniques and 'just in time' inventory management systems that reduce stock levels and the associated costs involved.

The Internet has also made it possible for intermediaries to operate and tailor products for individual needs. In doing so they do not need much in the way of capital for the business to operate, and yet they can still give the appearance of being a large, stable organisation. Insurance, utilities, and some forms of banking are prime examples of industries that have been transformed in this way.

Another phenomena affecting companies is 'people power' in the form of criticisms or endorsements on social networks that has significant influence on customer purchases. These kinds of comments, which often have nothing to do with the product or service being offered, are more to do with social attitudes to corporate responsibility, but they can be just as devastating as not keeping up with fast changing fashions.

Nike found this to their detriment when it was revealed that their shoes were manufactured by sweatshops in South Korea, China, and Taiwan. The resultant bad publicity greatly affected sales and Nike was forced to ensure those working for them were treated and paid better. Similarly, when it was reported that Starbucks had not paid any corporation tax between 2009 and 2012 on its UK sales of around £1 billion in the same period, a large number of customers boycotted the coffee chain and chose competitors who were seen to be more socially responsible. Of course Nike and Starbucks are by no means the only companies to be affected in this way, and the chances are that social pressure will increasingly affect organisational behaviour in the future.

At no other time in history has the business environment been so complex.

The Decreasing Planning Time Horizon

As a direct result of the speed and complexity of business, there has been a corresponding rapid decrease in the planning time horizon (that is, the ability to predict into future time periods with any degree of accuracy). Figure 1-2 outlines the impact of speed and complexity of business on a planning horizon.

In the past, the typical management processes of annual budgeting, quarterly forecasting, and monthly reporting were acceptable as changes in the market could be accommodated within the established planning timeframe. It is interesting to note that this timing was common place back in the 1920s and was written up by James McKinsey in his book, *Budgetary Control*, which sought to lay the foundation for effective management. However, the pace and complexity of the business world was very different, so it is strange to see those timings are still in place today when they are most unsuitable.

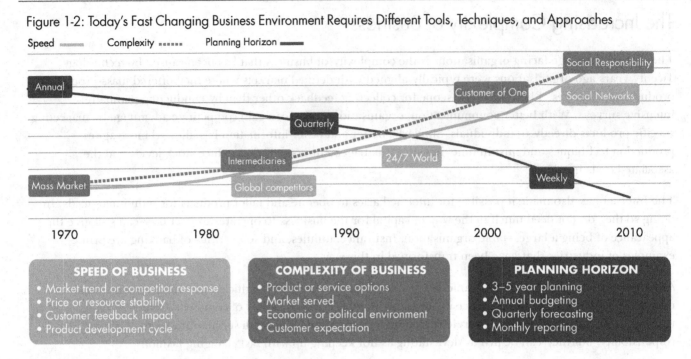

Figure 1-2: Today's Fast Changing Business Environment Requires Different Tools, Techniques, and Approaches

SPEED OF BUSINESS	COMPLEXITY OF BUSINESS	PLANNING HORIZON
• Market trend or competitor response • Price or resource stability • Customer feedback impact • Product development cycle	• Product or service options • Market served • Economic or political environment • Customer expectation	• 3–5 year planning • Annual budgeting • Quarterly forecasting • Monthly reporting

PLANNING CHALLENGES

In a survey of finance staff conducted in June 2013 by the Chartered Institute of Management Accountants in the UK and the American Institute of Certified Public Accountants in the US, over 53 per cent of the respondents said they were not satisfied with their organisation's strategic planning process for achieving its purpose. Most felt that too little time was spent in this key area of planning. Also, not surprisingly, almost 40 per cent were dissatisfied with their financial planning and budgeting process because participants felt that too much time was spent on these annual activities. Other findings from this survey can be found in Appendix I at the end of this book.

Combined these imply there is an imbalance toward where the emphasis should be—strategic planning over budgeting. The latter statistic reflects a growing awareness that the annual budget could be streamlined using driver-based expense modelling methods and possibly a bridge toward more use of rolling financial forecasts.

One unexpected observation was that over 50 per cent of the respondents do not perform scenario planning. This might indicate that they only have time to evaluate a single choice. Interestingly for those who responded on not using scenario planning, many commented that scenarios are not important. This begs the question, 'What is planning?'

Comments from respondents also indicate ominous concerns with their organisation's planning processes. When asked what one thing they would change in the planning process, the comments received fell into the categories outlined in the subsequent sections.

Dissatisfaction With the Planning Process

Many respondents thought that strategic, tactical planning and budgeting should be integrated and linked with goals, objectives, and accountability. That there should be more rolling forecasts and less annual processes such as budgeting. One participant emphasised that organisations should move toward an environment where the planning process is a part of our regular activities, not a periodic exercise. Comments were also made about placing more emphasis on strategy and not just financial projections.

Issues With the Planning Culture

Culture is something that is acquired over time through management attitudes that are allowed to operate. Respondents made a number of comments about the ownership of budgets and that there should be more focus on the long-term health of the company rather than the current month or short-term goals. Someone made the remark that planning should be based on real numbers and not what they want them to be, and that senior management should commit to being accountable on goals and objectives of the plan and the budget. The lack of accountability was seen by some to be a significant barrier that led to a lack of buy-in. This in turn leads to poor or no implementation, and a reduced desire to properly plan next time around.

Need for a Holistic Approach

The third area of improvement is in better performance measures that tie to critical organisational success factors. This requires a better awareness of how functions interact with each other and discussions around individual budgets and plans. To make this happen it was suggested that leaders of functional areas should be committed to the interrelationships required to meet overall corporate goals and to have a better follow-up on execution. One correspondent also commented that there should be a stop on having bonuses determined solely on earnings made, as depicted in the budget.

Need for Better Planning Technologies

The last area for improvement concerned the use of technology. Most participants still use spread sheets for planning, which they describe as being too manual and error prone, and wanted something more robust. A few made the comment that some planning systems are lacking key functionality, such as the requirement to produce cash flow forecasts and cash flow trending. By implementing enterprise planning systems, some thought opportunities would be offered for better analysis and personal skill set improvements.

In our experience, these planning issues have been known for some time. What management lacks is the exact knowledge of how these issues can be addressed, and in a way that the organisation can adopt in a timely manner.

PLANNING PRINCIPLES

The challenges outlined in our survey are fairly common, and are ones that we come across all the time. There is no simple solution to them; if there were then someone would have patented the idea and we would no longer be discussing these issues. Despite the hype you may read on business consulting and software vendor marketing literature, there is currently no widely accepted solution.

However, we believe many of the issues outlined in this chapter, particularly those that are specifically generated by today's complex and fast moving business environment, can be overcome; but it requires a radical re-thinking about the role of planning and how it is conducted within an organisation. The principles discussed in the following sections capture the core planning principles that help shape our business planning framework.

Principle 1: Planning Connects Inputs and Outputs and is Therefore Directly Related to Organisational Activities

At the heart of every organisation are a series of related activities through which goods or services are produced for its intended customers. It does not matter whether that organisation is a government department, not-for-profit, or a commercial entity. These activities exist in every industry and in every family unit.

How well they perform this chain of activities in the prevailing economic environment will determine the level of success it will achieve. Michael Porter's book, *Competitive Advantage: Creating and Sustaining Superior Performance*, published in 1985, described these activities as a value chain.

Each industry has a different chain of activities through which it delivers products or services to customers. For example, a manufacturer buys raw materials and, through a series of processes, will transform them into a finished product. Each process adds value to the raw materials so that at the end of each sub-process the original materials are now worth more than what they were at the start.

For a service organisation such as a software vendor, value is added in the form of knowledge, functions, and presentation capabilities, which transforms a computer into a more valuable piece of equipment. For example, a relatively low-cost computer with the right software is able to control a production facility that previously would either have been impossible or required a team of expensive staff to operate.

In both examples, the end result is that the finished goods and services are worth more than the collection of its individual parts to a prospective customer. That additional value came through a chain of activities defined by the business processes of the originating organisation.

With a not-for-profit organisation or government department, the business process or activity chain concept is just as valid. The main difference is that the focus will be on the delivery of a service that may be quantified in measures other than monetary. However, that service is still delivered through a range of value-add business processes.

Principle 2: Planning is About Maintaining a Shared Understanding of the Economics of a Business

Organisations operate in an ever-changing business world. They have to continually evaluate that their business processes—their chain of value added activities—are still able to sustain growth or at least allow them to survive. They also need to understand the demands being placed on these processes by products, customers, and business segments. As a result, according to Professor Andy Neely, Founding Director of the Cambridge Service Alliance and as published in a white paper, *Rethinking the Planning Process*,[1] organisational planning falls into one of three categories:

1. *To predict what may happen in the future.* This is achieved by making use of known facts, assumptions, and relationships to generate a forecast of future performance. For example, sales forecasts can be derived from past trends such as market growth and the organisation's conversion rates, which are then used to automatically calculate production and support costs.

2. *To challenge established theories on how the business operates.* This looks at generally accepted past (or current) relationships between business processes and the outcomes generated. This is used to model past performance and assess the accuracy of predictions to determine whether those relationships were valid predictors of performance.

3. *To innovate an established business model.* This type of planning allows management to assess changes to the way the business operates. For example, the way in which it is structured or funded and the new things the business would like to try out. Output from these different scenarios can then be used to make decisions on future changes to business processes.

Whatever type of planning occurs, all require a good understanding of how the organisation generates value.

Principle 3: Planning is About Shifting Focus From the Past and Onto the Future

Much management time today is spent in looking at the past. Monthly profit and loss reports, detailed sales analyses, and KPI variances all compete for management attention. By looking at such historic detail it is hoped that something about the future may be garnered. However, the business world is increasingly under major performance-impacting influences that have not been experienced in the past. As mentioned earlier, these influences include comments on social media that are able to add or destroy organisational value overnight, the ability for organisations to compete in markets around the world in a matter of months but without having to establish a local base, and the connected nature of the world where news of impending economic gloom in one area can produce a market-changing impact in others. In this new world, studying the past is unlikely to be of much help in predicting the future with any significant accuracy.

For planning to be effective, it has to shift focus away from the past and onto what is likely to happen in the future. That includes looking at all of the relevant influences, both in and out of the control of the organisation, which could potentially make a significant impact on planned goals and the way they are delivered. It is a future that may not align itself with past trends, and it is one that that will change quickly according to events that are currently unknown, but for which the organisation needs to be ready.

Principle 4: Planning is About Aligning Budgets With Strategy to Achieve Corporate Objectives

For the moment, imagine that you have been put in charge of a national sport whose aim is to compete at the highest level in the Olympic games. In taking on that responsibility, how do you think performance is going to be measured at the games? It could be by the number of gold medals won, the number of world records set, or the ranking of the team in comparison with other nations. All of these results are outcomes (that is, the things to be achieved).

Now let's go back a few years to when the team is preparing for the games. How is performance going to be managed? You can be sure it will not be solely in terms of the number of medals they hope to win. Instead the focus will be on the type of training to be given, the diets to be prepared, the way in which equipment and facilities are to be used. To ensure these activities can take place, budgets and other resources will need to be allocated appropriately. In short, the focus for managing performance is on the process of preparing athletes and not on the outcomes they hope to achieve.

To make a real difference, these organisational activities need to be better than what the competition does. If all you do is the same as everyone else, then there is no competitive advantage. This is where strategic planning comes to the front. How can we increase the efficiency or value of the things we do? Can we save some costs elsewhere and improve or introduce other new activities? Strategy is directly linked to budgeting and improving organisational effectiveness.

Now compare this approach to the way organisations typically plan and budget. Most tend to focus on outcomes—the gold medals of profit to be made and the total amount to be spent. Meanwhile the actions required to produce the 'gold' are left as a note in an operational plan document, only to be forgotten when actual results are produced. For the average company this process can take as long as four months and yet, as our survey shows, is usually devoid of any link to strategy and how it can be achieved.

Planning involves maximising the impact of organisational activities. This requires a process whereby management sets realistic corporate goals, chooses a particular course of action to meet those goals for a given business environment, communicates how those actions relate to individual departments, and ensures adequate resources are made available.

Principle 5: Planning is a Continuous Process

Planning is not something that happens just once a year. The business world is continually changing and organisations are never going to be able to predict or anticipate every twist and turn. This means some things will work as planned while others will need to change or be replaced.

To determine this, plans have to be monitored for execution against set milestones, and their impact on corporate goals. Plans must also be developed and monitored against assumptions made about the business landscape as these can affect what decisions are required.

Every decision made can have an impact on other areas, and so changes must always be assessed in the context of overall objectives. This assessment cannot be left to a date on the calendar and must be triggered when exceptions are detected, or events that could change the future take place.

For example, if a competitor introduces a competing product that is just as good but half the price as your product, then something will have to change. There is no point in telling sales representatives to sell more or threaten them with dismissal. The business world in which the organisation competes has just changed, and so the budgets and actions that were originally set may no longer be viable. As Gary Hamel famously comments in his book, *Leading the Revolution*

> Dakota tribal wisdom says that when you discover you are on a dead horse the best strategy is to dismount. Of course there are other strategies. You can change riders. You can get a committee to study the dead horse. You can declare that it is cheaper to feed a dead horse. You can harness several dead horses together. But after you've tried all these things, you're still have to dismount.

Because of this, planning is continuous. Continuous means you do it as often as required, rather than just by a date on a calendar. Trends and variances must be continually monitored, as well as changes in the business environment. Variances, events, and anticipated change become the trigger for plan revisions.

Principle 6: Planning is a Learning Process

All plans evolve over time. Planning systems that focus purely on results do not reveal the process that individual managers went through in setting targets, the actions that were going to be required, and, just as important, the reasons why.

Similarly, knowing what works in a plan and what does not is extremely valuable. Predicting outcomes requires plans to record what activities were carried out, who did them, how they were financed, and whether the assumptions made about the business environment were correct. All of this information must be available for future reference when reviewing past results. Even knowing where a course of action failed has worth, assuming that lessons are learned and history is not allowed to repeat itself.

OBJECTIVES OF THE PLANNING FRAMEWORK

It is likely that most of the issues raised in this chapter are well known and the principles that we have covered are common sense. The big question is how exactly do you overcome the issues and implement the principles? We have met many organisations that struggle with this question at a practical level, and that is why we have developed the planning framework outlined in chapter 4, 'Business Planning Framework'.

The aim is to help organisations create joined-up plans in an increasingly fast-paced, complex business environment. This framework combines the principles of planning while avoiding the issues that many organisations face, to provide a mechanism that will bring the whole organisation together where different departments are able to jointly act as a single entity. It is also a framework that challenges current beliefs and practices about the way performance is planned and managed.

It is important to recognise that the models defined within the framework are not about predicting numbers with high accuracy, but more about promoting a fact-based discussion. They allow management to think logically about the goals the organisation would like to achieve and the activities and resources required to get there.

By adopting the framework to be described in chapters 4–10, organisations will be able to realise a number of business benefits, including the following:

- Provide senior executives with a clear holistic view of what needs to be managed across the organisation.
- Provide an organisation-wide strategic focus within an adaptable planning time horizon.
- Help operational managers to overcome a myopic, departmental view of the business.
- Enable departments to create more accurate forecasts and understand their implications on corporate goals.
- Obtain a more effective use of working capital.
- Provide the basis for risk management.
- Help identify the planning technologies required and how to put them together to support performance management.

Having established the need for a business planning framework, many would question whether this is anything new. After all, there are countless methodologies in existence that are supposed to provide such a structure. That is what we will be looking at in the next chapter.

Endnotes

1 Corpeum. *Rethinking the Planning Process* (white paper).
  October – November, 2013. Corpeum.

2

PLANNING METHODS AND METHODOLOGIES

Over the years there have been many attempts to help organisations create better joined-up plans. This chapter will include an overview of some of these approaches and ways in which organisations can assess their planning maturity.

PLANNING: WHO, WHAT, WHEN, AND HOW

Planning is a simple concept to understand and yet can be difficult to perform. Part of the reason for this is its multi-faceted nature that, within a business context, can come in a range of types (for example, strategic, operational, financial), functions (for example, sales, logistics, production), and techniques (for example, top-down, bottom-up, driver-based). Plans include different combinations of these areas, depending on the purpose being served. As a consequence, it is easy to lose sight of what each is designed to do and organisations can end up with a mishmash of plans that have little or no connection to what they are trying to achieve.

To get a better understanding of how planning requirements evolve within an organisation, consider the following fictitious company, XYZ, Inc., as it grows into a large, multi-national concern.

Planning Within a Sole Trader

XYZ, Inc. was founded as a re-seller of ballpoint pens. The owner and workforce of four people started out by buying a small range of quality pens from different manufacturers and supplying them to a number of shops within their local area. For XYZ to grow they must ensure that their resale price is competitive with other suppliers and that the anticipated sales revenue covers the cost of buying, marketing, and distributing the pens along with paying wages and other administration expenses.

The planning requirements here are quite simple, and because there is only one person involved, they can be easily modelled in a spread sheet. This will include evaluating discount purchases from suppliers, as well as what discounts could be given to customers should they want to buy in bulk. Output from the model will include a target sales price, the volume to be sold each week, an associated budget for each activity (for example, marketing, travel, and so on), and a cash flow forecast so that adequate funding can be put in place.

Planning as a Small Manufacturer

Business is good. Pen sales increased and they are now sold through a number of wholesalers and large independent shops across the country. However, XYZ is experiencing supply problems in terms of delivery dates and quality, which they feel is vital if they are to retain customers.

To fix these issues and to be more competitive (and more profitable), XYZ believes they need to manufacture some of the pens themselves. This will require an investment in machinery and warehousing capabilities for both components—each pen typically consists of 26 different parts, some of which are purchased, and others are manufactured from raw materials—and for finished stock.

However, these changes will require an increase in the number of outlets they manage in a wider geographic area, and a move to becoming a manufacture, both of which greatly increase organisation risk. This is because the overhead costs to be covered would be much higher, and any miscalculation of variable costs (for example, price) can cause significant losses due to the high volumes involved. There is also a danger of losing customers (and hence revenue) if production does not meet demand, the possibility of wasting resources (which detract from profits) if more goods are produced than is required, and the capital investment for the machinery would need to be funded.

These risks greatly increase the complexity of the planning model(s) required, which now need to cover the following:

- *Marketing.* This will include a sales forecast broken down into each pen type, along with a budget for the promotional programme.
- *Pricing.* This needs to be competitive and generate sufficient margin to cover organisational costs and investment. It also needs to evaluate promotional pricing to capture market share.
- *Optimum production levels.* Management will need to decide which pens to manufacture, at what time, and the levels of stock to be held. This should be linked to the sales forecast.
- *Raw material purchases.* This will include what materials to buy, from which suppliers, and the levels of stock to be held. This will need to be linked to production levels, but XYZ may want to take advantage of any special offers that suppliers are willing to give.
- *Warehousing and logistics.* This cover the best way to deliver finished products to customers, which could either be by their own transport capability or via a third-party carrier, depending on location.
- *Cash flow and sources of funds.* This will need to show how much cash is required by the operation, and how any investment is to be funded.

It is unlikely that all of the preceding risks can be covered by one single model, and that multiple people will need to be involved. However, as the organisation is still relatively small in the number of employees and that they are all based in a single location, using a spread sheet to plan is still possible, although much care needs to be taken when setting up formulae, as an overlooked error could prove catastrophic.

If multiple spreadsheet models are used, then linking them becomes an issue. For example, cash flow will need to take into account sales forecasts by customer and the payment for raw material purchases, both of which could come from different planning spread sheets. As a consequence, the order of how the plan is constructed needs to be carefully managed. For example, production planning needs to be re-evaluated each time a sales forecast is received, and marketing promotions need to reflect what can be produced along with the lead times required for ordering materials.

Planning as a Listed Company

XYZ continues to do well. As part of its strategy for growth, it intends to expand the product range to include complementary stationery items such as pencils, rulers, rubbers, and ink. The management team also plans to expand to multiple locations throughout the country, with some having local manufacturing capabilities. This expansion will be partially achieved through acquisition, funded by becoming a public company and raising capital by selling shares on the stock exchange.

Planning has now become a more extensive process that not only has to cope with the new products and sites involved, but also with providing a clear, realistic strategy that communicates to investors how and when financial returns will be generated. As a result, the planning process includes all of the planning activities previously described, plus

- reviewing the market for writing products so management can decide where growth opportunities lie and how XYZ can take a major share (strategic planning);
- analysing what changes will be needed to the current operation in order to achieve the predicted market share (operational planning);
- assessing how much additional funding will be required for the planned infra-structure (capital planning);

Once these items have been agreed on, then the management team can then decide how

- it wants to allocate its resources (financial and human resources planning) to make the revised operation a reality; and
- how best to optimise its production and logistic capabilities (sales and operational planning) to maximise profitability.

As the plan gets implemented, it is now vital to

- track actual and forecast performance to see what is being achieved (forecasting).
- identify and mitigate risks that could derail the plan (risk management).
- reassess priorities so that adjustments can be made to either keep the plan on track or improve its performance.

As can be seen from this XYZ example, planning is now a multi-user activity that encompasses a range of tasks that are way beyond the capabilities of a spread sheet.

Planning as an International Group

XYZ has now made the big time. With help from the introduction of e-commerce and continued expansion, the company has gone international with a full range of stationery products. Because of this and the need to increasingly develop trade partnerships, decision making has become unwieldy. In response to this challenge, the company has been split into different legal entities so that each one can focus on the needs of individual countries and markets.

Planning has also become a challenge as it not only needs to take into account local trading conditions, but also has to include corporate requirements of tax planning, statutory consolidation, and regulatory reporting where required.

Further still, XYZ is now a recognisable brand and is easily exposed to risks, such as an attack by 'start-up' companies (like itself in the early days), who can provide a more personal service to customers, or by bad press on social media sites that dictate what is 'in' and 'out' of fashion. It will also need to act in a socially responsible way that smaller competitors can often ignore.

The main issue for XYZ is how do they plan and act like a single company when their planning activities are so diverse? How do they co-ordinate the different functions across geographic boundaries in a market that is continually changing? In this respect they are not alone.

THE RISE OF MANAGEMENT FRAMEWORKS AND METHODOLOGIES

As organisations (and the business world) become more complex and involve many people, planning must become better disciplined and organised. Every facet of the business needs to be considered, whether that means sales and operations, logistics, human resources, or tax. The company must be organised so that plans are complete and assembled in a logical sequence. There are dependencies. For example, there is no point in planning cash requirements unless sales forecasts and supplier orders are known with some degree of accuracy. To do this requires an analysis of market trends, competitor activity, and production capacity (and cost) of our own set up. Each part of a plan has the potential to impact another, and some method is needed to conduct planning in an orderly and efficient manner.

To help with this task, a range of management tools have been developed over the years that can be categorised as frameworks, methodologies, or processes. Figure 2-1 depicts examples of these.

Figure 2-1: Sample Management Tools for Dealing With Complexity

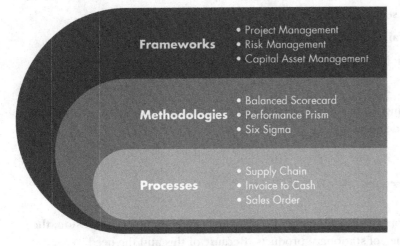

For this book we are using the following definitions to distinguish them:

A *framework* is a structured set of ideas and principles that provides direction on the preferred way of doing something. It is not prescriptive, but is more a set of guidelines that can be customised to suit a particular need or organisation. Examples of these include Risk management, Project management, and Capital asset management.

There are literally hundreds of management frameworks designed to help manage complexity. A recent LinkedIn discussion group listed over 940 as of February 2013, with the count rising on a weekly basis. Typically these frameworks are associated with a specific business area, as can be seen from the examples given, and so they can be considered complementary to the framework being described in this book.

A *methodology* by contrast is a set of practices that can be used to achieve a particular goal. They are typically more rigid and have a defined, proven set of rules, activities, and deliverables to solve a specific problem. Examples include the Balanced Scorecard, Performance Prism and Six Sigma.

Management methodologies tend to have their followers. An organisation will typically choose one and then adhere to it like a religion. Quite often the methodology will be tailored to the organisation based on their beliefs of what works for them. In the context of this book, methodologies fit within the planning framework as they tend to focus on improvement strategies rather than all aspects of operation.

Business processes are the activities an organisation does, typically across the functional boundaries of the organisation chart, to serve its purpose. These can be broken down into smaller tasks that are generally repeatable and could be automated if required. Examples include Purchase order processing, Invoice to cash, and Sales order to delivery.

Many processes, such as those that deal with payments and receipts, tend to be common across organisations and are carried out according to either a legal framework or as prescribed in the organisations' operating manual.

To enhance any framework, methodology, or process, management schools and leading business consultants have all contributed articles on how these should be conducted. They are typically grouped into popular topics such as strategy execution, change management, leadership, performance measurement, and so on. It is no wonder that there is confusion as each article seems to focus on a particular topic that expresses that their way is best, but leaves the reader to figure out how to put them all together.

Of course it could be argued that this book is coming up with yet another framework, methodology, and process, but we as the authors do not agree. Our approach is to learn from history and to set out what we believe is important for organisations to plan. To go with this we provide examples of how good practices, whether they are framework, methodology, or process based, can be implemented.

Before we do that, let's first look at some of the more popular management methodologies that have been shaping the way organisations plan today.

POPULAR MANAGEMENT METHODOLOGIES

Budgetary Control

Budgetary control is probably the most widely used method to plan and control organisational performance. It has been with us for nearly a century. In his book, *Budgetary Control*, published in 1922, James McKinsey put forward the concept of budgeting as a management framework—a concept that has dominated management practices for most of the 20th century. McKinsey stated that to effectively control an operation, it was necessary to set standards of performance, which should be described in the budget. As well as setting the standard, budgets were also seen as the means of co-ordinating activities between departments.

As Marvin Bower, former chief executive of McKinsey & Company, wrote in his book, *Perspective on McKinsey*, the concept of their top-management approach was based on the budget as 'a statement of policy, expressed in terms of future accounts delegated to units of an organisation'.[1]

Today, budgeting is still used as the main method of organisational control. Its strengths are that managers are restricted to spending levels that are not to be exceeded, and there are numerous technology systems that can streamline the process of producing the budget. However, results from the survey shown in Appendix I would indicate that budgetary control is increasingly under attack for a number of reasons:

1. *Absence of context.* Plans are based on underlying assumptions that are often outside of the control of the organisation. If assumptions made about market growth, price fluctuations, and actions of key competitors

are wrong, then any plan based on them will be misdirected. The issue is that these assumptions are rarely tracked or associated with the approved budget amounts, and when an assumption is no longer true, its consequence is lost and the amounts become meaningless.

2. *Inappropriate timing.* Plans are often seen as being financial in nature that last for a set number of months, typically 12. However, the markets in which organisations operate are continually changing and usually at a faster pace than can be predicted with accuracy at the start of the budgeting process. Some items such as fixed interest rates may be known for years in advance, but other items such as raw material unit cost may only be known for a few months in advance. Trying to put all of these different items onto the same planning time-frame is both unrealistic and diverts attention away from what is really important.

3. *Irrelevant content.* Plans are typically based around the financial structures and accounts found in an organisation's general ledger system. Although these structures are good for recording transactions, they are inadequate when it comes to describing actions and initiatives that are supposed to be linked to strategy. Planning and budgeting are not purely financial exercises. Their purpose is to help the organisation allocate resources and assets to achieve strategic goals, but all too often that strategic content is either vague or missing.

4. *Inadequate capability.* For planning to be of value, there must first be a process that allows management to explore alternative courses of action and to assess their impact on achieving the organisation's mission. Once those alternatives have been carefully evaluated, the best combination of activities can then be selected and resources allocated as appropriate. Unfortunately, planning is more like a guessing game where managers try to come up with a set of numbers that they think will be acceptable. These numbers are then ascribed to departments rather than projects or initiatives, mainly because the software solution being used does not allow a strategic focus. If the numbers are not acceptable, senior managers will arbitrarily adjust them so that they do add up to their own guess or expectations. However, who knows if any of these numbers make sense in terms of implementing corporate strategy.

Many organisations recognise that budgetary control falls far short of what they need to manage performance, but few companies seem willing to move away from them.

Quality Management Movement

The aim of the quality management movement is to continually improve the current operations of a business. It does this by analysing defects and coming up with ways to reduce or eliminate them. The methodologies associated with the movement all have their roots in manufacturing and include the following:

- Total quality management (TQM) started about the same time as budgetary control, and involved applying statistical techniques to detect and fix problems on production lines to reduce the number of faulty products. These techniques were developed further by William Deming, Joseph Juran, and Armand Feigenbaum during the 1940s and were systematically applied to Japanese manufacturers during the 1950s. In addition to training management, workers were also encouraged to meet regularly to discuss and suggest ideas on how things could be improved. These became known as quality circles and ensured that the methodology was pushed down to all staff levels.

  Because of the success of Japanese companies in the 1980s and 1990s, organisations in the West started to take a closer look at improving quality. This launched a range of quality-focused strategies, programmes, and techniques that became the focus for the TQM movement.

TQM is defined as 'management philosophy and company practices that aim to harness the human and material resources of an organisation in the most effective way to achieve the objectives of the organisation'. It places customer satisfaction at the centre and looks at how all of the processes in the organisation can better work together in serving them.

- Six Sigma came out of Motorola in the 1980s and is based on the tools they developed to improve manufacturing. It became famous after Jack Welch introduced the techniques into General Electric during its period of rapid growth and profitability. The term *sigma* has its basis in statistics and refers to the deviation from perfection, the idea being that if you can get rid of the deviations, then you have perfection. The sixth sigma is a defect level of less than one in 99.99966 per cent.

What sets Six Sigma apart from TQM is the approach, which looks at improving all of the operations within a single business process. There is a defined set of management and statistical methods overseen by teams of people that go under the dubious titles of champions, black belts, green belts, orange belts, and so on, who are experts in these complex methods. Improvement initiatives are set up as six sigma projects that follow a defined sequence of steps with quantified value targets (for example, process cycle time reduction, customer satisfaction, profit increase).

Like any other methodology, those related to quality management are not perfect. There will be issues that can derail the spirit of what the methodology is trying to achieve, including

- *Quality versus results.* Focusing on improving quality does not necessarily produce profits. As we have seen, the impact of social media and competing with organisations that have a fundamentally different business model can invalidate the output of any improvement initiative.

- *Focus on short-term goals.* Quality improvement is a long-term process. Organisations that drive and reward staff on this month's, quarter's, or year's goals will never be able to implement the practices required in an efficient and effective manner.

- *Alignment with strategy.* Quality improvement is the total strategy. Anything else is outside of the methodology and can adversely impact the goal of any existing improvement project.

- *Staff motivation.* TQM and Six Sigma are surrounded in technical terms and practices that require months, if not years, of training to perfect. As such this generates elite teams whose presence can cause those not involved to feel devalued and their expertise ignored.

- *Complexity.* TQM and Six Sigma techniques include a variety of analytical tools such as fish bone diagrams, the Define, Measure, Analyze, Improve, Control (DAMIC) improvement cycle, measuring Defects Per Million Opportunities (DPMO), and Pareto analyses. The volume of data required is often immense and finding suitable and reliable sources can be a real problem.

Lean Management

Traditional management is often results oriented. Did we achieve the target? Did we stay within budget? Is our performance better than competitors? The only trouble is that when these objectives are achieved, people tend to relax as if the company has made its goals. But this can lead to a situation where resources could have been put to better use, or whose cost could have been avoided altogether.

Lean management is a companion of the quality movement previously mentioned. Its focus is to provide value to customers and ensure that the processes put in place to deliver goods and services, continually add value. Lean management also promotes minimising or eliminating all forms of waste.

The term *lean* was coined by a research team headed by Jim Womack, Ph.D., at MIT's International Motor Vehicle Program. It was used to describe Toyota's business during the late 1980s, which at the time was considered to be one of the best at generating customer value.

To be a lean organisation is to have adopted a new way of thinking about the way the business is managed. This changes the focus of management away from vertical departments and assets to one that optimises the flow of products and services through the organisation's business processes (that is, how raw materials are acquired and turned into added-value products for customers).

As a consequence, lean thinking is claimed to

- eliminate waste along entire business processes instead of at isolated points.
- create processes that need less effort, space, capital, and time to make products and services at less cost and with fewer defects, compared to traditional management systems.
- make companies more responsive to changing customer desires for high variety, high quality, low cost, and short delivery lead times.
- enable information management to become simpler and more accurate.

Lean management techniques are being used by organisations in all industries and services, including healthcare and governments. Not all choose to use the word lean, but label what they do as their own system, such as the Toyota Production System or the Danaher Business System.

The main issues around the methodology is that it is often seen as a way to make cuts in costs that can often destroy an organisation's value chain. It also requires a complete transformation of the way in which the business is measured and managed, something that cannot be achieved in the short-term.

Balanced Scorecard

The Balanced Scorecard is one of the more modern management methodologies around, although it was introduced over 20 years ago. It first appeared as a series of articles by authors Robert Kaplan and David Norton in the *Harvard Business Review* in the early 1990s, although it was based on the work of General Electric on performance measurement reporting in the 1950s.

The aim of the Balanced Scorecard is to continually improve results by providing feedback on internal business processes and their link to external outcomes. It is promoted as a management system and not just a measurement system. By adopting the methodology, it is hoped that organisations will be able to clarify their vision and strategy, which can then be translated into action.

Two of the more notable facets of the Balanced Scorecard include the following:

1. *Perspectives.* The methodology views organisations from a number of linked perspectives. The more common being the following:
   - *Learning and growth.* This includes the activities that help the organisation to develop in meeting customer needs both now and in the future.
   - *Business processes.* This includes activities on how the business operates in meeting customer needs.
   - *Customer.* This includes the activities that lead to satisfied and loyal customers.
   - *Financial.* This includes how the organisation is funded and the financial rewards that emanate.

   Each perspective has a series of measures that are used to plan and report performance.

2. *Strategy mapping.* Strategy maps are a visual representation on how the organisation generates value. They link strategic objectives in each perspective with measures in the form of a cause and effect chain, with the perspectives determining what measures contribute to meeting the overall goals of the organisation. For example, a profit-motivated company will have the financial perspective as its goal, whereas a not-for-profit organisation may see the customer perspective measures as the goal.

Given that the Balanced Scorecard methodology was developed at a time when executive information systems and supporting technologies were making real headways into an organisation, there are many software tools that claim to provide management support. However, many of these appear to be limited to ways of generating and disseminating scorecards throughout an organisation.

The issues caused by the Balanced Scorecard include the following:

- It is often seen as just a reporting system and not a planning system.

- Quite often the measures used are backward looking and either not directly related to corporate objectives or they are outside of user control.

- Measures are rarely balanced across the different business perspectives. The financial perspective tends to be overly represented, mainly because of the amount of available data or the one of highest interest to the executives.

- Targets are generally negotiated rather than what is required in order for the business to survive and thrive

- There is no mechanism for improving organisational processes

Beyond Budgeting

Beyond Budgeting is the latest of the methodologies described here, although it is more of a movement with a set of principles than a set of prescribed rules. Those who adopt beyond budgeting concepts tend to choose the ones that they think will work best for them. Despite the title, and the mantra chanted by some advocates that they have 'dumped the budget', the method still retains budgets. What has changed, though, is that the traditional budget process has been replaced with a more dynamic and adaptable way of allocating resources that focuses on delivering organisational value.

The Beyond Budgeting Round Table (BBRT) was established at the turn of the century and was brought to a wider audience in an article published in 2003 in the *Harvard Business Review*. Titled 'Who Needs Budgets', the authors Jeremy Hope and Robin Fraser discussed the problems with traditional budgeting and asked why organisations still cling to inflexible planning practices. It then went on to cover the beyond budgeting principles.

For them, beyond budgeting means moving beyond command and control and towards a management model that is more adaptive and empowering for employees. It is about rethinking how organisations are managed where 'innovative management models represent the only sustainable competitive advantage'. They go on to say that it is also about 'releasing people from the burdens of stifling bureaucracy and suffocating control systems, trusting them with information and giving them time to think, reflect, share, learn and improve'.

The common principles of the methodology have been set as follows:

- Governance and transparency

    o *Values.* Bind people to a common cause, not a central plan.
    o *Governance.* Govern through shared values and sound judgement, not detailed rules and regulations.
    o *Transparency.* Make information open and transparent, do not restrict and control it.

- Accountable teams

    o *Teams.* Organise around a seamless network of accountable teams, not centralised functions.
    o *Trust.* Trust teams to regulate their performance, do not micro-manage them.
    o *Accountability.* Base accountability on holistic criteria and peer reviews, not on hierarchical relationships.

- Goals and rewards

    o *Goals.* Set ambitious medium-term goals, not short-term fixed targets.
    o *Rewards.* Base rewards on relative performance, not on meeting fixed targets.

- Planning and controls

    o *Planning.* Make planning a continuous and inclusive process, not a top-down annual event.
    o *Co-ordination.* Co-ordinate interactions dynamically, not through annual budgets.
    o *Resources.* Make resources available just in time, not just in case.
    o *Controls.* Base controls on fast, frequent feedback, not budget variances.

The BBRT (www.bbrt.org) provides resources and case studies on organisations that have embraced the beyond budgeting concepts and the success they have achieved.

The issues with beyond budgeting are related to changing the culture of an organisation. It is assumed that everyone is working for the good of the organisation, when other pressures such as rewards and 'hitting targets' encourage people to take short cuts or 'fudge' the results. This is true of any methodology but more open to abuse with beyond budgeting.

PLANNING AND SUCCESS

In reviewing the planning needs of our company outlined at the start of this chapter, with the aims of management methodologies, it would seem that the two should go hand-in-hand. After all, XYZ's management wants to be able to better plan (that is to connect its resources with maximising its outputs) and be more reactive when things change. The promise of a management methodology is to facilitate that planning and review process by offering a set of practices that, if followed, will ensure a more reactive process tied to the implementation of strategy.

However, few organisations seem to achieve the methodology promise. It is interesting to note from our own survey that despite most organisations' claims to use a methodology, most have fundamental issues in the linkage to strategy. In general, there is really nothing wrong with the concepts of each methodology previously described. They are all a product of their time and strive to fix glaring weaknesses in an organisation's management processes. They all have good points as well as weaknesses inherent in their structure. If they did not have weaknesses, then one of them would triumph over the others and stand the test of time. In our experience, some methodologies tend to fail for the following reasons:

- *The need for a quick fix.* Quite often management will look to a methodology as a way of fixing a problem in a short period of time. However, quite often what needs fixing is the culture of the business or organisation, and that takes time. It is easy to announce the introduction of a new methodology and to arrange training classes, but to get the principles engrained in every manager's mind in a way that changes their way of working is far from easy. Change requires a consistent message from senior management, clear communication on why change is necessary, and unwavering support for the principles being established. Changing course part way through the implementation of a methodology is guaranteed to bring failure to any new method being introduced.

- *Hype over substance.* Organisations may choose to adopt a methodology to solve an issue that cannot be defined or solved. For example, having a vague strategy that cannot be measured is not going to be fixed by introducing a balanced scorecard. Similarly, consultants quick to see an opportunity may contribute to the propagation of hype by promising unrealistic savings or goal attainment.

- *Inappropriate systems.* In this case, systems refer to the technology solutions designed to support the methodology. It is not uncommon for spread sheets to be promoted as the underlying solution, but they are far from ideal as an enterprise wide system. Additionally, most systems focus on just one aspect of the methodology, such as the scorecard. These methodologies require links to budgets and forecasts, and they involve both financial and non-financial key performance indicator (KPI) measures, which quite often are supported in different, unconnected solutions.

- *Lack of success.* There is an underlying belief that implementing a methodology will guarantee success. Similarly, there is also a belief that a lack of success means that the methodology has failed. Neither are true. Organisations can 'get lucky' despite the methodology being used, or they may just fall victim to catastrophic circumstances, none of which could be predicted or managed by the adopted management system.

The aim of a management methodology is to bring management together around the topic of managing performance and that is it. Success is dependent on the right information being displayed, at the right time and in making the right business decisions. Oh, and a bit of luck is helpful.

However, it is unlikely that an organisation can jump from where it is today into a fully-fledged, continuous planning process. It will require a number of smaller incremental steps that gradually introduce changes over time. Because not everyone is at the same stage, we have developed the following maturity model that describes the different levels of planning being exhibited within organisations today. These different levels can then be used to assess the next steps in developing the planning process.

PLANNING PROCESS MATURITY

Planning Objectives

The overriding factor in developing an effective (and successful) planning process is to assess the level of maturity required by the organisation. Planning maturity can be defined as two sets of objectives that an organisation should desire to achieve: (1) those that relate to the outcome of process itself and (2) those that relate to the behaviour of those involved. These planning objectives are outlined in figure 2-2.

Some of these objectives will be easy to achieve, depending on the complexity of the organisation. For example, in an organisation containing just a few employees that work closely with each other, the behaviour objectives of

Figure 2-2: Planning Maturity Objectives

Process Objective	The Nature of the Objective
Optimisation	Optimise resource allocation across functions and business units
Executability	Identify operational issues and risks affecting plan executability
Adaptability	Enable organisations to quickly react to change
Alignment	Maintain strategic alignment and manage expectations
Visibility	Provide forward visibility into potential performance issues
Profitability	Forecast the profitability and cash flow of business segments

Process Objective	The Nature of the Objective
Ownership	Establish front line ownership of plans and forecasts
Accountability	Establish effective accountability for outcomes
Communication	Establish open and honest communication about resource needs
Efficiency	Reduce the cost of planning and forecasting processes
Consistency	Establish one plan across the organisation

ownership, accountability, and communication do not require much consideration. These can be assumed to occur as part of a conversation and without recourse to the development of a specific technology. However, in a large organisation containing large numbers of people, spread out over broad geographic areas, these same objectives need to be carefully considered and achieved through the careful design of a supporting planning system.

As a result, these objectives become more relevant to the design of planning solution as organisations exhibit more of the following complexity characteristics:

- *Large scale.* Many and diverse products, services, customers, employees, vendors, purchased parts, and commodities.
- *Variability.* In demand volume, product and customer mix, inventory and service levels, product pricing, and input costs.
- *Rapid change.* To products, suppliers, services, processes, projects, operational constraints, and organisation structures.
- *Organisation structure.* Multiple legal entities, business units (BUs), channels, geographies, and product groups.
- *Interdependence.* BUs share customers, suppliers, production, and back office services, thereby obscuring profit drivers.
- *Globalisation.* Lead times across global supply chains, inventory levels, and material availability.

The more that these objectives and complexity characteristics apply to an organisation, the more likely it is that they should consider moving to a more mature planning model.

Planning and Forecasting Maturity Levels

The maturity of planning and forecasting processes is driven by the level of model integration. As models become more integrated, they support faster processes that yield greater forward visibility and reduce uncertainty. Figure 2-3 outlines two broad categories that comprise our maturity model: fragmented and integrated planning approaches.

Figure 2-3: Fragmented and Integrated Planning Approaches

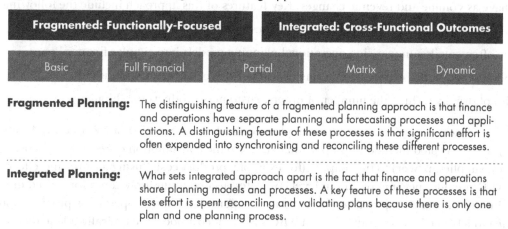

Fragmented: Functionally-Focused		Integrated: Cross-Functional Outcomes		
Basic	Full Financial	Partial	Matrix	Dynamic

Fragmented Planning: The distinguishing feature of a fragmented planning approach is that finance and operations have separate planning and forecasting processes and applications. A distinguishing feature of these processes is that significant effort is often expended into synchronising and reconciling these different processes.

Integrated Planning: What sets integrated approach apart is the fact that finance and operations share planning models and processes. A key feature of these processes is that less effort is spent reconciling and validating plans because there is only one plan and one planning process.

These approaches can be further broken down into five stages of planning and forecasting maturity: basic planning, financial integration, partial integration, matrix planning, and dynamic planning. A key feature that separates each of these stages is the type of driver-based planning approach that it employs. Being driver-based means that variables affecting performance or resources can be related to one another. The dependencies between the variables can be modelled. For example, production costs could be related to volume made, which in turn could be related to sales success, and so on. By entering a few numbers, the planning model can make use of these relationships to predict future results. As driver-based planning becomes more mature, organisations are also able to support more sophisticated scenario planning.

Basic Planning

At this stage, organisations employ traditional bottom up budgeting approaches that are augmented by very basic models. These models are typically based on financial relationships where a planning line is expressed as a per cent of another line item or period. The following are examples of this:

- Sales are expressed as a per cent increase or decrease over the prior year.
- Cost of sales is expressed as a per cent of sales.
- Expenses (for example, salaries and travel) are expressed using either approach.
- Cash flow is expressed as per cent of receivables and payables.

The following are some the classic characteristics of these models:

- Any analysis that supports them is often maintained in off line systems or spread sheets.
- Operational reconcilliation is done on an ad hoc basis, if it is done at all.
- There is a loose connection between objectives, targets, budgets, and forecasts.

The effectiveness of these models depends on the complexity of the business. For smaller and less complex organisations, they may support all of the analysis required. However, as complexity rises, these models are not as useful because they are not accurate and they do not support consensus.

Financial Integration

The financial integration stage is one where organisations use operationally-based driver models that estimate how costs behave as volume and revenue changes. Key features of this approach include the following:

- The role of finance is to determine which drivers best quantify the impact of changes.
- This role often entails summarising operational planning models into simpler financial ones.
- The models are typically expressed in terms of cost per driver or per unit of output.
- Examples of drivers include the number of orders, customers products, or shipments.

These models are typically developed for financial planning and cost estimating purposes only. Activity-based costing (ABC) is the accepted method to proportionately trace the consumption of resource expenses (for example, wages, supplies, power) to the outputs (for example, product costs) using a cause-and-effect relationship. ABC provides per unit of output level cost rates needed to multiply times forecasted unit of output volume quantities to calculate projected resource capacity expenses. Although operations provide input into developing the models, the level of granularity of ABC's activity cost pools are typically adequate for strategic insights by having high cost accuracy, but may not be sufficiently detailed to enable operational managers to make operational decisions.

Gary Cokins, co-author of this book, has written a popular book, *Activity-Based Cost Management: An Executive Guide,* that explains how to construct, implement, and apply ABC for strategic and operational analysis, projections, and decision support.

At this stage, many organisations start using balanced scorecards and other performance measurement approaches. However, target setting, budgeting, forecasting, and scenario planning processes are only loosely connected. This is primarily because the planning models are not sophisticated enough to connect KPI targets to resource requirements.

In organisations that experience little change or variability, these models can be very effective. However, more complex ones often experience the following:

- Maintaining models can be time consuming, often resulting in models that are inaccurate.
- Embedded operational assumptions are often only valid across a narrow range of scenarios.
- Models often have to be manually updated to examine the impact of outlying scenarios.
- As a result, organisations can only run a limited number of scenarios, thereby exposing them to potentially unidentified risks.
- Scenario planning can be costly, as significant time and effort goes into validating and reconcilling financial and operational scenario planning efforts.

Partial Integration

At this stage, finance and operations start sharing models and processes in parts of the organisation. Other parts continue to operate processes at level 1 and 2. They do this because it

- reduces the cost of processes and systems.
- results in greater clarity because there is only one plan.
- supports more effective scenario planning in these parts of the business.
- provides greater forward visibility into risk as a result of scenario planning.
- improves process speed by eliminating non-value added activities.

This stage of planning maturity can take many forms. Demand planning is a classic example of where a single model can be used to support more effective processes. The manufacturing sector has led the way in leveraging such integrated models that, at a basic level, provide the means to connect the number of units sold to revenue and average selling price. Beyond that, they enable organisations to

- establish more collaborative demand and revenue planning processes.
- automate the analysis of volume and mix variances on revenue and average selling price.
- support a more effective rolling forecast process that adapts faster to change.
- co-ordinate new product development and promotion planning into demand and revenue forecasting.

Manufacturing has also led the way in developing models that integrate planning of direct costs or cost of sales. Planning bills of materials are used to define the commodities and components of the products they sell and how they are made. This results in a process that simultaneously forecasts

- cost of goods manufactured and sold, together with inventory balances.
- production capacity requirements, together with capacity constraints.
- commodity purchase requirements and related cash flow impact.
- purchase price and production cost variances from standard.

From an indirect perspective, integrated models translate KPI targets, along with departmental volume into the following:

- Staffing requirements
- Departmental budgets and forecasts
- Productivity (cost per outcome) targets

Multiple planning models and systems still exist for organisations at this stage of maturity.

Matrix Planning

At this stage of maturity, organisations shift from traditional functionally-based planning approaches to more horizontal cross-functional and outcome-based approaches. To support this, finance and operations share models and processes across the organisation. The following are key features of this stage:

- Profit and cash flow forecasting is explicitly linked to KPI and revenue targets
- Plans are expressed from both functional and process perspectives

- Budgets and forecasts are expressed in relative terms (cost per output)
- Planning and target setting cuts across functions and BUs

One of the key reasons that organisations shift to such an approach is to optimise performance across functions and BUs. In so doing, they are also recognising the limitations of traditional budgeting processes because they reinforce functional silos and thereby sub optimise performance.

Dynamic Planning

Organisations employ highly sophisticated models that integrate all aspects of planning and forecasting at this stage of maturity. One of the primary motives for doing so is to enable organisations to more effectively manage complexity, uncertainty, and risk, a key component of which is more effective scenario planning.

These organisations also conduct integrated scenario planning. This includes the ability to simultaneously evaluate the impact of different scenarios on all aspects of performance. Four specific capabilities arise at this level of maturity:

- Dynamic models that self-adjust to changes in volume and mix
- Forward looking (activity-based) product and customer profitability and cash flows
- Capacity constrained cash flows, whereby models forecast capacity constraints, along with their impact on cash
- Project and portfolio return on investment whereby models quantify the impact of operational changes on the cash flow of project portfolios

As mentioned earlier, the levels of planning maturity described can be used to assess where an organisation is today and the level at which it needs to be.

As we come to the end of this chapter, we recognise that the reader can be easily overwhelmed by the array of methods that all seem to point to an idealistic approach to planning. It's an approach that seems to be devoid of internal politics, where everyone is working for the good of the organisation, and there is ample time in which plans can be carefully crafted. In the last part of the chapter we looked at the levels of planning maturity that organisation's achieve, irrespective of their chosen management methodology.

The reason for doing this is to show that planning is a complex topic and more than just predicting a set of numbers on future performance. However one thing that is missing is in explaining just how does an organisation go about putting a more focused plan together? Well that's something we will do starting at Chapter 4 'Business Planning Framework', but before then we need to cover the role of planning technology which is the subject of the next chapter.

Endnotes

1 Marvin Bower, *Perspective on McKinsey*, 1977.

3

PLANNING TECHNOLOGIES

Technology has allowed organisations to plan at ever-increasing levels of detail, and the use of e-mail and network capabilities means that managers at all levels can be involved. However, with these capabilities come problems that can derail the very plans they were meant to enable.

SUPPORTING THE DECISION-MAKING PROCESS

Because of today's complex and fast changing business environment, technology plays a key role in the development and tracking of plans. There is just too much data to consider and people involved to rely on intuition or gut feel. Imagine for a moment communicating with customers but without the use of email or a website. Other methods could be employed but the speed and cost efficiency of Internet based technologies create significant advantage for those companies that do use them over those that don't.

Since the advent of the spread sheet, which is arguably the most important business tool created, planning models have become a way of life. In just a few minutes, any planner can quickly construct a simple model that shows the amount of resources expenses to be consumed and the revenues that can be expected by month. The results can be embellished with formulae to generate key performance indicators, perform currency conversions, and create consolidations of different departments. Reports can then be presented to management in the form of grids, tables, and charts.

The spread sheet has transformed planning, or rather, it has transformed the way numbers can be generated, massaged, transposed, redefined, accumulated, and presented. In the past, planners had to rely on manual tabulations or complex computer languages to compute totals and associated ratios, but today a spread sheet can perform all of these tasks easily and without the need for specialist staff.

So it is with other planning systems. All hold the promise of streamlining the planning process through the creation of models that try to mimic the business world. These models are then able to predict what may happen in the future based on a number of assumptions about the market and the anticipated relationships between business processes, inputs, and outcomes.

Streamlining the generation of numbers has given planners a number of benefits, including the following:

- Quickly assessing a range of likely outputs that reflect changing assumptions. By doing this management can be made aware of likely consequences and be prepared should they happen.

- Helping managers to focus on the future, rather than on the past. Models are there to predict what could happen and what needs to be done if the desired performance is to be realised.

- Challenging current business processes. They help management to think through the company operating structure, the drivers of risk and value, and the funding that will be necessary. They provide a concise, logical view that can be contested and ultimately proved, through which the organisation can learn more about the way it operates.

Just one word of caution—no matter how sophisticated a model becomes, it can never reflect the true complexity of the world in which we operate. Models are poor substitutes for reality which is subject to a range of unknowable forces that cannot be codified. However, their true value is in assessing changes to the organisation's business processes. In other words, their purpose is to support business decisions.

It was in the 1960s that decision making became more of a science with Ronald Howard, a Stanford University professor, coining the term *decision analysis*. He was instrumental in developing practices and tools in support of organisational decision making that recognises the world is neither rational nor predictable.

In *The Rational Manager: A Systematic Approach to Problem Solving and Decision-Making,*[1] published in 1965, the decision-making process was defined as the following set of management processes:

1. Establish objectives first.

2. Classify objectives and place in order of importance.

3. Develop alternative options.

4. Evaluate alternative options against all of the objectives.

5. Make a tentative decision based on the option most likely to achieve all of the objectives.

6. Evaluate the chosen option against potential consequences.

7. Implement the chosen option and additional actions required to prevent any adverse consequences from becoming problems.

To adopt a consistent, systematic approach, decision making requires organisations to use planning systems that are able to model their business processes in sufficient detail, and that can provide a number of analytical capabilities that support the seven steps previously mentioned. For many organisations this will mean moving away from using spread sheets as their primary modelling language to more robust software applications.

Eventually decision analysis will advance to decision management, relying on business rules including algorithms as promoted by James Taylor (www.decisionmanagementsolutions.com), but that is in the future.

PLANNING TECHNOLOGIES: THE SPREAD SHEET

When using any technology to plan, the organisation must first be translated into the world of the chosen planning solution. With spread sheets this world consists of three dimensions: sheets, rows, and columns. Typically, sheets are used to represent the organisation structure, columns are used to show version and time, and rows represent accounts. To these, cell formulae and macros add business intelligence such as the calculation of sub-totals, Key Performance Indicators (KPIs), and currency conversions.

Business intelligence in this context applies to the way in which relationships are defined to transform raw data into meaningful and useful information for decision making. For example, the cell containing the measure 'gross profit' is calculated by subtracting the cells that represent 'direct costs' and 'total revenues'. Similarly, the cell representing the measure 'net profit' is derived by subtracting the cell that has the total of all related expenses, which itself has to be calculated, from the cell containing 'net profit' that has been previously calculated. From this management can decide whether the level of profit was adequate, and if not, what areas (that is, revenue or costs) are responsible.

When it comes to consolidating results from different processes or departments, assuming they have been set up as separate sheets, then multiple cell formulae will need to be defined that accumulate the cells from all of the measures on those departmental spread sheets. Of course not all of these formula will be simple additions, as those that calculate ratios will need to be recalculated at the summary level.

Calculations like these are easy to write, but given the number of them that need to be written and checked for anything but the smallest of organisations, the sheer volume becomes unmanageable. If we then start to add complexity in the form of currency conversions, cash flow, and balance sheet calculations that need to take into account prior periods, and dealing with lines of business, the resulting spread sheets become a major liability in that you cannot be sure the numbers are adding up correctly. This is only made worse as they are modified to cope with new requirements.

The problems caused by a spread sheet are down to fundamental flaws in their design when applied to organisational planning. These flaws are outlined in the following sections.

Two or Three Dimensional

As already mentioned, spread sheets are made up of rows, columns, and individual spread sheets that are used to represent the different elements of an organisation. However, organisations are not three dimensional; at a minimum they have at least five dimensions: department, measure, version, period, and year. (We will explain the concept of dimensions shortly, so just bear with us for the time being.) If an organisation also wants to plan by line of business, or by product and customer, then the number of business dimensions has just increased to eight.

In order to handle this level of detail, either the rows, columns, or spread sheets must represent more than one dimension. So typically an annual plan will consists of rows representing measures and another dimension (for example, sales being subdivided into customers, products, and lines of business). Columns will be used to represent periods, years, and version (quite often there is a comparison to last year actual when collecting next year's plan). Of course these dimensions can be presented differently, but the point here is that the rules need to be carefully managed, as inserting any new rows, columns, and spread sheets could have a major impact on any rules already defined. This brings us to the next point.

Cell Meaning

All data held in a spread sheet is typically referenced by an intersection of row, column, and spread sheet. A particular cell reference 'C23' has no particular meaning; it is only by applying rules or macros that the content of any cell takes on its meaning. (It is true that Microsoft's Excel software has the capability to define range names that can then be used in rules, however this facility involves a high degree of maintenance and cannot be used to track how Excel calculates a particular value.)

Using cell references in formulae are fine when the system is dealing with a relatively simple analysis, such as displaying the profit and loss (P&L) statement for a single company for one year. However, when the data has to deal with multiple companies, with multiple versions of the data (actual, budget, forecast) over multiple years and a mixture of balance sheets, P&L, and statistical accounts, then controlling the meaning of a particular cell and the way it should be treated within a calculation becomes increasingly difficult.

For example, calculating a variance or adding up accounts over time requires knowledge about the account type in order to create the correct formula. Balance sheet accounts cannot be accumulated over time. Creating a budget or actual variance with P&L accounts is not a simple subtraction because you need to know whether the account is a debit or credit. Copying formulae between types will give the wrong answer, so it is not even safe to drag formulae between rows and columns.

If a new row or column is inserted to cope with a new service or product line, there is a real danger that the rule logic will be compromised. If you are lucky, you will get a '#VALUE' error message to let you know there is an issue. If you are unlucky, the error will go undetected until a crucial decision is taken and the error becomes apparent.

Limited Business View

Spread sheets only hold one view of the data, unless that data is duplicated via cell links. This view is fixed by determining what the rows and columns represent when first setting it up. For example, columns may be set up horizontally as time periods, with accounts displayed vertically as rows and the different sheets that represent departments. Of course you can mix dimensions such as displaying actual and budget values within a particular time period as columns.

The way the spread sheet is laid out gives you one view of the business. But what if you want a different view from the way the data was collected? For example, the budget or cash forecast will typically be entered with the columns representing each period next year. However, when reporting actual results, we will want to pick up just one of those budget periods (the current period) and then compare it with actual and forecast results. Of course things are never simple, as the forecast month that is picked will change each month and so any cell references to the original budget will have to change.

What if you want to analyse expenses by market sector or by product? To do this requires a different view of the data, where row and columns represent different items, but that involves either duplicating content or creating a large number of error-prone cell links to switch the data around.

Single User

Single user means that only one person can update the contents of a spread sheet file at a time. That is not a problem for personal use, but when used as an enterprise application where data is to be collected and consolidated from across the organisation, this presents a major problem. To get around this limitation, spread sheets are typically split into multiple files so that users are provided with just their portion of the data for updating. However, even with small organisations, the number of spread sheets can rapidly increase to tens or even hundreds of files.

This proliferation of files now causes its own maintenance and control issues. For example, if you give someone a spread sheet to fill in a budget or forecast, how do you know that the version they send to you is the latest one, and that it has the same contents as the one they are viewing now? The short answer is you do not know, as you cannot control when they are no longer allowed to change values entered and what version they send to you.

Similarly, if you want to consolidate the answers, you will need a spread sheet that links to all of the other spread sheets to get the latest data. However, if that latest data is not actually the latest data (and you would not know), the integrity of the consolidated result is always in question. What happens if you issue a new spread sheet with new rules or accounts? What happens if they do not use that version? For these reasons version control becomes an unmanageable nightmare.

Lack of Workflow Capabilities

Most planning applications require a distinct set of operations to be carried out in a set order. For example, in a manufacturing company, there is no point in planning for the purchase of raw materials and components until after the sales forecast has been entered and approved. In modelling terms, the amount of sales is the independent variable and its required purchases are the dependent variable. As previously mentioned, when a forecast has been generated it should not be changed until the next round of planning. Similarly, data on current actual expenses should be loaded before we ask departments to review and forecast expenses into future periods.

The order in which things take place needs to be carefully controlled and orchestrated so that everyone knows what they need to do and when. Those overseeing the process need to know what the status is and where there may be capacity constraining 'bottlenecks' that are holding up production throughput located elsewhere in the chain. None of these capabilities exist within a spread sheet-based system.

As mentioned earlier, these limitations are caused by the fundamental architecture of a spread sheet, and they are the direct cause of a number of major issues when used for enterprise planning and reporting. Issues like these will lead to wrong results, many of which will go undetected. So why do organisations still use spread sheets? In our and other surveys, it is estimated that around 50 per cent of organisations still use them for planning. Part of the reason may simply be due to their availability, low cost, and apparent ease of use, although these last two reasons are easily refuted in anything but the smallest of organisations. The reason could be due to the lack of knowledge about modern planning systems. It is true that in the past planning systems were expensive and complex, but as you will see in chapter 11, "Latest Developments in Planning and Analytics Technologies," things have changed quite a bit over the past few years. Affordable software is available.

PLANNING TECHNOLOGIES: MULTI-DIMENSIONAL DATABASES

In response to the limitations imposed by spread sheets and other two- or three-dimensional planning applications, specialist software vendors working in the 1970s developed the concept of the multi-dimensional database. These can be viewed as being spread sheet-like in that they can display data in the same way as a spread sheet, but underneath there are some fundamental differences that make them ideal for building complex planning and reporting models.

Multi-Dimensional

Figure 3-1: Schematic of a Multi-Dimensional Planning Cube

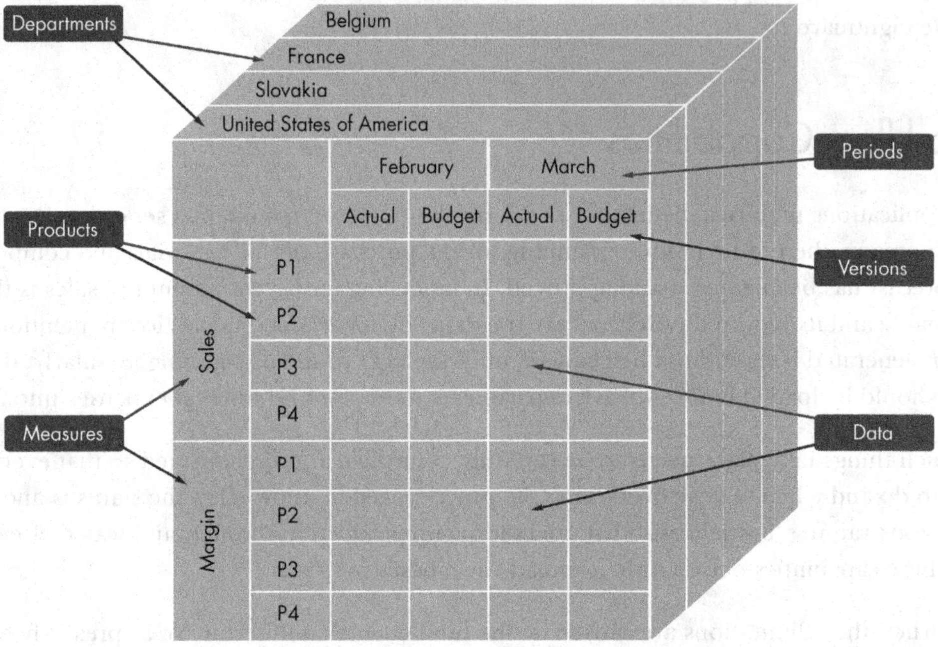

Multi-dimensional planning systems are set up in terms of the business dimensions to be modelled. This will almost certainly include the organisation structure, the accounts used to plan and report results, the time periods to be covered (for example, weekly, monthly, season), the years, the versions of data to be held (for example, actual, budget, forecast), any line of business or major product grouping, and so on.

Each of these business dimensions is defined separately and uses common user-recognisable names. It is the intersection of these dimensions that defines a particular value (for example, actual sales of product P1 by department United States of America in March 2012). Figure 3-1 provides an example of how a multi-dimensional database holds data. Each underlined item is a member of a different business dimension, which in this example includes the version, measure, product, department, month, and year.

New dimensions and members can be added at any time by simply defining them to the system. These new members are then automatically available for planning.

When it comes to reporting, different slices of the database can be selected and displayed (figure 3-2). These views, as they are known, access the same database and so data is not duplicated.

In order to display these views on a two-dimensional screen or paper, the different dimensions are selected to form the columns and rows of the report. These dimensions are then known as the on grid dimensions, which can also be nested, so that, for example, versions can be displayed for each period being shown on the report. The remaining dimensions of the model are then known as the off grid dimensions and can be used to control what data is selected for the on grid dimensions. This is exactly the same concept as when using pivot tables in Excel.

Not all members need to be displayed and so they can be restricted to what makes sense for the report being produced.

Figure 3-2A: Different Views of the Same Multi-Dimensional Cube

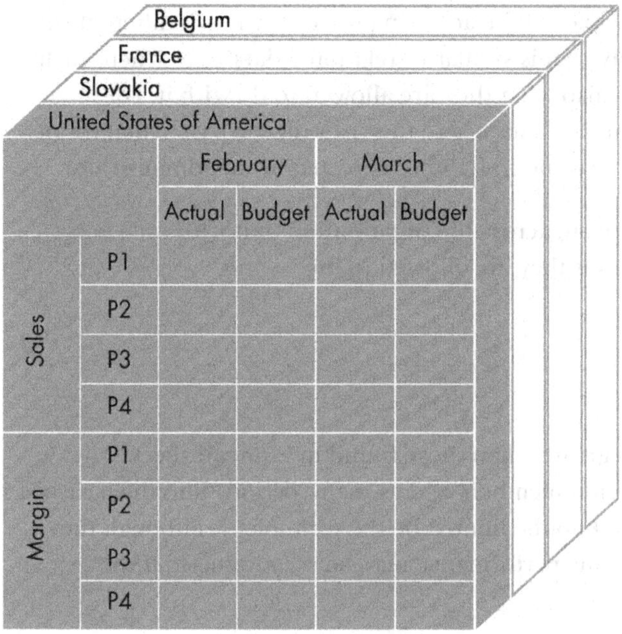

Figure 3-2B: Different Views of the Same Multi-Dimensional Cube

Slice 1

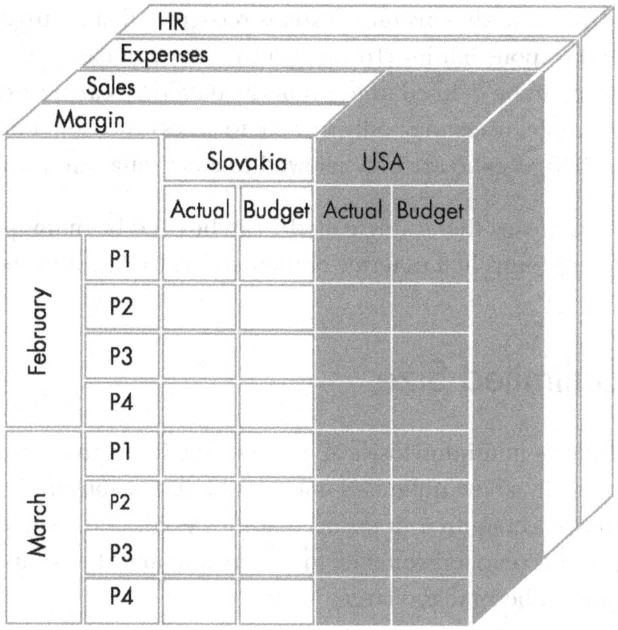

Slice 2

As well as providing fixed reports, analytical reports can be set up to allow the users to swap the rows and columns of the report. This enables them to view performance from a range of business perspectives without having to duplicate the data or ask for new reports to be developed.

Business Hierarchies

Unlike Excel pivot tables, dimension members in a multi-dimensional database can be arranged as one of more hierarchies. For example, the total company member can be defined as the aggregation of four divisions, which themselves can be defined as the aggregation of other departments. These hierarchies can then be used to consolidate data from those entities at the bottom of the structure to give intermediate consolidated results.

Some of the more advanced systems can store multiple hierarchies. For example, this year and last year's organisation structure can be displayed. This then enables results from last year to be consolidated according to this year's structure and still preserve results in last year's format.

Name-Based Rules

Rules can be defined for each member of a business dimension. This typically happens on the measures dimension where rules can be set up to calculate sub-totals and ratios. These rules can access members in other dimensions and at different hierarchy levels, allowing the creation of allocation rules that span multiple structures. What makes these rules different from a spread sheet is that each rule uses specific member names, so users and administrators alike can easily understand what is being calculated. It also means that as new members are added, existing rules do not change and the integrity of results is preserved.

Multi-User, Role-Based Security

Most multi-dimensional systems recognise that a range of people will be accessing them, each with different roles and responsibilities. To support this, the database has security that is similar to relational databases where each user can be defined in terms of the data they can access, and also what they are allowed to do with it. For example, users may only be able to access their own department's data where they can review past actual results or budgets and are only allowed to enter data into future forecast periods, when directed by an administrator.

This means that a single model can be used by many people from across the organisation, but with each person being controlled in terms of their access to data and the features they are allowed to use.

Unlimited Size

Today's multi-dimensional models have limits that are much greater than those found in a spread sheet. They typically allow unlimited numbers of dimensions and dimension members and as many periods into the past and future as required. It means that the design of the system need not be limited by the technology, although they may become too complex to understand and the computing time performance may be compromised if the models become too large.

Financial Intelligence

Some of the more sophisticated multi-dimensional databases have built-in financial intelligence. This intelligence relates to the way in which measures that represent finance values are treated for consolidation, when aggregating time periods, or when used within a formula.

To invoke this intelligence, financial measures will require attributes that identify the following:

- Their natural sign (for example, debit or credit). This allows cash outflows such as expenses to be shown as a positive number and yet will be subtracted when being summed with a revenue number to calculate a net position.

- The type of account (for example, is it a balance sheet measure such as 'cash at bank', a P&L measure such as expenses, or is it a statistical value such as staff numbers). These types have significant implications when consolidating data. For example, when aggregating monthly data into quarters, you cannot just add up all of the cash at bank items for each month. The cash at bank value is whatever was there at the end of the last month, although the expense items must be summed. Similarly, measures such as staff numbers cannot be translated into a base currency. Ratios will need to be recalculated at consolidated levels, and other calculated measures, such as revenue = number of units sold × price, must be calculated at a department level and then consolidated.

- Financial measures (for example, what type of exchange rate is to be used when converting from local to base currency; is it the average, opening, or closing rate). Where subtotals are derived from measures that are converted at different rates (for example, closing stock value = opening stock value + additions − sales), an exchange gain or loss will occur so the system can be directed on what to do with the difference in the converted value.

Having this built-in financial intelligence greatly simplifies the set-up of calculation rules. Rules do not have to test the type of measure as this will be done automatically by the system. This ensures that calculations are performed in the right way and at the right time. For this reason alone, errors in setting up rules are far less likely.

Spread Sheet Access

In general, users like spread sheets. They like the formatting, charting, and note making capabilities but they dislike the limitations covered earlier. Fortunately, Microsoft has given Excel the ability to view and manipulate data within multi-dimensional databases that support the OLAP standard (OLAP is short for On-Line Analytical Processing and is sometimes used in reference to a multi-dimensional database). This means users can create reports where they can decide which dimensions make up the rows and columns on the spread sheet.

Data is filtered in two ways. First, Excel respects the database security system and so will only allow users to view data that has been assigned to them. Second, users themselves can filter out what is displayed on the report. To the data that is displayed, users can then add normal spread sheet formulae, formatting, charts, and colour coded exceptions. This means that anything Excel can do with data stored inside a spread sheet, it can do with a supported, external database.

It is important to stress here that the data is coming from the multi-dimensional database, which means as data gets updated in the model, the results in the spread sheet reports are also updated.

MULTI-DIMENSIONAL SYSTEM ISSUES

Given these capabilities, you may wonder why multi-dimensional databases are not universally employed for modelling. This isn't due to a lack of marketing effort where many millions have been spent on promoting such solutions. Similarly, it's probably not due to a lack of awareness as many leading analyst firms such as Gartner continually track and publish reviews on software vendors that produce multidimensional planning applications.

In our experience there are a number of issues that prevent their widespread use.

Comprehension

The first issue is one of comprehension. Just getting your head around multi-dimensional views can be a bit of a challenge if you have not come across the concept before. With spread sheets you can see the structure of three dimensions—rows, columns, spread sheets—but after that the dimensions have to be imagined. Although Excel now has pivot tables that simulate some aspects of multi-dimensionality (for example, dynamic swapping of rows and columns with business dimensions), they still fall a long way short of what a true multi-dimensional database does.

It is interesting to note that back in the early 1990s, Lotus (later acquired by IBM) introduced a multi-dimensional spread sheet called Improv. This involved the use of names for defining measures and rules, which could also be grouped into different categories that could represent years, products, and departments in the same way as multi-dimensional systems do today. It still made use of cells as in a normal spread sheet, but these were only used to enter and view data and not to store data as in a conventional spread sheet.

Lotus Improv was a powerful tool but it did not take off. This is because many users just did not understand how to approach the building of models that have multiple dimensions. For example, when using a spread sheet you tend to start with what the report looks like, including the mix of the different dimensions on the page after which you can start to add the business rules by making reference to what is on the screen. Multi-dimensional models typically cannot be built this way. You need to first define the business dimensions and the relevant members before you can place them on a report page. Business rules are defined by going back to the dimensions definition and cannot be accessed from the report layout.

Complexity

The second area of concern is the apparent complexity of multi-dimensional databases. Some of this complexity is due to a misunderstanding of the concepts of multi-dimensionality as previously mentioned, but others are due to the age of some systems being offered by vendors.

Many of the systems around today still require some knowledge of information technology (IT) as they abound in the use of IT terms (OnLine Analytical Processing or OLAP for short, Extract, Transform and Load more commonly referred to as ETL), and in some cases model rules have to be written in a language known as MDX (MultiDimensional eXpression), which can be difficult for non-IT users to learn. The underlying technology also comes in a range of flavours such as relational star schema, multi-cube, in-memory, or hybrid, each with their own particular merits depending on what kind of model is to be built. These flavours then determine the way that user access profiles or backup procedures are set up, which may require an in-depth knowledge of the underlying database technology.

Some will require other software components to deliver a complete solution. For example, most will provide reporting as an optional extra, and few provide any form of process management.

Things are improving, particularly with the introduction of cloud-based solutions (see chapter 11, "Latest Developments in Planning and Analytics Technologies," for more details), but most systems available today still require a good knowledge of the IT infrastructure in which a model is to be built and accessed by users.

Data Uniformity

The third area of concern that has challenged multi-dimensional systems is that problems to be solved must have some degree of data uniformity. This means they must be described in terms of common dimensions and members that are then deemed to apply to all other dimensions and members. For example, defining the year dimension to have the members 2012, 2013, and 2014 means that these years apply to all versions of data, all departments, and all measures. This is because the cube created by the multi-dimensional database assumes that all dimension or member combinations apply to all others.

With the years example this is not a problem, but this is not always the case. For example, sales may be collected by product and customer as well as by operating unit, but balance sheet items such as fixed assets will not. Similarly, some expenses may only be assignable to the operating unit and have no connection with either products or customers. To store these values in a multi-dimensional database requires the set-up of members in both the customer and product dimensions which are basically ignored, but whose reference must be given when accessing the value in a formula.

There are ways around this problem, but the resulting solution can be more complex to set up. Recent developments in multi-cube and star-schema architectures have helped to alleviate this problem, but they are only typically found in the newer systems.

Effort and Price

The last area of issue is the administrative effort involved in setting up a multi-dimensional system. Unlike a spread sheet where Microsoft Excel is dominant (or at least sets the standards that other spread sheet vendors follow), there are different vendors offering different products at different levels of capability.

Most of these are relatively expensive to buy and typically involve an up-front purchase price that depends on the number of users, an annual maintenance fee that is around 10–20 per cent of the software purchase price, training costs for administrators that can run into weeks, and an implementation fee where the vendor helps to design the initial model that can cost as much as the software fee. These costs provide a formidable barrier for organisations that have never used multi-dimensional systems.

The good news is that prices have been coming down and are likely to fall more as multi-dimensional software becomes more of a commodity product. More and more vendors now offer these systems as a service commonly known as Software as a Service (SaaS), where systems are rented rather than purchased. Microsoft has started to do this with their popular Office suite that avoids up-front costs and allows new users to try out the system before committing the company to an on-going level of expense.

For most of this book we will remain technology agnostic. That is, we will be describing the suggested planning models in terms that can be implemented with a range of solutions including a spread sheet, although the latter will challenge developers due to the inherent weaknesses that were outlined earlier.

MODELLING TOOLS

Most specialised planning systems come with a range of tools that can speed up the way in which plan data is generated. These tools are more than a set of rules that you would find in a spread sheet. They include a number of techniques that are often marketed as being essential for planning. They can be applied as required (that is, they do not have to be thought about when building a model), and can be used in combination with other tools.

Some of the more common tools and the buzzwords that go with them include the following:

- *Extrapolation.* This is where the system employs statistical techniques to analyse historic trends in the data and use them as the projection basis for automatically generating a forecast. The more sophisticated systems allow users to select the extrapolation method (for example, the use of least squares to fit the data to a set pattern) and whether or not to ignore abnormal exceptions, known as outliers.
- *Allocations.* Cost allocations are used to take a value and apportion it across the organisation according to existing values. For example, the cost of the human resources (HR) department is sometimes seen as something that should be shared by all departments based on the number of staff each have. To calculate this, the cost allocation module must first capture the expenses of HR and the total number of people in the organisation, excluding those in HR. The system will then create a value in a selected measure (typically referred to as cost allocation factor) for each department except HR, which is calculated as:

$$Allocated\ Cost = \frac{Number\ of\ staff\ in\ department}{Total\ number\ of\ staff} \times Total\ expense\ of\ HR$$

Ideally, this calculation should use activity-based costing (ABC) as the method to proportionately trace and assign the consumption of the resource expenses into calculated costs based on a cause-and-effect relationship. This provides higher cost accuracy and visibility to the drivers of costs. Most software vendors offer ABC features. Alternatively, commercial ABC software can be integrated with the financial system.

- *Spread.* This is a short cut method of entering a series of data, typically into the periods of a year. For example, by entering an annual amount the system is then apportioned into each period. The method of apportion can usually be chosen from a range of profiles (for example, 4–4–5, which says the last month in a set of 3 is to have an additional amount). The apportionment can be spread evenly across all periods, or it can be based on values that already exist (for example, sales volume to be sold).

- *Bottom up or top down.* This relates to how data is to be entered. Bottom up refers to departments at the lowest level entering values that are then consolidated to give a total company position. Top down is where a value is entered at a total level for a selected measure, which is then apportioned to all the units that consolidate to it. The apportionment is typically done in proportion to the existing values.

- *Goal seek.* Goal seek allows a user to select a particular measure that is typically a function of other measures at a consolidated level. The value that the user desires is entered and the supporting measures that can be changed are also selected. The system then works back through any calculations and consolidations, amending the selected measures in proportion to one another, in order to achieve the set target. If the target cannot be met, a warning is given.

This type of analysis can be quite sophisticated as it may require several consolidations in order to achieve the target. For example, setting a contribution level of 30 per cent may involve buying more materials that in turn may increase direct costs due to additional storage being required, and at the same time lessening the purchase price because of volume discounts. This type of analysis may also cause circular references, which the more sophisticated systems are able to detect and solve through the use of simultaneous equations.

- *Lock.* In addition to the previously mentioned techniques, some systems allow users to lock values from being changed. For example, when performing a spread, extrapolation, or allocation, selected measures can be marked so that the system knows it cannot change these values. Similarly, if some of the data is there for reference (for example, displaying last month's actual results while collecting a forecast), this can also be locked against the change.

- *Thresholds.* The more sophisticated systems allow the setting of thresholds on measures. That is, the measure can be changed but there are lower and upper limits that cannot be exceeded. This is useful when modelling things like production capacity, as there will be limits on what can be produced in any given time period.

- *Approval process.* This last tool is more of a system capability that can be applied to when and how data can be changed. For example, when setting budgets it is quite common to allow data to be entered by users for a set period of time, during which they can submit their final numbers for approval. Once done, they can no longer enter or change data—they are effectively locked out.

Those users designated as approvers will now be able to review what was entered and either approve or reject the submission. Rejected submissions are usually unlocked so that users can make changes in order to comply with any directive, after which they are resubmitted and relocked against further change.

This completes Section 1 of the book where we set out to provide a background to the state of planning within organisations. We have looked at the challenges managers face generated by the business environment, and outlined some of the more popular management methodologies that are employed to overcome the issues faced. And in this chapter we have touched on the role of technology and the capabilities of modern planning solutions.

We are now going to build on this foundation in Section 2 by focusing on what types of planning models an organisation requires and how they can be put together in an efficient and effective framework that truly helps organisations manage performance.

Endnotes

1 *The Rational Manager: A Systematic Approach to Problem Solving and Decision-Making*. Charles H. Kepner, Benjamin B. Tregoe. McGraw-Hill, June 1965.

Section 2

BUSINESS PLANNING FRAMEWORK

4

BUSINESS PLANNING FRAMEWORK

The framework we are about to describe provides organisations with a holistic way of planning and managing performance that links resources to workload and the achievement of business objectives.

LOGICAL OVERVIEW OF THE FRAMEWORK

Back in chapter 1, 'Planning Fundamentals', we established that the role of planning was to achieve an organisation's purpose by managing what can be controlled within an uncontrollable and unknowable external environment. As a direct consequence of this, the focus of the planning framework is on cross-functional business processes, resources, and outcomes and how they link to business objectives.

The framework translates the six views of business processes as shown in figure 1-1, into a set of linked planning models and components (figure 4-1).

Figure 4-1: Key Components of the Planning Framework

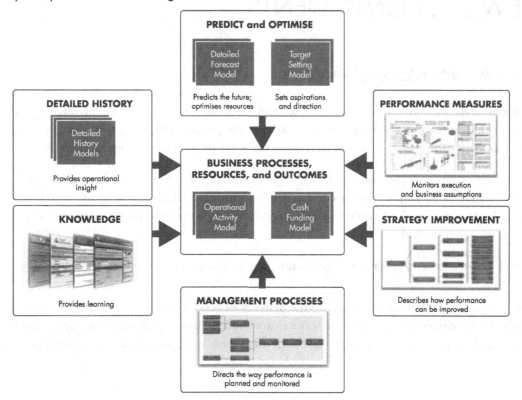

At the heart of the framework is the operational activity model (OAM) that describes an organisation's business processes. This can be used to assess workload and resources required to meet objectives. The model also provides input to the cash funding model (CFM), to determine cash requirements and funding sources.

Around these two models are a series of other models and related components that provide different but linked views of performance

- Detailed history provides backup information on what actually happened
- Performance measures view results in comparison to the external business environment
- Predict and optimise looks at future targets and gathers realistic forecasts
- Strategy improvement assesses and monitors changes to business processes
- Knowledge holds management intuition and insight about the future
- Management processes direct and control those involved in planning and monitoring performance

As also mentioned in chapter 1, 'Planning Fundamentals', these areas are not independent of each other as they each provide a different view of managing performance that must be brought together in context for any decision that is made. Similarly, these areas do not necessarily mean that the individual models shown in the schematic are separate and disconnected physical models, as this will depend on the complexity and size of the organisation.

In the rest of this chapter we will present an overview of each area, while chapters 5–10 will go into practical details of how these models and components are set up. In these descriptions we have tried to keep the planning framework technology agnostic, but we will keep in mind the capabilities of modern planning technologies as discussed in chapter 3, 'Planning Technologies'.

FRAMEWORK COMPONENTS

Operating Activity Model (OAM)

The central focus of the planning framework is on business processes. These typically involve departmental activities that work together in generating outcomes to meet the purpose of the organisation. In doing so, these business processes will consume resources, which could be in the form of knowledge or finances.

It is only by managing business processes and their related activities that things get done, and only by monitoring their effect along with the resources deployed can informed decisions be made with regard to future performance. This monitoring can involve real-time decisions based on useful information and an approach that is forward-looking, not historical.

The end-to-end business processes for any organisation can be grouped into core processes and support activities:

- *Core processes* are those that directly relate to the delivery of products or services to the intended customer. This includes how products or services are sourced, developed, manufactured, marketed, sold, delivered, and supported. It is typically these activities where most organisational value is generated.

- *Support activities* are those that enable the organisation to operate legally and in an effective manner. This includes how suppliers and employees are paid, monies collected from customers, the way the organisation is financed, and how it meets its legal and statutory responsibilities.

Sometimes the boundary between a core process and a support activity is not always clear. For instance, meeting satisfactory minimum standards of health and safety fosters compliance with the law (support) but also ensures an orderly production process and maintains commercial brand reputation. The key point to understand is that an organisation needs both types.

Core processes tend to be similar within an industry, but support activities are often common to all organisations. Figure 4-2 provides an example of the high-level activities of our fictious manufacturer that we introduced back in chapter 2 'Planning Methods and Methodologies'.

Figure 4-2: Sample Activities Through Which an Organisation Creates and Supports Value

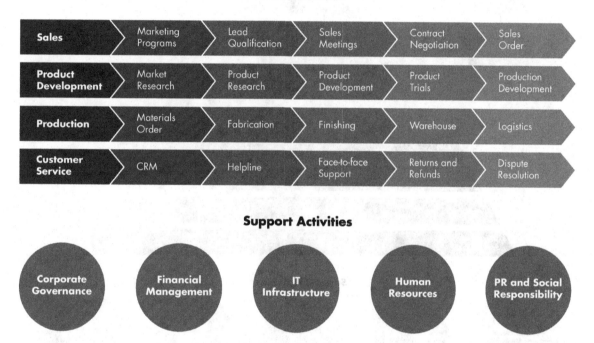

The example in Figure 4-2 shows four core processes, many of which can be expressed as a chain of linked work activities and tasks. The sales process is responsible for the way products or services are promoted, how sales inquiries are handled, and the tasks that lead to a sales order. The product development process is where the organisation ensures it has a pipeline of new products it can sell, which in our example includes tasks for conducting market and product research, through to designing and conducting product trials. The production process is concerned with how raw materials and purchased components are converted or assembled into products that are then delivered to customers. The customer service process determines how the organisation interacts with customers and clients once they have received the products or services.

Supporting these core processes are a number of support activities that include how the organisation ensures regulatory compliance, how it generates funds to operate, the information technology (IT) infrastructure required, and so on. Each support activity has a number of tasks (not shown in the graphic) that may or may not form a chain, however each provides a vital service that enables the core processes to operate effectively.

Not all activities or tasks have to be fulfilled by the organisation. For example, some aspects of production could be outsourced to another company, as could Helpline and IT support functions. Competitive advantage is gained when these activities (for now we will categorise tasks with activities) are either performed more effectively or help to generate a higher level of value for customers.

Activities are typically implemented (or managed when outsourced) by operational departments that have specific responsibility for carrying them out (figure 4-3).

Figure 4-3: Relationship Between Operational and Organisational Departments

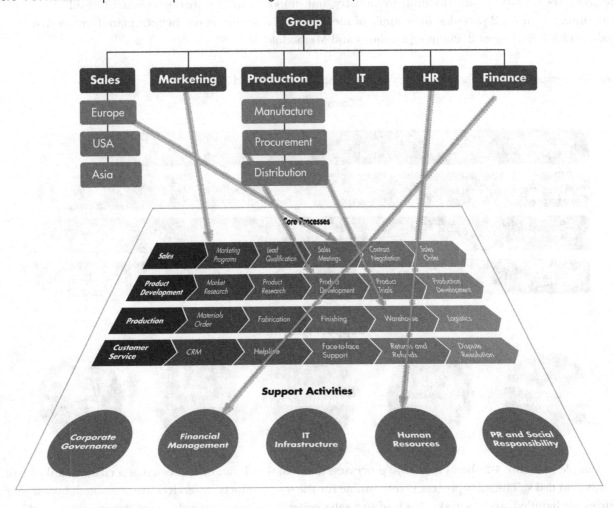

With the preceding information in mind, the OAM is where the relationships between organisational objectives, business process activities, resources, and outcomes are defined. The OAM is comprised of structures that identify business processes and contains a range of measures through which departmental activities and outcomes can be judged. A detailed view of this model is provided in chapter 5, 'Operational Activity Model', along with the steps to follow in its creation.

The OAM holds a number of versions of data that can be used to assess whether the operation is functioning well and whether the resources allocated to activities represent good value. These versions include the following:

- *Target.* This is set by senior management as part of the strategic planning process and establishes the level of performance management desires for a given perceived business environment.

- *Budget.* This is an operational manager response that breaks down strategic targets into shorter-term departmental goals along with the expenses for resources required and the outcomes that are expected.

- *Forecast.* This is the current, realistic outlook that management believes will be delivered if the business processes continue as planned.

- *Actual.* This is taken from the organisation's transaction systems and reliably reports with precision what was achieved.

- *Benchmark.* This final version holds industry or competitor data for some measures and can be used to compare and judge the organisation against the market or peer groups.

These versions are not fixed and may be extended to monitor, for example, best or worst case estimates and comparing multiple scenarios.

Cash Funding Model (CFM)

Sitting alongside the OAM is the CFM. Cash is the life-blood of an organisation that enables business processes to operate. It cannot be ignored. It can be both a resource and an outcome, which from time to time will need to source from outside the operation (for example, when first starting out in business or in funding strategic initiatives).

Businesses typically fail, not through a lack of profit, but through a lack of cash. This disconnect between profit and cash is sometimes due to operational factors like the failure to timely and accurately bill customers or collect cash, and sometimes through strategic factors such as the high cost of entering a market. As a key resource, cash needs to be carefully monitored and managed because once it is spent, it cannot be re-used.

Knowing when cash is available has benefits that can directly impact overall performance. Having a surplus means strategic initiatives can be brought forward. If cash is not going to be available as planned, then decisions can be delayed so that unbudgeted financing costs are avoided. Similarly, maximising the flow and availability of cash can result in securing low rates of bank funding when required, and it can help with lower operational costs by being able to take advantage of bulk buy discounts such as inventory purchases.

When you look at the three financial statements organisations rely on, it could be said that the

- cash flow statement is the most objective as it represents what money has come into an organisation.

- profit and loss income statement is the least objective as it is based on human estimations by applying interpretations of accounting standards.

- balance sheet statements are derived as a result of the estimations of profit, loss, and the truth of cash.

Because of its importance, cash and the source of funds is a key model when planning and monitoring business processes.

Detailed History Models (DHM)

The second area of the planning framework are the detailed history models (DHMs). These provide management with detailed analyses of what actually happened. They can be used to investigate abnormal variances in the OAM, as well as to confirm underlying trends and assumptions that were made when creating forecasts.

For larger, complex organisations the detailed history will probably consist of multiple models, each having a focus on a particular measure. The summary from those models is then transferred to the actual version of corresponding measures in the OAM. For example, a commercial company may have a more detailed history model in which total sales in the OAM are broken down by customer, product, channel, and so on. Similarly, the DHM may contain a list of general ledger transactions behind a departmental expense line that appears in the OAM.

The subject matter of these DHMs and the level of detail are typically determined by the industry and activities being performed by the organisation. Not every measure in the OAM has to have a supporting model. It may be sufficient just to hold actual results within the OAM, with the supporting history models being added over time as required.

Within each DHM, users should be provided with analytical capabilities that allow them to search, filter, and produce additional summaries in different formats for their own investigative purposes. From a technology point of view, these models can be stored in a variety of formats, such as relational, multi-dimensional, and unstructured forms, and can come from external sources as well as internal systems.

DHMs tend to fall into the following categories:

- *Transaction data sets.* These come in the form of a tabular list containing fields that are often unique to each record. Examples include expense transactions or client purchases where the content has come directly from an existing system. In this case, the model can be used to support individual queries on actual results. Capabilities should also exist that allow the data to be summarised, sorted, and filtered.

- *Business intelligence (BI) analytical models.* These store data in a multi-dimensional format that allows users to conduct analyses rather than query individual records. These analyses create cross-tabulations that are able to

  - view data from different business dimensions (for example, show all actual sales for product X by location, or show actual versus budget for all locations by product).
  - compute new measures (for example, the per cent of total sales made for each product or location).
  - identify trends (for example, show the annual average sales growth by period for all locations).
  - show exceptions (for example, show just the top ten products whose actual sales were greater than budget).

  The benefit of a BI model is it provides the user a wide range of analytical capabilities that cannot be produced from a transaction set.

- *Unstructured models.* These models consist of information that is not organised in a predefined manner. In other words, it is not possible to categorise the data in terms of fields or records, as you can with transaction sets and BI models. This data will typically include dates, text, and numeric information, and tends to come in the form of electronic documents, website content, comments, audio, and video. This type of data can be stored and analysed through specialist software that can then be used to back up data within the OAM.

Whatever type of history model is chosen, not all dimensions need to be represented in the OAM. There are cases when the supporting model will have a lot more detail, such as invoice number, customer, product, location, transaction ID, sales representative, and so on. However, there must be a minimum number of key fields that link it directly with the OAM. These keys should include a member of each business dimension used in the OAM, which will typically include measure, department, period, year, and version.

Linking a DHM to the OAM causes designated values to be summarised and transferred so that the number reported in the OAM is exactly the same number as the summary of the detail provided in the supporting model. If a change occurs in a supporting model it should automatically feed through to the respective measures in the OAM.

Target Setting Model (TSM)

The aim of the target setting model (TSM) is to allow senior management to set aspirational goals and strategies for the organisation to achieve in the medium- to long-term. This model will be at a summary level and include a mixture of financial and operational measures. Input will come from current actual and forecast data, typically stored in the OAM, and structures that represent the future operation of the business for a given business environment. The model is also typically driver-based and links operational activities to long-term objectives. This allows management to quickly assess changes to business assumptions and the driver variables.

The TSM is used extensively when setting the long-term direction of an organisation and may come in multiple versions as different structures and objectives are evaluated. Once an agreement has been reached on goals, the model that generated them is used to populate the target version in the OAM for later comparatives. Other model versions may be kept for reference as part of organisational knowledge.

Detailed Forecasting Model (DFM)

In contrast to the TSM, the detailed forecasting model (DFM) is used to collect information on what is likely to happen,. Again, depending on the complexity of the organisation, there may be multiple models involved, each having a focus on a specific business area. In manufacturing, this could include a sales and operational planning model that seeks to balance demand with production so that the manufacturing process is run efficiently in terms of the resources it consumes. In the service sector, this could include modelling the type of customer interaction with the level of skill required in order to determine the appropriate staffing levels.

In both cases the DFMs must first acquire the latest forecast information along with the current business structures in place. For many organisations, the data is likely to be at a lower level of detail than found in the OAM, and so a separate model is required to collect and hold it.

Optimise Resources Model (ORM)

The optimise resources model (ORM) shows how assigned resources can be optimised in line with the forecast. In a complex organisation this may require specialist algorithms that can iterate through a range of scenarios before coming up with the most effective outcome or use of resources.

Summaries from the ORM are then passed to the OAM for comparison with actual, budget, and target data.

Performance Measures Model (PMM)

The planning framework is able to provide reports and analyses that help management assess current and projected performance. Most of the data in these reports is likely to come directly from the OAM as this holds much of the key information regarding performance, although supporting history and forecasting models may be able to provide some specific insights.

However, to fully understand performance, some data will need to be combined with external information. For example to assess the efficiency of business processes in comparison to competitors. As to whether this area needs its own model, to some extent, will depend on the technology system being used and the complexity of the organisation. For our purposes, we will envisage this area as being a separate model—the performance measures model (PMM)—that has direct links to the other models as well as external market or social media data. This model is then enriched with calculations and analyses.

Output from the PFM can be in a variety of formats including grids, charts, colour-coded variances, strategy maps, dashboards, scorecards, and combinations of all of these. The latter point is important, as the way in which data is displayed will determine how the information is assessed and any actions that it may trigger. To this, reports must also be able to handle notes, comments, attachments, and more.

Strategy Improvement Model (SIM)

Organisations should never stand still or rest on their laurels. Alternative solutions, technologies, and competitors with better business models will constantly chip away at the organisation's ability to achieve its goals. For this reason, senior management is charged with a continual quest to improve established business processes, as well as to consider alternative markets or products that it could move into to achieve its mission.

This is where strategy comes in, which forms the next component of the framework. Strategic and operational planning processes are typically focused on the development of projects or initiatives that seek to improve the organisation's capabilities or existing business processes. Strategy impacts all parts of the organisation; it is not simply a financial concept.

According to Michael Porter, each organisation's business model should be unique as it forms the basis on how it gains a competitive advantage over other companies operating in the same market. For example, if company A is in the same business as company B, for one to gain an advantage over the other, there must be more value on the offer to a prospective customer for the price, compared to what is being offered by the other company. The only way they can do this in a sustainable way is by improving the way they add value, and hence the operation of the business.

There are many methodologies such as the balanced scorecard that can help organisations choose the most appropriate initiatives. Although each methodology has its own specific terminology, they tend to have a common approach, and that is to view initiatives as a cause and effect or strategy map (for example, figure 4-4). Whatever method is chosen, they will need to be linked to the OAM and CFM, as together they form the overall plan of how the organisation intends to meet its objectives.

Figure 4-4: Strategic Initiatives are Typically Focused on Improving the Organisation's Established Business Model

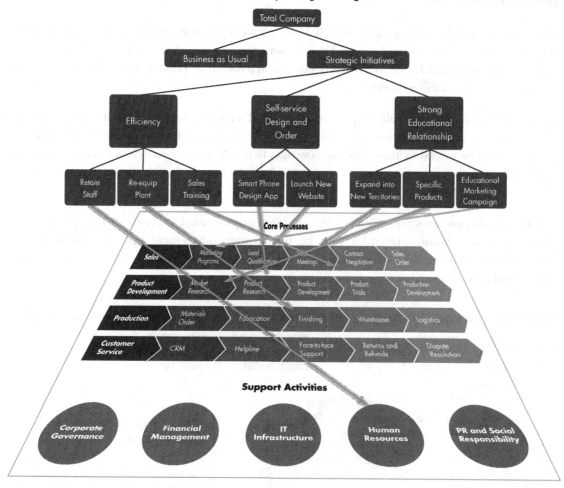

In the book titled *Best Practices in Planning and Performance Management*, author David Axson cites that a planning characteristic of high performing companies is that they separate sustaining current operations from improving current operations and embarking on new ventures or initiatives. The planning framework with its strategy improvement model allows this separation to continue, but also to bring them together to see the overall impact on resources and outcomes.

A natural way of viewing initiatives is to consider them as new projects that consist of a number of activities not currently being performed by the organisation. Unlike a budget, initiatives (throughout this book we will refer to projects as initiatives) will be continually proposed and form a wish list of what an organisation could consider to choose to do, but may not necessarily do.

To assess which initiatives are to be adopted requires a planning system to model them in isolation and in combination with other initiatives. This allows managers to optimise the impact of initiatives with the resources available while taking into account the market opportunity and competitor activity.

Once chosen, initiatives will need to be tracked in terms of their impact and the resources being consumed. This will be for both past performance to assess if they achieved what was planned, and for future performance to assess if they are going to achieve what was planned. Depending on the answers to these questions, initiatives may need to be reviewed, modified, replaced, or even cancelled.

Management Processes

Management processes are the mechanism by which performance is planned, resourced, and monitored. They are primarily concerned with 'what' and 'when'. From a user point of view, they determine when users interact with the different planning models previously described. From a data flow point of view, they determine what and when data flows between those models.

For example, the budget process typically requires departmental managers to plan expenditure by month for the upcoming year, whereas forecasting sales may be required by week for cash flow purposes. To monitor performance, there will be a need to automatically flow data between transaction systems and the planning models on a weekly or daily basis. However, to review funding, the flow of data to the funding model may only be required on a quarterly basis.

In general, management processes are typically seen and often implemented as the six distinct processes of strategic planning, tactical planning, financial planning, forecasting, management reporting, and risk management. However, as figure 4-5 shows, these six processes consist of a number of interconnected sub-processes that together form the basis for managing performance.

Figure 4-5: Performance Management Processes Combine to Form a Single Process Aimed at the Execution of Strategy

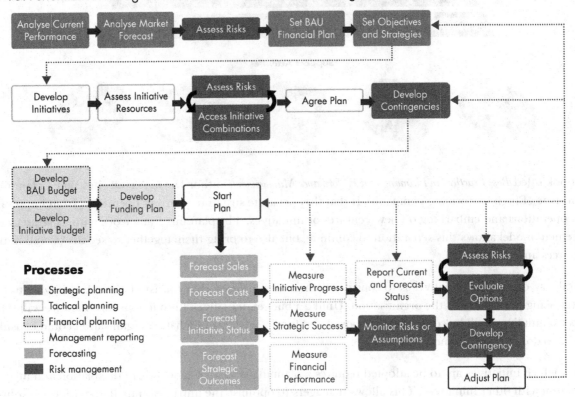

Each sub-process is critical to the management of the organisation, none can be left out. They need to be performed in a particular order and by different parts of the organisation. Even within an activity, there are interconnected tasks that each department has to perform, in a specific order and at specific times.

For example, budgeting may start off with the setting of a high-level target to which sales respond on how this will be delivered throughout the year. To do this they may need to work in collaboration with marketing and production. Once this has been completed, other areas of the organisation can start allocating resources that fit in with the sales and marketing plan.

In the past these planning and reporting activities were run according to the organisation's planning or reporting calendar, and they focused on a particular period of time such as the current or next year. But as we have seen, the volatility of today's business environment means that organisations are now unable to reliably predict events even a few months out, and so it makes little sense to wait for the next annual planning process when dealing with unexpected issues.

In the book *Best Practices in Planning and Performance Management,* research into high-performing companies found that

> Best Practice companies decouple their internal management processes from the calendar and provide a set of planning and reporting processes that utilise continuous processing and monitoring of activity. The passage of time becomes (just) one of many criteria for triggering the reporting of information or the initiation of planning or forecast activities.

The report goes on to say, '[a]spects of strategic planning are not once-a-year events but a continuous process. The pace of change is so great that management needs to monitor the strategic implications of new developments on a continuous basis'.

As a consequence of this, the planning framework recognises the following:

- Although planning is seen as a discreet process, in reality it is comprised of multiple activities that have strong links to activities within other processes.

- Planning and monitoring activities need to act as a single continuous process triggered by events and exceptions.

- For effective performance management, none of the six management processes can be left out.

- What goes on within these processes and how they are interconnected will determine whether performance is effectively managed.

Knowledge

The last part of the planning framework is knowledge. Knowledge can come in many forms, much of which is not easily stored or retrieved through electronic systems. In the context of the planning framework, knowledge that is related to business processes exists in the following questions:

- What actions have been tried before and how did they perform and succeed?

- What would we do differently if we knew what we now know?

- What trends do we think are occurring in the business landscape and how are we positioned to make the most of them?

Knowledge is continually acquired and can be a valuable resource if a way is found to capture it and make it available in an easily accessible format.

REPORTING FROM THE PLANNING FRAMEWORK

All of the models within the planning framework can be used for reporting. These are not discrete views of performance, but are linked with a focus on answering the following questions:

- *OAM.* What did we achieve against the plan in relation to resources, workload, and outcomes for each business process? Is performance getting better or worse? How do each of these look for the future?

- *CFM.* What is the cash outlook and from what sources can this be funded?

- *DHM.* What is the detail behind the resources, workload, and outcomes reported by the OAM? How does this compare to previous periods?

- *TSM.* How accurate are the relationships between resources, outcomes, and business processes in predicting future performance?

- *ORM.* How are business processes best optimised to produce planned outcomes?

- *SIM.* What changes do we need to make and are they on track?

- *PMM.* How does performance relate to what is going on in the business environment and in comparison to competitors or peers?

That completes the framework overview. In the next few chapters we will look at how each of these models are derived and the way in which they can be put together.

CASE STUDY OVERVIEW

To help explain the concepts within the planning framework in more detail, we have created a fictitious company that we will use as the main example. For continuity purposes, XYZ, Inc. will be our stationery manufacturer, as introduced in chapter 2, 'Planning Methods and Methodologies'. Although we have chosen a commercial organisation, hopefully readers from other industries will see how these can be made to apply where they work, including those from the services sector, government, and not for profit agencies.

About the Case Study Organisation

XYZ, Inc. is an international manufacturer of quality, personalised stationery products that are sold through different channels and in different locations around the world.

The market for personalised stationery products is undergoing rapid change as interactive websites and smart-device applications provide organisations with the ability to self-service the design and ordering of products that are unique to their particular brand.

XYZ's senior management is determined not to be left behind and has introduced a radical change programme that protects both its existing business streams and allows it to take advantage of intelligent web applications. As this is a volatile and fast changing environment, traditional annual budgets assigned to cost centres are inadequate to support the organisation's strategy.

To succeed, it is vital that XYZ's management understands their corporate strategy and their involvement in its implementation, and that its management processes are agile so that adjustments to operational plans can be made quickly as market conditions dictate.

Company Structure

From an operational point of view, figure 4-6 shows how XYZ, Inc. is split into business units.

Figure 4-6: Case Study Organisation Structure

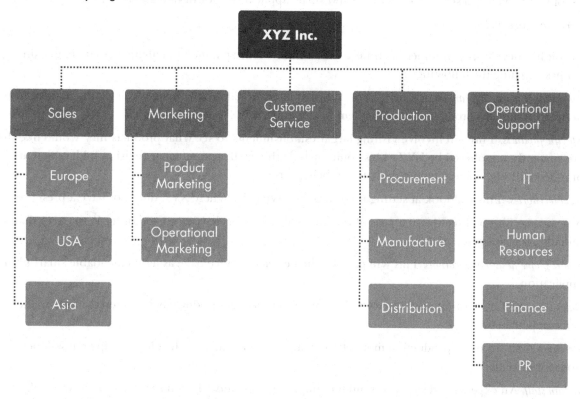

The core business processes are controlled by the following:

- *Sales departments.* These are organised by geographic location and include orders taken via the Internet. Sales are planned by product and by major client, where appropriate.

- *Marketing.* This department is responsible for deciding which products are promoted in each location (operational marketing) and evaluating future products to be developed and sold (product marketing).

- *Customer service.* This department is responsible for dealing with customer queries once a product has been sold.

- *Production.* These departments are responsible for the procurement of raw materials and components, the manufacture and assembly of products based on sales orders, and in delivering products to customers.

There are a number of departments supporting these core processes that include IT, human resources, finance and public relations.

Company Strategy

The overall aim of XYZ is to grow by adopting the following objectives:

- Develop strong relationships with educational establishments
- Become involved in a self-service website and smart applications for design and order
- Become more efficient

To do this it has developed a number of strategic initiatives that are planned to enhance its current business model. These include the following:

- *Educational marketing campaign.* This will be aimed at educational establishments to encourage them to buy branded stationery products and offer them to students.
- *Specific products.* This will involve visiting larger establishments to see what products they would like that are currently not offered by XYZ. This could include things like exam paper revision folders that are branded with the university and department being served.
- *New territories.* This will look at setting up offices to serve cities where XYZ does not have a presence.
- *New website.* This will see the first pass of the interactive self-service design and order Web pages that will initially focus on pens.
- *Smart phone design applications.* This will provide the new self-service page as a downloadable smart phone application.
- *Sales training.* The existing sales force will be trained on the new products being offered and how they can compete better.
- *Re-equip plant.* To make production more efficient and 'green', much of the older equipment will be updated or replaced.
- *Retain staff.* An experienced staff is essential to improve sales rates. This initiative looks at ways of improving morale to prevent good staff from joining competitors.

Versions and Other Information

XYZ, Inc. plans and tracks performance in four separate versions:

- *Target.* This is where management set aspirations for the future performance of the company.
- *Budget.* This is the bottom-up response from operational managers to the targets set.
- *Actual.* This is used to track what actually happened.
- *Forecast.* This is used to predict what is likely to happen should things continue as they are.

There is also a fifth version—benchmark—that is used to track performance against the market or major competitors should the relevant information be available.

Other details such as measures and processes to be supported can be found within the appropriate chapters.

So let's take a look at how this case study can be implemented within the planning framework.

5

OPERATIONAL ACTIVITY MODEL

This chapter is concerned with the creation of an operational activity model that was described in Chapter 4 'Business Planning Framework'. Its purpose is to monitor departmental workload, resources, and outcomes. To illustrate how this is done, examples have been based on the XYZ, Inc. case study outlined at the end of the last chapter.

OVERVIEW

Model Structure

The operational activity model (OAM) is central to the planning framework that, as its name suggests, has a departmental activity focus. Its purpose is to monitor business processes with regard to departmental workload, resources, and outcomes. This is achieved through a range of measures that allows management to evaluate the following:

- What activities are carried out by each department
- How departmental activities contribute to organisational objectives
- What resources are consumed

The model holds different versions of data, much of which flows from other models in the planning framework (figure 5-1). For example, the target version holds values that represent targets to be achieved as supplied by the

Figure 5-1: Graphic Showing the Flow of Data Between the Operational Activity Model and Other Framework Models

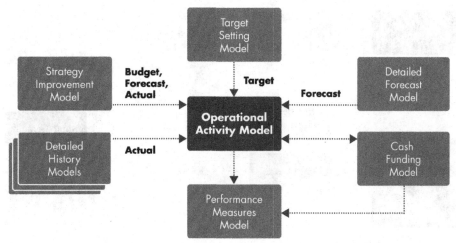

target setting model (TSM). When monitoring performance, the actual version represents what was actually achieved, much of which is supplied via the detailed history models (DHM). The forecast version contains values that represent what is most likely to happen should the current plan continue within the predicted business environment, which comes from the detailed forecast model (DFM).

Output from this model is used to generate a cash flow forecast within the cash funding model, as well as provide information to the performance measures model. This interconnected nature of the OAM brings together all performance data in the context of business processes, and therefore should be the first model that is developed.

Measurement Types and Relationships

In looking at the measures within the OAM, there is a structure that links operational activities with corporate objectives. Figure 5-2 depicts the relationship between different types of measure. These cover different areas of the plan and can be classified into the following types:

- *Objectives.* These define what the organisation is trying to achieve in the long-term.
- *Business process goals.* These measure the success of an organisation's core business processes and support activities that directly lead to the achievement of objectives.
- *Performance measures.* These break down business process goals into measures that can be directly related to activity outcomes.
- *Activity measures.* These can come in three types:
  - *Workload* types are those that measure the volume of work done by a particular department (for example, the number of mailings sent out by the marketing department as part of its lead generation activity).
  - *Outcome* types are those that measure what an activity should directly achieve (for example, the number of people that respond to the mailing).

Figure 5-2: Operational Activity Model Measurement Relationships for Planning and Monitoring Business Processes

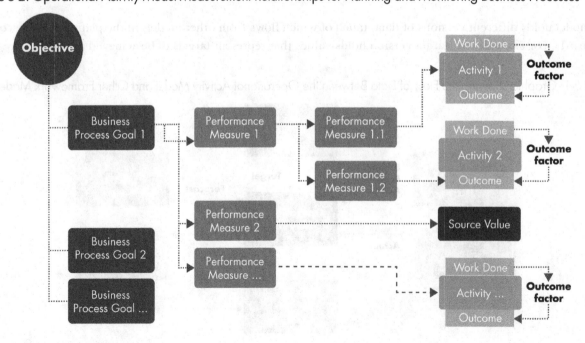

- o *Outcome factor* is an optional measure that can be derived from the first two activity measures by linking the work done with outcome. For example, by dividing the outcome (number of people responding to a mailing) by the work done (the number of mailings sent), one can calculate the outcome factor, in this case the response rate.

- *Source measures.* These are values that are either derived from existing data (for example, last year actual sales) or manually entered (for example, annual salary growth).

There are four other types of measure worth mentioning here:

- *Risk measures.* Every activity, or set of activities, carries a risk. For example, outsourcing logistics carries a risk that the chosen vendor may go out of business or be bought by a competitor. To manage any risk it must be quantified in terms of the likelihood of the risk materialising and the impact it would have on revenue or costs. From this, management can decide on actions to minimise the risk.

- *Assumption measures.* These monitor key assumptions made about the prevailing and forecast business environment. For example, the interest rate and the purchase price of raw materials, each of which could have a direct and severe impact on the volume of business or profitability. By monitoring these assumptions, results can be assessed in relation to external influences that are beyond the control of the organisation.

- *Income measures.* These track income that comes into the organisation.

- *Resource measures* These track expenditure that flows out of the organisation.

The reason for mentioning these types is that when defining a measure, we will also be indicating what category of measure it belongs to (note that some measures may belong to multiple categories). When creating a report, a data capture screen, or an analysis, we can quickly select the measures we want by referencing the measurement type. We will see more of this as we go through the chapter.

To define the OAM, the following steps are recommended.

Step 1: Define High-Level Objectives

The starting point in designing the OAM is to define the ultimate high-level objective(s) that the organisation wishes to achieve in the long-term. For a commercial organisation, this will consist of a financial target that represents some return to shareholders and may also include a related non-financial measure that quantifies the organisation's impact on its target market (for example, its position within the market). This long-term view helps management retain focus on the reason why the organisation exists rather than on short-term 'quick wins' that could be of detrimental value to the company in later years.

For our case study, the high-level objectives have been set as the following:

- Return on equity (ROE), as measured by (net income/shareholder equity) × 100. The aim is to have the highest ROE in the industry within the next 5 years.

- Market leadership, as measured by total sales of personalised stationary and associated equipment. To go with ROE, the aim is to become the market leader; the current position is number 5.

There is no set limit on the number of objectives an organisation can have, but experience shows that the more measures involved, the more confusing it is for others to understand the purpose of the organisation and, hence, in prioritising activities.

Step 2: Define Core Business Processes and Assumptions

The next step is to consider how the organisation's core business processes contribute to the established long-term goals. For most organisations (commercial and not-for-profit entities), these business processes relate to the following:

- How income is generated
- How products or services used to generate income are created and delivered
- How customers are supported in their use of products or services
- How products or services are developed to sustain future business

The output of each process will be measured by one or more quantifiable goals that management considers to be essential if the long-term objectives are to be achieved. Each core process is typically represented by a chain of activities that are under the control of management. Activities that directly impact organisational objectives. Associated with these goals are assumptions that may not be under management control, but whose values determine the level of success that each process can deliver.

For the XYZ, Inc. case study, the business process goals and assumptions set included the following:

- *Sales growth.* Measured by the increase in sales revenue year-on-year. The assumption used for setting target values is the forecast market growth.
- *Production.* Measured by gross product margin per cent (that is, the cost of materials, manufacturer, and warehouse divided by total sales). The assumption is a stable energy price.
- *Customer service.* Measured by support costs as a per cent of sales and customer retention rate. The assumption measure is the rate of inflation as this dictates salary and related costs.
- *Product development.* Measured by the average order size per customer. No assumption has been set for this measure.

Planning models will cover an extended period of time, and so the values assigned to goals (as well as the objectives) define success at certain points in the future, providing all goes to plan and that the assumptions made about the business environment prove accurate.

The measures used in the preceding list are examples from our case study, but these will differ between organisations depending on the mission, the industry in which it operates, the customers being served, and the way in which it values success. For example, a not-for-profit company may place customers as its reason for being, whereas another commercial organisation may see discounted cash flows as the goal. These would then require different measures from the core business processes in order to provide the link to long-term objectives. Table 5-1 shows an example of one way to operationalise measures with specific attributes.

Table 5-1: XYZ, Inc. Objectives, Goals, and Assumption Measures

CODE	MEASURE	ATTRIBUTES	
		DEPARTMENT	ACTIVITY
High-Level Objectives			
HL00510	Return on equity	Total company	
HL00520	Market leadership	Total company	
Business Process Goals			
OM01110	Year-on-year sales growth	Total company	Sales
OM01120	Product gross margin %	Total company	Production
OM01130	Support costs as % sales	Total company	Customer Support
OM01140	Customer retention rate	Total company	Customer Support
OM01150	Average order size per customer	Total company	Product Development
Assumption Measures			
AM01210	Market growth	Total company	Sales
AM01210	Inflation rate	Total company	Customer Support
AM01210	Energy price index	Total company	Production

In table 5-1, the attribute 'department' indicates at what level in the organisation the measure can be evaluated. In those shown it is at the consolidated total company level. The 'activity' attribute denotes the core process being measured. The important point is that this table shows that the attainment of objectives is to be achieved through the goals set by the organisation's business processes.

Step 3: Identify Core Business Process Activities

Defining Operational Activity Relationships

Core business process goals such as those set in table 5-1 (sales revenue, customer retention, and product margins) are typically delivered through a chain of operational activities. For example, manufacturing a product requires raw materials and components to be purchased, fabricated, packed, and shipped to buyers. Similarly, selling a service requires it to be promoted and potential customers to be contacted, sold to, and billed.

These core operational activities are usually assigned to one or more departments to carry out, which should be performed in an ordered, continuous sequence. If departmental activities are not aligned, performed badly, or the department gets distracted from completing them, then resources are being wasted and the business process goals (and hence organisational objectives) are in danger. It only takes one department to fail in its role to adversely impact performance, no matter how well the rest of the company performs.

With all of this in mind, the next step is to describe how each department—the key activities they perform and the outcomes that result from each—contributes to individual business goals. This exercise is best done by individual business processes and involves taking the goal assigned and breaking it down into performance measures. These in turn are broken down into further measures until we arrive at either the outcome of an activity, or where source data is referenced.

To see how this works in practice, let's use the XYZ, Inc. case study. In our example we are going to look first at the sales business process whose goal is measured by sales growth. Sales growth is a simple year-on-year calculation, and so it is sales revenue that becomes our focus. We now ask the question, 'What drives this value'? In other words, what are the factors that determine the amount of sales revenue? This could either be a performance measure or the outcome of an activity. In our case study the answer is three performance measures linked by a straightforward mathematical relationship:

$$\textit{Sales revenue} = (\textit{Number of customers placing orders} \times \textit{Average order amount}) + \textit{Web orders}$$

In this example we are keeping things simple to show the concepts involved in modelling, but there is no reason why the formula could not take into account different calculations depending on sales channel or product. The second question we need to ask about this relationship is whether there is any time lag involved. That is, is there a delay in the number of customers placing orders and the sales revenue that emanates? In this particular case, there is not.

At this stage it is worth pointing out that the relationships defined here are those that can be used in the target setting model that we will define in chapter 8, 'Predict and Optmise Planning Models'. For example, by capturing data for the number of customers and the average order amount, we can get the model to automatically calculate sales revenue. However, when monitoring actual performance or collecting forecasts, these modelling relationships will be invalid and other rules will need to apply. For example, when reviewing actual results, we would collect data for sales revenue and number of customers placing orders from the appropriate internal ledgers, but would then use this information to calculate the following:

$$\textit{Average order amount} = \frac{\textit{Sales Revenue}}{\textit{Number for customers placing orders}}$$

For the time being we are only considering what relationships exist so that we can identify the measures we need to collect and their time lag. Similarly, we are not concerned with setting values for these measures, which will be achieved later on through a management process.

Having established the first relationship to the core business process goal, we now take the component parts of the performance measure—number of customers placing orders and average order amount—and ask what drives them. Again, in our case study we have the following:

$$\textit{Number of customers placing orders} = (\textit{Total number of customers} \times \textit{Customer retention rate}) + \textit{New customers}$$

In our example, the management at XYZ, Inc. believes that the number of orders is dependent on two things: (1) the number of customers they had last year adjusted by the customer retention rate, and (2) the number of new customers they acquire.

The customer retention rate is affected by a sales activity: the number of times a customer is contacted. For our case study, the retention rate is entered by management, which is then compared with the number of customer interactions by sales staff.

The number of new customers is believed to be an outcome of an activity performed by the operational marketing department. This is determined by the number of mailings made and the mailing response rate. Both of these measures are entered by operational marketing management, along with a time lag factor that signifies the expected delay between sending out a mailing, getting a client as a new customer, and receiving their first order.

And so the process continues; what drives Web sales, what drives the re-order rate, and so on. At some point the base component of any relationship in the OAM model should be one of the following:

- The outcome of a departmental activity
- A number that is based on past performance
- A value supplied by management as a guesstimate

For the sales stream of XYZ, Inc., the complete list of measures, activities, and relationships are shown in figure 5-3.

Figure 5-3: Operational Activity Measurement for XYZ, Inc. Sales Business Process

Business Process Goal	Performance Measures	Source or Outcome	Activity Workload	Department Responsible	Time Lag
SALES BUSINESS PROCESS					
Sales Growth	= (sales revenue/last year sales revenue) x 100				0
Sales Revenue	= (No. placing orders x customer reorder rate) + web sales				0
No. Placing Orders	= No. customers + mailing response rate				0
No. of Customers	= No. customers last year + retention				0
		No. Customers Last Year			0
	VISIT EXISTING CUSTOMERS				
		Customer Retention Rate	No. of Customer Contacts	Sales Depts	0
	VISIT NEW CUSTOMERS				
		No. New Customers	No. of New Sales Leads	Sales Depts	2
	LEAD GENERATION				
		Mailing Response Rate	No. Mailings	Op. Marketing	1
Customer Re-order Rate	= Last year re-order rate x customer spend growth factor				0
		Last Year Re-order Rate		Op. Marketing	0
		Customer Spend Growth Factor		Op. Marketing	0
Web Sales	= No. online orders x online order rate				
No. Online Orders					
	SOCIAL MEDIA CAMPAIGN				
		Website Hits	No. Social Media Articles	Op. Marketing	1
			No. Google Adwords	Op. Marketing	0
			No. LinkedIn Ads	Op. Marketing	0
Online Re-order Rate	= Last year re-order rate x online				0
		Last Year Online Re-order Rate		Op. Marketing	0
		Online Spend Growth Factor		Op. Marketing	0

Figure 5-3 shows the connection between the business process goal and supporting measures. The bold boxes indicate particular activities within the business process such as 'visiting existing customers,' 'visit new customers,' and so on.

This exercise in connecting departmental activities to business process goals is repeated for each core process. Let's take a look at the production business process of XYZ, Inc. In this case, production is measured by the gross profit margin made from each product. This figure is determined by three factors:

- Purchase price of materials used in each product
- The cost of manufacture, which includes the days lost due to the unavailability of purchased raw materials or components, and where production machines have failed due to faults
- Warehouse profit margin that is influenced by the number of days that each product is held in stock before being shipped

As with the sales process, each of these are analysed to see what impacts those measures and the time lag that occurs. The list of measures for the case study is depicted in figure 5-4.

Figure 5-4: Operational Activity Measurement List for XYZ, Inc. Production Business Process

Business Process Goal	Performance Measures		Source or Outcome	Activity Workload	Department Responsible	Time Lag
		PRODUCTION BUSINESS PROCESS				
Gross Product Margin %	= (material + manufacture + warehouse costs) / total sales					0
	Materials Cost Margin	= total procurement costs / volume shipped				0
			SUPPLIER RELATIONSHIPS			
			Procurement Cost	Research Suppliers	Procurement	1
	Manufacturing Margin	= (product standard cost x volume shipped) / total sales				1
			Product Standard Cost	= Last year manufacture costs / volume shipped		0
		Volume Shipped	= total made – products lost to poor quality and lack of materials			
			Volume Lost Due to Machine Reliability			0
			MAINTAIN MACHINES			
			Machine Reliability	Machine Maintenance	Manufacture	0
			Volume Lost Due to Machine Reliability			0
			JUST IN TIME MANUFACTURING			
			Material Stock Levels	Avg. Raw Material Stock Days	Procurement	0
	Warehouse Cost	= total cost of warehouse dept / volume shipped				0
			REVIEW WAREHOUSE NEEDS			
			Material Stock Levels	Avg. Raw Material Stock Days	Distribution	0
		Average No. of Days Products Held in Stock				0
			JUST IN TIME MANUFACTURING			
			Product Stock Levels	Avg. Raw Material Stock Days	Manufacture	1

Note that one of the activities (just in time [JIT] manufacturing) has two sets of outcome and workload measures.

Figure 5-5 shows the list of measures found in the customer service business process.

Figure 5-5: Operational Activity Measurement List for XYZ, Inc. Customer Service Business Process

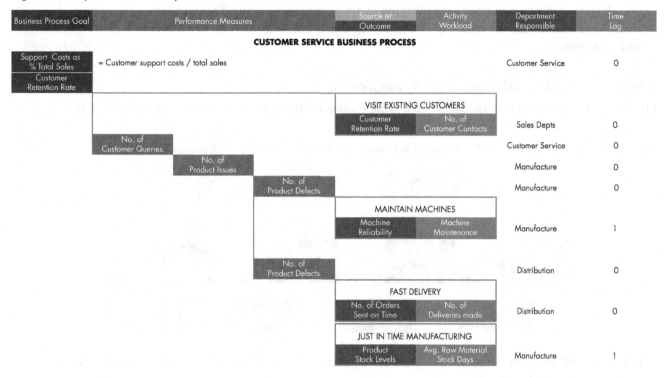

In this case, three of the activities—visit existing customers, maintain machines, and JIT manufacturing—have already been defined in other business processes. However, they are repeated here as they directly impact the customer service goals.

To complete the case study, the measures for product development are outlined in figure 5-6.

Figure 5-6: Operational Activity Measurement List for XYZ, Inc. Product Development Business Processes

Business Process Goal	Performance Measures	Source or Outcome	Activity Workload	Department Responsible	Time Lag
PRODUCT DEVELOPMENT BUSINESS PROCESS					
Average Order Size	= Sales revenue / No. of orders			Product Marketing	0
% of Products With Sales Over 5,000				Sales Depts.	0
	No. of Products on Sale			Product Marketing	0
		IDENTIFY NEW PRODUCTS			
		No. of New Products Proposed	No. of Customers Surveyed	Product Marketing	3
		IDENTIFY NEW PRODUCTS			
		No. of Products to Launch	Assess Production Costs	Manufacture	1
			Assess Material Costs	Manufacture	1
		LAUNCH NEW PRODUCTS			
		No. of New Products Proposed	No. of Customers Surveyed	Op. Marketing	3

When this task is complete we should have a list of core business process goals broken down by performance measure(s) where most are linked to the outcome of a departmental activity. Our website (www.BusinessPlanningFramework.com) has the complete list of measures and departmental activities defined for our case study.

Things to Note When Defining Activity Relationships

There are a few things to take note of when linking business process goals to operational activities (figure 5-7):

Figure 5-7: Relationship Between Activity and Outcome in the Product Development Business Process

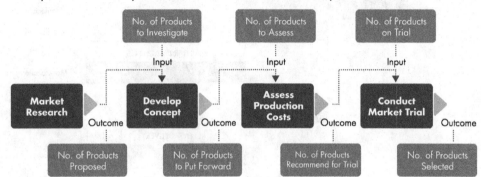

1. Within a chain of activities, the measures between the outcome of one activity and the input to the next activity are closely related.

   For example, the activities shown in figure 5-7 are part of the product research business process. As you can imagine, there are many measures that could be chosen. However, in this example, the outcome of the market research activity is the measure of the number of products proposed, which is closely linked to the input of the next business process activity, develop concept. In this activity, the measure of work is the number of products to investigate and its outcome is set at the number of products to put forward for a full cost assessment. Once the assessment activity has been completed, successful product candidates are then placed in a product trial, from which the best are chosen to become part of the standard product offering.

   This linkage can be used within the forecast and target setting models (to be defined in chapter 8 'Predict and Optimise Planning Models') to create driver-based planning models. This is done by applying a series of outcome factors to generate forecasts and through which the changing nature of these relationships can be explored.

2. It will not be possible to do this at a detailed activity level (unless an activity-based costing system is being used), so you will likely find that some activities may support multiple goals and objectives. If an activity is found to support many goals, then consider whether they should be defined as a general support activity or sub-divide the activity associated with each goal. The aim here is to keep relationships simple. This is not an exercise in creating a detailed representation of the business, but in understanding the key drivers of value. The result should convey how the organisation operates and the levels of activity that are needed

3. Business process goals and operational activities do not always line up with the organisation structure. Some have a one-to-one relationship (for example, marketing), but others may go across multiple departments (for example, sales or corporate governance). Often this mismatch is driven by regional or business line matrix structures that can result in conflicting metrics and performance measures. In some organisations this clash can produce sub-optimal goals as well as the wrong behaviour for achieving corporate objectives.

4. It is unrealistic to link every activity. In some cases you may only be able to present the work that has been done with no obvious mathematical link to the outcome or the performance measure it supports. For example, customer retention is influenced by many factors, some of which may not be measurable (for example, social impact or JIT manufacturing) and where the mathematical link is unknown. However, there is still value in presenting a goal and the supporting work being done along with its cost, so at least management can make an informed judgement as to whether they are linked.

5. With any relationship it should be noted that
   a. they do not take into account unpredictable external influences (for example, weather or impact of social media posts).
   b. they can only model what has happened in the past, which may not be a reliable indicator of the future in a volatile market or where product life cycles are relatively short.

   As a consequence, relationships should, where possible, be validated against both past behaviour and assessed as to their accuracy in predicting the future. Often this requires the finance professional to blend formal modelling techniques with sound commercial judgement.

6. Finally, you will not get this linkage or the measures right the first time around, or even the second time. The point is to keep iteratively refining the measures by challenging management beliefs about organisational drivers, risk, value, and reward, and how they can be better leveraged to drive success.

As an interesting exercise, try to write down the activities currently being performed within your organisation and then see if they can be linked back to the stated corporate objectives. You will likely find that some objectives have many activities, others will have few or none, and one or two activities will be left unconnected.

Step 4: Identify Support Activity Measures

To enable the core business process activities to deliver their designated outcomes, a number of support activities will be necessary:

- Financial administration activities will be required to ensure customers are billed, suppliers are paid, and that the in-flow and out-flow of monies are correctly recorded.

- In today's online world, an up-to-date information technology infrastructure is essential through which the organisation can conduct its business and stay in contact with all of its stakeholders.

- Corporate governance is playing an increasing role in how the organisation is perceived by customers and investors alike. This means pro-active steps must be taken to ensure the company complies with regulatory directives as well as in its social responsibilities.

These types of activities may not be essential to the way in which value is directly added for customers; they may not form a business process chain and so cannot be linked. It also may not be possible to directly relate them to the business process goals. However, they are essential and must be conducted in an efficient and effective way if value is not to be lost.

As with the core business process activities, it should be possible to define the key workload measures that go on within the respective departments, as well as the outcomes that are to be expected. This information will help management judge a range of conditions, such as whether the departments are underfunded, delivering good value for the resources they consume, or whether they should be outsourced.

For our case study, measures were defined for the support activities, and outlined in table 5-2.

Table 5-2: Support Activity Measures

CODE	MEASURE	ACTIVITY TYPE	ACTIVITY	DEPARTMENT
SA05110	eCommerce website errors reported	Outcome	Website maintenance	IT
SA05120	Number of Web pages reviewed or updated	Workload	Website maintenance	IT
SA05130	Number of positions vacant (%)	Outcome	Recruitment campaign	HR
SA05140	Number of candidates being interviewed	Workload	Recruitment campaign	HR
SA05150	Number of leavers (%)	Outcome	Skills training	HR
SA05160	Number of people attending training	Workload	Skills training	HR
SA05170	Debtor days outstanding	Outcome	Prompt payment campaign	Finance
SA05180	Number of invoices raised	Workload	Prompt payment campaign	Finance
SA05190	Number of governance issues encountered	Outcome	Corporate governance	Finance
SA05200	Number of guidance notes tested	Workload	Corporate governance	Finance
SA05210	Number of days to report	Outcome	Billing accuracy	Finance
SA05220	Number of billing errors made	Workload	Billing accuracy	Finance
SA05230	Number of positive reports	Outcome	PR Investor campaign	PR
SA05240	Number of investor communications	Workload	PR Investor campaign	PR

Step 5: Define Profit and Loss and Other Financial Measures

So far we have defined measures as they relate to objectives, business process goals, performance measures, and activities. Some of these may be financial, but no matter what kind of organisation is being modelled, it will have to produce a summary set of financial statements. The first of these that will be considered here is the profit and loss (P&L) statement.

The P&L statement is made up of two types of accounts: income and expenditures. Income is more likely to be a function of a few activities from specific departments, whereas every department and activity incurs expenditures.

When defining the accounts that are used to produce the P&L statement, we need to split them up into two categories:

- Those that are common across most activities or departments (for example, salaries or expenses)
- Those that are specific to certain departments or activities (for example, marketing spend)

We also want to keep the number of accounts to a minimum. In his book, *Best Practices in Planning and Performance Management*, author David Axson cites that high-performing organisations typically only budget around 40 accounts in total, compared with an average of 220 accounts for other companies.

What this indicates is a focus on what is really important, rather than a quest for detail. The survey on which the book is based also reveals that it was not unusual for companies to develop a budget item for spending on photocopier paper in the third quarter of next year, but have little or no idea how much business it expects to generate with its 20 best customers. Similarly, the survey found that the more detail contained within the budget, the less time managers had for investigating more relevant issues. After all, do you want people to spend time looking at minor expenditure variances or in identifying the key value drivers that are critical to ensuring corporate objectives are achieved?

Consider this example. An organisation hires an additional procurement staff member to extract an additional 2–3 per cent savings in the cost of global office overheads. The bulk of these costs are real estate, facilities maintenance, and equipment that are driven by the number of staff. A better approach would be to build an accurate sales forecasting system so it can correctly predict the number of staff it will need and therefore its facilities requirements.

Put simply, overemphasising structure shifts decision-making time away from the 'why' of financial performance to merely 'what' happened.

When reviewing actual results, there may be a requirement to look at P&L in detail, such as provided by the chart of accounts. This type of analysis is where a supporting detailed history model (DHM) would be used to hold expenditure down to the transaction level. To set targets at this level of detail though makes no sense. So for the purposes of the OAM we will only define summary accounts.

For our case study, the following income accounts were created (table 5-3).

Table 5-3: Sample Income Accounts

ACCOUNT CODE	DESCRIPTION	NOTE
SR10100	Gross sales	Total lined to detail within a history or forecast model
SR10200	Discounts	By sales department
SR10300	Returns	By sales department
SR10400	Delivery charges	By sales department
SR10900	Total sales revenue	= SR 10300 – SR 10400 – SR 10500 – SR 10600

When defining accounts we would suggest that you use the code found in the general ledger (if it exists), as this will help some systems when loading data. They also provide a short cut to referencing a particular measure in describing relationships. Table 5-3 also has a note indicating at what level of detail these accounts are held (in our case study, this is by sales department, and gross sales is linked to a detailed history [for actual results] or forecast model). As we will discover in chapters 7, "Detailed History and Performance Measures Models," and 8 "Predict and Optimise Planning Models," support models allow the holding of data at a more detailed level when that level of detail is specific either to just a few measures or to a particular department. For XYZ, Inc. the detail held behind gross sales includes volume and price by product, as well as sales made to individual customers.

For our case study, table 5-4 has accounts that are common across each department, while table 5-5 has those that are for specific departmental activities.

Table 5-4: Sample Common Accounts

ACCOUNT CODE	DESCRIPTION	NOTE
Staffing		
GS21010	Salaries and wages	Total linked to detail within a history or forecast model
GS21020	Commissions	By department
GS21030	Overtime	By department
GS21040	Contract labour	By department
GS21050	Social welfare	Total linked to detail within a history or forecast model
GS21060	**Total salaries**	**= Sum GS21050–GS21050**
General Expenses		
GE22010	Rent	By department
GE22020	Heat, light, and power	By department
GE22030	Water	By department
GE22040	Telephone	By department
GE22050	Insurance	By department
GE22060	Vehicle	By department
GE22070	Travel and entertainment	By department
GE22080	Hotel and living	By department
GE22090	Equipment hire	By department

Continued on p. 83

Continued from p. 82

ACCOUNT CODE	DESCRIPTION	NOTE
GE22100	Office supplies	By department
GE22110	Postage	By department
GE22120	Cleaning and office services	By department
GE22130	Other expenses	By department
GE22140	**Total general expenses**	**= Sum GE22010–GS22130**

Table 5-5: Specific Departmental Accounts

Procurement:		
PR23110	Raw materials used in products	By products
PR23120	Wastage	By products
PR23130	**Total procurement**	**= PR23110 + PR23120**
Manufacture:		
MA23210	Manufacturing costs	By department
MA23220	Waste disposal	By department
MA23230	**Total manufacturing**	**= MA23210 + MA23220**
Distribution:		
DI23310	Warehouse costs	By department
DI23320	Delivery costs	By department
DI23330	**Total distribution**	**= DI23310 + DI23320**
Product Marketing:		
PM23410	Agent fees	By department
PM23420	Trial fees	By department
PM23430	**Total product marketing**	**= PM23410 + PM23420**

Continued on p. 84

Continued from p. 83

Operational Marketing:

OM23510	Advertising	By department
OM23520	Shows and exhibitions	By department
OM23530	Promotional aids	By department
OM23540	Sponsorships	By department
OM23550	Printing	By department
OM23560	**Total operational marketing**	**= Sum OM23510–OM23550**

Customer Service:

CS23610	CRM maintenance	By department
CS23620	Vouchers	By department
CS23630	**Total customer service**	**= CS23610 + CS23620**

Information Technology:

IT23710	Website fees	By department
IT23720	Computer software	By department
IT23730	Hardware maintenance	By department
IT23740	**Total IT-related costs**	**= IT23710 + IT23720 + IT23730**

Finance:

FI23810	Legal fees	By department
FI23820	Audit and accountancy fees	By department
FI23830	Bank charges	By department
FI23840	**Total finance-related costs**	**= FI23810 + FI23820 + FI23830**

Human Resources (HR):

HR23910	Recruitment costs	By departments
HR23920	Training	By departments
HR23930	**Total HR-related costs**	**= HR23910 + HR23920**

The final step in completing the measures list is to see what other accounts are required to produce the P&L statement and balance sheet for the entire company (for example, overheads or stock levels). As we identify them we also need to note the departments assigned to manage them.

In reviewing the final measurement list we should identify the source of any measure that is not calculated and its availability. It could be that not all values are available when required. In this case it should be noted that either an educated guess needs to be made (and broadcast as such) or consideration should be given to creating a system that can collect at the appropriate level. The business case for its development is the benefit of knowing those facts and their relationship to the overall objectives.

PUTTING THE MODEL TOGETHER

Armed with the information described in this chapter, we are now ready to build a computer model that can monitor business performance. For most organisations this will require a technology system that can deal with the concept of business dimensions when defining the model, however we will continue to remain technology agnostic and try to describe this in terms that those using spread sheets can understand.

Measures and Attributes

As we have seen, the OAM consists of many measures that serve different purposes. Some are limited to particular activities or departments, and others describe outcomes, the amount of work done, or the resources consumed. To simplify the set-up of a model that will automatically display the right combination of measures for any particular activity, we can assign each with one or more attributes.

An attribute is simply a label that denotes what the measure represents. In our case study, each measure has the following three different types of attributes:

1. *Measurement type.* This is set to one of objective, business process goal, assumption, performance measure, workload, outcome, outcome factor, income, or resource. These types were explained in Measurement Types and Relationships at the start of this chapter.

   Where a measure can be assigned to more than one of the preceding attributes (for example, sales revenue can be both a value chain goal and an income measure), then the measure may need to be duplicated depending on the sophistication of the modelling system.

2. *Department.* This attribute identifies which departments are responsible for the measure and whether it is to appear in a particular departmental plan or report

3. *Activity.* This final attribute identifies whether the measure is linked to a specific work activity and its appearance in any report where that activity is included.

These attributes make it easy when setting up reports or data capture screens in that they can act as an automatic filter to define what measures are to be shown. For example, show all measures designated as resource or outcome for the customer support department, or show measures for the market research activity or any combination of attributes.

Model Dimensions

As mentioned in chapter 3, 'Planning Technologies', most planning systems allow models to be defined by specifying the individual business dimensions to be used, and the members that make up each dimension. For most organisations, the OAM will consist of the following five business dimensions:

1. *Measures.* These hold values and have been covered in detail throughout this chapter.

2. *Organisation.* This dimension contains the departments and how they consolidate into the total company. Given that hierarchies change over time, it is important that these can be tracked and made available for reporting purposes. It is likely that most organisations will not be able to track departmental activity separately except by reference to the department that carries it out and the associated measures. This means budgets cannot be assigned to an activity unless the department itself is broken down into sub-departments within the organisation structure, or activity is considered to be a separate dimension. For the purposes of our case study we have assumed the former (that is, activities can only be tracked at a departmental level).

3. *Periods.* This defines the organisation's operational calendar to be applied within the model. Some data may be held at a day level and others held at a month and quarter level. For retail organisations this grouping can include seasons and take note of public holidays. This definition also describes the period groupings on how data is to be accumulated over time so that reports can be produced for a selected period in both year-to-date and periodic format.

4. *Years.* This defines the time span to be covered by the model, which can be either a true calendar year or a fiscal year.

5. *Version.* This is used to separate the different versions of data. In our case study this is set at target (to hold high-level goals), budget (to hold agreed bottom-up plans), actual (to hold actual results), and forecast (to collect the latest estimate of what the future holds).

Where more dimensions are needed (for example, to plan and monitor sales by product, line of business, and so on), these extra dimensions can be defined within the corresponding detailed history, target setting, or detailed forecast models, rather than applying them to all of the measures within the OAM.

Model Rules

The final part in setting up the model is defining the rules that govern measures. Although we identified measures as having relationships, particularly between performance measures and business process goals, the OAM does not use them. They will be used in the respective target setting and forecast models to predict future performances, which are then transferred into the relevant version within the OAM.

The rules that are set up are as follows:

- Sub-totals (for example, to calculate total expenses).
- Where measures such as ratios need to be calculated from base data.
- Those governing currency conversion.

- Those required to monitor drivers. In step 3 we identified the relationship between activities and objectives or financial measures. As mentioned, when collecting actual results we will want to change the way that formula works so that items such as outcome factors can be calculated.

- Those that are involved in consolidating results to give a total company picture.

REPORTING FROM THE OAM

The OAM provides management with an internally focused view of performance. It relates resources with outcomes as produced by the organisation's business processes. There are many types of reports that can be produced, but for now we will look at just a few examples.

Departmental Outcomes, Activity, and Resources

From a budgeting point of view, it is important to see what kind of performance is expected, which requires measures of workload to be contrasted with outcomes along with budgeted resources. The OAM is able to produce this by department by using the attributes defined on the measures. These are able to filter measures so that only those that apply to the department and its assigned activities are shown. Table 5-6 is an example of a filtered report for XYZ, Inc.

Table 5-6: Sample Departmental Report With Measures Filtered by Activity and Department

Department:	**Operational Marketing**
Month:	**July**
Year:	**2014**

	Budget	Actual	% Var	Last Year
Outcome measures:				
Mailing response rate (%)	2%	2%	1.30%	2%
Responses from social media sites	1250	1253	0.25%	1065
No. of new products selected	25	27	8.00%	23
Website hits	145000	157615	8.70%	132450
Avg. gross margin per new product	28%	28%	1.70%	24%
Workload measures:				
No. of mailings sent	35	34.72	-0.80%	29.52
No. of active campaigns	13	13	0%	11
No. of new potential products trialed	14	38	-5%	32

Continued on p. 88

Continued from p. 87

Resource measures

Staffing:

	Budget	Actual	% Var	Last Year
Salaries and wages	$115,000	$112,988	1.75%	$96,039
Commissions	$15,000	$15,035	-0.23%	$12,779
Overtime	$45	$45	0.05%	$38
Contract labour	$36,000	$36,270	-0.75%	$30,830
Social welfare	$24,000	$23,981	0.08%	$20,384
Total Salaries:	**$190,045**	**$188,318**	**-0.92%**	**$160,070**

General expenses:

Rent	$3,200	$3,176	0.75%	$2,700
Heat, light, and power	$600	$556	7.30%	$473
Water	$200	$200	-0.08%	$170
Telephone	$1,100	$1,100	-0.01%	$935
Insurance	$1,600	$1,549	3.20%	$1,316
Car	$800	$800	0%	$680
Travel and entertainment	$1,950	$1,995	-2.30%	$1,696
Hotel and living	$1,600	$1,580	1.23%	$1,343
Equipment hire	$2,300	$2,415	-5%	$2,053
Office supplies	$750	$767	-2.30%	$652

	Budget	**Actual**	**% Var**	**Last Year**
Postage	$40	$39	3.20%	$33
Other expenses	$5	$6	-12%	$5
Total General Expenses:	**$14,145**	**$14,183**	**-0.27%**	**$12,056**

Dept. specific resource measures

Advertising	$54,000	$57,024	-5.60%	$48,470
Shows and exhibitions	$48,000	$45,936	4.30%%	$39,046
Promotional aids	$37,000	$36,223	2.10%	$30,790
Agent fees	$5,000	$5,300	-6%	$4,505
Sponsorships	$1,950	$1,866	4.30%	$1,586
Printing	$32,400	$30,586	5.60%	$25,998
Total Marketing specific expenses:	**$178,350**	**$176,935**	**0.80%**	**$150,395**
Total department:	**$382,540**	**$379,436**	**0.82%**	**$322,520**

This report shows, by department, outcomes that it has generated from the activities it performed and the resources those activities consumed. Actual results are contrasted with the budget that also shows variances and last year's performance. What matters most are the outcomes, as these have a direct impact on organisational objectives, or they should have, as we will see in the next report.

Outcome Versus Activity

In this next report (table 5-7) we have selected the corporate objectives and the business process goals (although only the sales process is shown due to lack of space). For each goal, the list of associated activities is displayed, along with the measures of workload and outcome. Actual performance is compared to what was expected in the budget. From this management can assess the relationship between workload and outcomes to judge whether the focus is on the right activities.

Table 5-7: Sample Report Showing Activity Versus Outcome

Month: **May**
Year: **2013**

	Business Process: Sales		
	Activity	**Outcome**	**Vs. Target**
Corporate Objectives			
Return on Equity		7.9%	-3%
Market Share		13.5%	-2%
Goal: Direct Sales:		$435,700	-$34,670
Visit Existing Customers:			
Outcome: Customer retention rate		85%	5%
Activity: No. of customer contacts	120		2%
Visit New Customers:			
Outcome: No. new customers		175	-6%
Activity: No. of new sales calls	75		-8%
Lead Generation:			
Outcome: Mailing response rate		3.5%	3%
Activity: No. mailings	15680		2%
Total Cost:	$263,000		-$12,000
Goal: Web Sales		$174,500	$14,500
Social Media Campaign			
Outcome: Website hits		134630	14300
Activity: No. social media articles	7		0%
Activity: No. Google adwords	17		0%
Activity: No. LinkedIn ads	15		0%
Total Cost:	$73,500		$2,100

Outcome Versus Assumptions and Resources

This last report (table 5-8) contrasts the business process goals with assumptions and costs. If the assumptions were not right, then doubt must be placed on whether the success of affected actions and the associated costs are appropriate. The aim of the report is to start a debate around whether the level of success being achieved is worth the costs that were assigned.

Table 5-8: Sample Report Showing Success Versus Assumptions and Cost

Outcomes Vs. Assumptions and Resources

		Target	Actual	%Var.
Sales:	Market position	3	2	66.7%
	Sales contribution by channel	28%	27.60%	98.6%
	Total cost	$234,500	$263,000	112.2%
Assumption:	*Market growth*	14.50%	13%	89.7%
Customer Support:	Support costs as % sales	18%	17.50%	97.2%
	Social media ranking	5	6.5	130.0%
	Total cost	$325,000	$315,000	96.9%
Assumption:	*Inflation rate*	2.30%	2.50%	108.7%
Production:	Average unit cost of production	2.97	2.99	100.7%
	Cost of shipping as % total costs	8%	8.30%	103.8%
	Total cost	$974,000	$990,000	101.6%
Assumption:	*Energy price index*	12	14	116.7%
Product Development:	No. of products being developed	65	65	100.0%
	% of products with orders	85$	87%	102.4%
	Total cost	$265,000	$255,000	96.2%

These reports have just touched the surface of what can be displayed from the OAM. Interestingly, most organisations have much of this data already, although it is typically split into separate budgeting and scorecard or dashboard models that focus on the performance of individual departments. When treated in this way, the data cannot be used to model organisational value and much of its worth is lost.

As mentioned at the start of this chapter, the OAM is a key model in the planning framework. It shows how everyday business processes consume financial resources to produce outcomes that will enable the organisation to achieve its goals. However, this view does not take into account where those financial resources come from and whether they will be available at the right time. This is the role of the cash funding model, which will be described in the next chapter.

6

CASH FUNDING MODEL

Closely connected to the operational activity model is the cash funding model, which calculates cash requirements based on future revenues and expenses. This chapter explains how to create this model, with examples based on the XYZ, Inc. case study.

MODEL PURPOSE

The purpose of the cash funding model (CFM) is to assess the organisation's need for financial resources. Some of those resources will be used to support operating expenses, and others will be required for capital investment or strategic initiatives. This model is intrinsically linked to the operational activity model (OAM) and detailed forecasting model (DFM) in order to predict future cash flows. This can help management to assess the best source for any cash shortfalls.

Although it is true that most internal financial systems can hold data relating to the actual flow of cash, what they do not allow is for management to 'play around' with the data from a planning point of view (for example, to see a revised cash flow based on new supplier credit terms or a change to customer payment profiles, to consider the cost of funding an increase in production capacity to meet the projected demand for new products, or to assess the impact on resources by outsourcing a particular function).

Similarly, financial systems do not hold the key assumptions that affect cash flow. For instance, inflation has a major impact on cash resources, yet the underlying data supporting any inflation assumptions is not contained within those systems.

This is where the CFM comes in; it lets management gauge the impact of change on financial resources without having to commit to those changes within the supporting transaction systems.

The versions held by the model include the following:

- *Actual.* This enables a historic view of cash balances and will be directly loaded from an organisation's general ledger.
- *Budget.* This is generated as part of the budget process to gain an idea of cash requirements.
- *Forecast.* This takes a realistic, forward look at the best estimates for cash in the short term (that is, the next couple of months). Depending on the complexity of the organisation, the data used will come either from the DFM or the OAM.

DEFINING THE MODEL

Model Content

Modelling cash flows and balances require different sets of information, as depicted in figure 6-1.

Figure 6-1: The Flow and Sources of Cash Within the Planning Framework

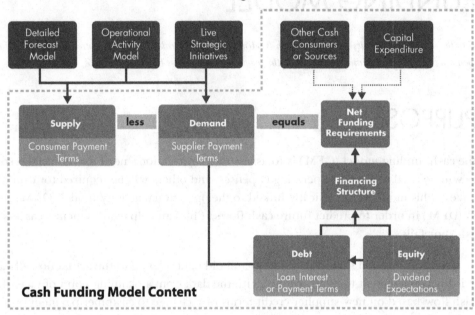

The dotted line indicates information stored within the CFM, and the data flows from other models in the framework. These can be summarised as follows:

- *Customer and supplier payment terms.* The CFM contains details about each major supplier and customer where the cash flow effect is to be calculated. Depending on how payment terms are defined (for example, in weeks or months), the time intervals in this model may be at a shorter increment than that of the OAM.

- *Cash supply.* Cash is modelled for budgets and forecasts. The supply side of cash is taken from the OAM and the DFM. Data from these models will need to be at a level of granularity where individual supplier or customer movements can be identified so they can match up with the appropriate customer details.

- *Cash demand.* Similarly, the demand side for cash is also taken from the OAM and the DFM. This takes into account all operational expenses, which for a manufacturer would include the supply of raw materials and manufacturing costs. It also includes any cash flows that arise in relation to capital expenditure. As with supply, these outflows should be at a level where they can be linked to the payment profiles held within the CFM.

- *Net funding requirements.* Rules within the CFM are used to 'time-shift' the imported cash supply and demand data into the time periods in which cash will flow in and out of the organisation's treasury bank account(s). To this other cash consumers and income streams not covered are added. This may include items such as interest payments and dividend accruals. To capture these, we could either create a separate support model or they can be entered directly into the CFM. By subtracting the demand for cash from the supply, management can review the financial resources required.

To address any cash shortfall, or to reduce the amount of borrowings, budget and forecast data within the OAM can be reassessed to see what activities might change. The model would also allow management to gauge the impact of changing customer and supplier payment terms. Assuming this has been done, the model can now be used to assess how any cash shortfalls should be financed with the two obvious financing sources being debt and equity.

When reporting actual results, much of the data within the cash flow model will be entered directly from the underlying transaction systems, so there is little need for modelling other than to produce a comparison between budget and forecast versions.

Additional Data Requirements Within the OAM

Generating a cash flow from the OAM and DFM as previously defined requires two things:

1. New information will need to be held in those models that links individual suppliers or customers to the P&L data.

2. Data held within these models will need to be at the level of detail where interactions with major suppliers and customers can be identified. With this in mind, a few comments need to be made on the practicalities of designing the CFM and associated models.

Depending on the industry, it may not be possible to forecast sales by individual customer. In this case, grouping customers into categories, such as sales channels, that reflect their payment profile is adequate for our needs.

Similarly, it could be that invoices are only raised at the end of the month with a standard payment profile of 30-day terms. In this case, from a planning point of view, cash will theoretically be received 1 month following the invoice date. As this is equivalent to a 1-period delay between P&L and cash flowing, there is no point in calculating this at a day level.

The level of detail in both content and time should be determined by the impact severity that any time delay on a particular measure has on overall cash flow. For example, if invoices for particular customers or suppliers are raised mid-month that have a 1 per cent or greater impact on cash flow, then it could be argued that it is worth modelling cash flow by week, and worth modelling at that customer or supplier level. This will almost certainly warrant a more detailed forecast model for the measures involved.

If there is no such requirement, then modelling cash flow could be accommodated within the OAM.

Identifying Cash Payment Profiles Within the OAM

In order to generate the cash flow from P&L data, the model will need to identify the payment profile for both customers and suppliers. Where it is not practical to identify these at a third-party organisation level, such as with office expenses where the supplier may vary from month-to-month, then some broad assumptions can be made as to when cash flows out of the organisation. For example, we could assume that cash involved with personnel costs will always be in the same period in which the costs are incurred from a P&L standpoint. Other items could be assumed to have a one-period delay from when they are incurred.

To identify individual profiles, we can add a new attribute against the measures in the OAM where that P&L data is held. This provides a 'look up' inquiry capability that indicates who the third party is for the related income or expense. Remember, these are for income and expenditure items that do not have a DFM. Consider the following example from our case study, depicted in table 6-1.

Table 6-1: P&L Third Party Measure Example

ACCOUNT CODE	DESCRIPTION	CUSTOMER OR SUPPLIER ATTRIBUTE
GS21010	Salaries and wages	Employee
GS21010	Commissions	Employee
GS21010	Overtime	Employee
GS21010	Rent	S. Atkins
GS21010	Heat, light, and power	EDF
GS21010	Travel and entertainment	General expenses
GS21010	Equipment hire	AV supplies

In this example, the attribute 'customer or supplier' is used to forge the link between an account and the third party involved. Salaries and wages, overtime, and travel and entertainment have the customer or supplier attribute of 'employee'; rent is linked to 'S. Atkins'; heat, light, and power is linked to the supplier 'EDF'; and so on. These attributes appear as members within the CFM as will be explained in the next point.

Defining Payment Profiles Within the CFM

One of two methods can be used to store and calculate the cash effect of individual payment profiles within the CFM:

- When there are only a few suppliers or customers, each could be set up as individual measures in the CFM. These measures directly relate to the individual customer or supplier attributes as defined in the OAM, and the value contained within the measure is set to the period delay (that is, the number of periods that occur between order and cash flowing). Table 6-2 gives an example.

Table 6-2: P&L Period Delay Measure Example

ACCOUNT CODE	MEASURE DESCRIPTION	MEASURE VALUE
Supp0010	EDF	+ 1
Supp0020	Employee	0
Supp0030	S. Atkins	+ 1

In the table 6-2, the value in measure 'EDF' and 'S. Atkins' signals that cash flows out of the organisation one period after any expense that has this attribute. However, any expense associated with employee occurs in the same period.

- Where there are multiple suppliers or customers, each could be set up as individual members of a new dimension within the CFM. These members directly relate to the individual customer or supplier attributes as defined in the OAM. Using the preceding example, this dimension (table 6-3) would consist of the following:

Table 6-3: P&L Individual Member of New Dimension Measure Example

DIMENSION MEMBER	DESCRIPTION
Supp0010	EDF
Supp0020	Employee
Supp0030	S. Atkins

To go with this dimension, we require a measure within the OAM that indicates the time delay between the value appearing in the P&L and cash flowing into a bank account. The value of this measure is set for each dimension member to reflect the payment term.

Other Cash Measures and Rules

As well as the P&L measures identified so far, additional measures may be required to cover other cash flows not contained within the OAM (for example, loan repayments, dividends, bank balances, interest charges, and interest rates). A measure will also be required to hold exchange gains or losses, should the organisation be involved with multiple currencies.

The attributes, dimension members, and measures as they relate to customers and suppliers are used to ensure that the correct data is pulled through from the OAM to the right place within the CFM. They are also used in rules to calculate the cash impact on any pulled-through values, ensuring they are suitably time-shifted.

For the XYZ, Inc. case study, these measures and rules were set at the following:

Table 6-4: Additional Cash Flow Measures Example

CODE	NAME	SOURCE OR RULE
CF10900	Total sales revenue	From support model shifted by payment attribute
Staff costs:		
CF21010	Salaries and wages	From OAM shifted by payment attribute
CF21020	Commissions	From OAM shifted by payment attribute

Continued on p. 96

Continued from p. 95

CODE	NAME	SOURCE OR RULE
CF21030	Overtime	From OAM shifted by payment attribute
CF21040	Contract labour	From OAM shifted by payment attribute
CF21050	Social welfare	From OAM shifted by payment attribute
CF21060	Total staff costs	Sum (GS21010–GS21050)
General expenses:		
CF22010	Rent	From OAM shifted by payment attribute
CF22020	Heat, light, and power etc.	From OAM shifted by payment attribute
CF30010	**Total direct costs**	**Sum of all general and department-specific expenses**
Other cash flows not covered:		
CF40010	Interest charges	Entered
CF41020	Dividends paid	Entered
Capital expenditure:		
CF41010	Interest paid	From capital expenditure model
CF41020	Capital paid	From capital expenditure model
Bank balance details:		
CF50010	Opening cash balance	= CF50010 in prior period
CF41010	Interest rate on overdrawn balances	Entered
Cash summary calculation:		
CF50040	Cash balance	= CF50010 – sum (CF30010–CF41020) If CF50040<0, then calculate charge as CF50040 × CF41010
CF50050	Overspend interest charges	CF41010
CF50060	Closing cash balance	= CF50040 – CF50050

As table 6-4 shows, there needs to be a process that transfers the data from the OAM and other models into the CFM. How this is done depends on the planning technology being used. In a spread sheet, this would be via cell links that reference both the model and the attribute so the CFM receives the appropriate values.

Although this example has concentrated on the link between the OAM and the CFM, the same concept also applies to any DFM and strategic improvement models.

REPORTING FROM THE CFM

By implementing the CFM as described, it is possible to track how individual P&L items impact cash flow, as can be seen in the following examples.

Displaying Cash Requirements by Department

For our case study, we have defined customers and suppliers as a separate dimension member. Customers have also been linked to particular organisation departments by adding an attribute to the customer member that identifies which department is responsible for them. This is then used to filter the customer list depending on the department selected on the report. We could also have gone one step further and introduced products into the profile, which would then allow us to have multiple prices and payment profiles.

In the first report, shown in figure 6-2, the user can select the department (provided they have the correct security access rights), the version (that is, budget or forecast), and the year to be displayed. This then selects the appropriate measures, which in our example is the US sales division. The values shown are the cash effect of P&L data taken from the OAM. Alongside each account, we have displayed the customer or supplier attribute and the payment term that was used to time-shift the P&L data. The report then shows the cash supply and demand as being forecast for the next six periods. At the bottom is a summary of individual month requirements and a cumulative view.

Figure 6-2A: Report Showing Cash Requirements by Department

Department: USA Sales
Version: Forecast
Year: 2014

	Account	Customer or Supplier	Payment Term	Period 1	Period 2	Period 3	Period 4	Period 5	Period 6
Cash Supply									
Revenue:									
	Sales	J Bright & Sons	2	$13,400	$5,000		$43,600		
	Sales	J Smith Inc.	2		$17,500	$17,800			$3,400
	Sales	Other sales	1	$23,400	$22,500	$237	$25,000	$23,450	$22,300
Total Cash Supply				**$36,800**	**$45,000**	**$18,037**	**$68,600**	**$23,450**	**$25,700**
Cash Demand									
Staffing:									
	Salaries	Employee costs	0	$18,321	$18,321	$18,321	$18,321	$18,321	$18,321
	Labour taxes	Dept of social security	3	$2,750	$2,750	$2,750	$2,750	$2,750	$2,750
	Welfare costs	J Investments	1	$1,210	$1,210	$1,210	$1,210	$1,210	$1,210
Total Salaries				**$22,281**	**$22,281**	**$22,281**	**$22,281**	**$22,281**	**$22,281**
General Expenses:									
	Rent	S. Atkins	1	$3,200	$3,200	$3,200	$3,200	$3,200	$3,200
	Heat and light	Beyer Heat & Light Inc	2	$600	$600	$600	$600	$600	$600
	Water	Southern Utilities	2	$200	$200	$200	$200	$200	$200
	Telephone	Bell Telephone	1	$1,100	$1,100	$1,100	$1,100	$1,100	$1,100
	Insurance	G Sedgwick Insurance	1	$1,600	$1,600	$1,600	$1,600	$1,600	$1,600
	Travel	Personnel expenses	0	$1,950	$1,950	$1,950	$1,950	$1,950	$1,950
	Hotel and Living	Personnel expenses	0	$1,600	$1,600	$1,600	$1,600	$1,600	$1,600
	Office supplies	General	0	$750	$750	$750	$750	$750	$750
	Other expenses	General	0	$5	$5	$5	$5	$5	$5
Total General Expenses				**$11,005**	**$11,005**	**$11,005**	**$11,005**	**$11,005**	**$11,005**
Total Cash Requirements				**$3,514**	**$11,714**	**-$15,250**	**$35,314**	**-$9,836**	**-$7,586**
Cumulative Cash Requirements				**$3,514**	**$15,228**	**-$22**	**$35,293**	**$25,457**	**$17,871**

Figure 6-2B: Report Showing Cash Requirements by Department

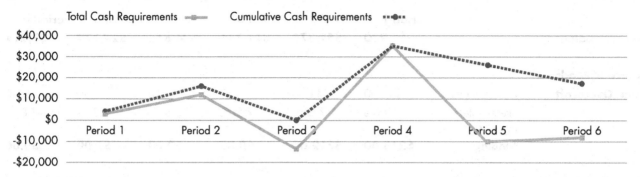

In the report, payment terms are stored as periods. If the CFM was set up as a weekly model, then the values would represent the number of weeks between supply and receiving cash. Payment profiles are kept by month and version. This allows the profiles to be modified over time and to be applied to different budget or forecast scenarios.

By selecting total company as opposed to an individual department, the report would accumulate the cash impact from individual departments to give a total cash picture.

Evaluating Sources of Cash

This next report, shown in table 6-5, has the total cash requirements as produced in the last report, which is then compared with potential cash sources. The user can select budget or forecast versions.

Table 6-5: Report Showing Cash Requirements and Sources

Version: Forecast
Year: 2014

	Period 1	Period 2	Period 3	Period 4	Period 5	Period 6
Cash from operations						
Current cash balances	$54,200	$68,250	$65,205	$52,905	$65,995	$51,401
Income from ongoing operations	$193,450	$184,300	$142,300	$202,430	$195,640	$121,340
Expenses from ongoing operations	$179,400	$187,345	$154,600	$189,340	$210,234	$124,350
Net cash from operations	**$68,250**	**$52,905**	**$65,995**	**$65,995**	**$51,401**	**$48,391**
Other cash movements						
Interest	$1,420	$1,420	$1,420	$1,420	$1,420	$1,420
Dividends		$75,400				
Loan repayments	$17,600	$17,600	$17,600	$17,600	$17,600	$17,600
Other cash movements	**-$16,180**	**-$91,580**	**-$16,180**	**-$16,180**	**-$16,180**	**-$16,180**
Investments						
Capital expenditure	$55,000	$25,000	$25,000	$25,000	$60,000	$25,000

Continued on p. 100

Continued from p. 99

		Period 1	Period 2	Period 3	Period 4	Period 5	Period 6
Net cash balance		-$2,930	-$51,375	$11,725	$24,815	-$24,779	$7,211
Source of Funds							
Bank Overdraft	Amount funded	$3,500	$4,000	$0	$0	$0	$0
	Interest rate	7.80%	7.80%	7.80%	7.80%	7.80%	7.80%
	Cost of funding	$273.00	$312.00	$0.00	$0.00	$0.00	$0.00
M Capital Inc	Amount funded		$50,000				
	Interest rate		3.50%				
	Cost of funding		$1,750.00	$1,750.00	$1,750.00	$1,750.00	$1,750.00
B Investments	Amount funded					$30,000	
	Interest rate					4.20%	
	Cost of funding					$1,260.00	$1,260.00
Net cash requirement		$298	$2,625	$11,725	$24,815	$5,221	$7,211

The report displays the forecast bank cash balance along with projected cash income and expenditure to give the net cash flow from operations. From this the other cash consumers and cash needed for capital expenditure are deducted. This calculates a net cash balance. If positive, the organisation has enough cash to operate. If negative, cash sources need to be found unless forecast expenditures can be reduced (or income increased).

The source of funds section contains various ways of funding any cash shortfall. Here management can enter the amount to be funded, which can be split amongst a number of providers. These sources also have an impact on cash flow and the net cash requirement at the bottom of the report calculated to take into account.

Scenario Analysis

By using versions within the CFM, we are able to run different payment scenarios as well as try out alternative sources of funding. For example, we could set up a forecast version to show a worst position (for example, low revenues and high expenses), and a best forecast version (for example, high revenues and low costs).

Data from the current forecast version can be copied into these versions where revenues and expenditures are adjusted. The resulting cash impact for each version can then be displayed side-by-side so the extent of any borrowings can be seen and compared.

We have now completed the description of the two central models of the planning framework. Supporting these are a range of models that provide detail behind the OAM and CFF. The first two we will examine—detailed history model and performance measures model—are the subject of the next chapter.

7

DETAILED HISTORY AND PERFORMANCE MEASURES MODELS

The detailed history and performance measures models are created to make sense of results being achieved. The detailed history model does this by drilling down into a particular result to reveal the detail behind the numbers. The performance measures model takes a high-level view by combining summaries of internal performance with external data to create industry related comparisons.

REPORTING PAST AND FUTURE PERFORMANCE

Relevance

Field Marshal Arthur Wellesley, otherwise known as the Duke of Wellington, was one of the leading military and political figures of the 19th century. He was commissioned into the British Army in 1787 and rose to the rank of general. One of his more prominent campaigns resulted in the defeat of Napoleon in the Battle of Waterloo in 1815. He is famous for his extensive planning before battles, which left him able to score victories against larger superior forces at minimum cost to his own troops.

According to various online encyclopaedias, the Duke of Wellington is regarded as one of the greatest defensive commanders of all time, with many of his tactics and battle plans studied in military academies around the world. He is also known for his disregard of ineffective and inefficient bureaucracy, as can be seen from the following letter he is said to have written in 1812 while leading an army in Spain:

Gentlemen

Whilst marching from Portugal to a position which commands the approach to Madrid and the French forces, my officers have been diligently complying with your requests, which have been sent by HM ship from London to Lisbon and thence by dispatch rider to our Headquarters.

We have enumerated our saddles, bridles, tents and tent poles and all manner of sundry items for which His Majesty's Government holds me accountable. I have dispatched reports on the character, wit and spleen of every officer. Each item and every farthing has been accounted for, with two regrettable exceptions for which I beg your indulgence.

Unfortunately the sum of one shilling and nine-pence remains unaccounted for in one infantry battalion's petty cash and there has been hideous confusion as to the number of jars of raspberry jam issued to one cavalry regiment during a sandstorm in Western Spain. This reprehensible carelessness may be related to the pressure of circumstances, since we are at war with France, a fact which may come as a bit of a surprise to you gentlemen in Whitehall.

This brings me to my present purpose, which is to request elucidation of my instructions from His Majesty's Government so that I may better understand why I am dragging an army over these barren plains. I construe that perforce it must be one of two alternative duties, as given below. I shall pursue either one with my best ability, but I cannot do both:

1. To train an army of uninformed British Clerks in Spain for the benefit of the accountants and copy-boys in London, or perchance

2. To see to it that the forces of Napoleon are driven out of Spain

Your most obedient servant
Wellington

Whether Wellington actually wrote the letter or not does not concern us here, but as this book's authors, we suspect that many of you have wanted to write something similar to your boss. It seems that the focus of management reporting is often on the insignificant, and the real issue of achieving the organisation's purpose is forgotten. What is more important: being over budget on stationery by 10 per cent this month or beating the competition? It is an issue of materiality versus relevance.

You can tell a lot about an organisation's priorities by looking at the management reports through which people and departments are judged.

Context

A natural consequence of any kind of plan is the variances that arise when monitoring what actually happened. The more detail kept within a plan, the more variances that will be generated. The more variances there are, the more management time and effort will be required to analyse and interpret what they mean.

Herein lies the problem. Technology has allowed vast amounts of detail to be planned and tracked. Computer systems can quickly and effortlessly go through a sea of data, spitting out variances and trends. They can then sort, rank, and chart that data in many weird and wonderful ways. But systems typically require management skills to assess what is relevant and what is not. To determine relevance requires results to be placed in context of what really matters.

As an example, take a report that shows we are over budget on travel expenses by 15 per cent. Is this a good or bad performance? Well, it depends. If that overspend was due to visiting 20 key customers in trying to secure future sales orders, then it was probably well worth the cost. But if it was spent attending a range of internal meetings, then who knows?

The trouble is that quite a lot of management decisions are made on variance reports that have no context. How many readers have had their expenses cut (or expected revenues increased) simply because actual results disagreed with budgets? Indiscriminate cost cutting can easily result in key initiatives that are crucial for future growth to be starved of essential resources. Or how about a report that shows that a department is 20 per cent under on costs? It is easy to assume that there is nothing to worry about, and so no action is required. The result of this decision (deciding to do nothing is still a decision) means that allocated resources that could be better used elsewhere are wasted. It could also mean that key activities are not being carried out, or not carried out to the level that is required for future goals.

Connected to this question of relevance is the standard to which performance is compared. In most organisations, this will be against the numbers negotiated when the budget was set. However, is this standard good enough in the real world? Let's suppose for a moment that the budget was based on an assumed business environment. What if those assumptions turned out to be wrong? For example, if when setting a revenue target an assumption was made that the market growth was 10 per cent, but the growth turned out to be 20 per cent. It would mean that an on-target performance could be bad, as market share would be lost.

Too often, organisations compare their performance with numbers they established at the start of the year. If these are not presented in the context of what the market is doing, then variances become at best meaningless, and at worst can cause the organisation to make decisions that are wrong.

Data Issues

It is essential for those making decisions based on past performance to recognise that the data being presented may not tell the whole story. Ignoring the issues of relevance and context mentioned previously, the data may also incorporate one or more of the following issues:

- *Data accuracy.* Actual results are typically held in other systems, such as the general ledger. To transfer these into the planning models for reporting will require values to be summarised, translated, and mapped into the right measures. Depending on the source system and the data acquisition capabilities of the planning technology, this may not be a simple task. Even when the transfer routines have been set up, changes within the source systems (for example, adding new measures or changes to operational structures) could invalidate how results appear within reports.

  Then there is the issue that the source data itself may be in error, all of which can lead to data integrity issues. The only way to check is to have some kind of validation procedure that gives confidence that results being reported are of the highest data quality. This will almost certainly mean that a user should be able to interrogate any number in a report to see how it has been translated from its source to the appropriate planning model.

- *Timing issues.* Variances are calculated at a moment in time. Although data may be correct within a model, because there is a delay between what is held and what may now be the truth, the data can lead to unexpected results. Of course, models could be set up so there is a dynamic link to the source systems, but this leads to another problem: the result someone saw yesterday that sparked a conversation with other managers has mysteriously changed overnight. Assuming that only some people noticed the change, it appears that the data is randomly changing and is therefore unreliable. After all, how can managers be sure it will not change again in the next few minutes and therefore cause people to doubt what the numbers are actually revealing?

  A solution to this dilemma is to have a cut-off point in time that everyone agrees to. This assures that reports are made of detailed data that existed within the transaction systems at that point in time. To complement this, comparisons should be allowed between the results that exist now and the cut-off point. This would indicate that any variances between the two versions are either down to errors being corrected or were subject to timing issues when recorded.

- *Hidden horrors.* Variances may show that a particular measure is on track against plan, but hidden beneath the value may be individual items that mask what is really going on. For example, there may not be a variance on a particular revenue stream, but when looking at the detail there could be some customers or donors whose revenues are way under what was expected and is being offset by other revenue items that are unexpectedly way over. The only time this is discovered is when the good variances become on target, leaving the bad performing results with nowhere to hide.

Of course, you could print out every conceivable variance, but two issues then arise. First, it may not be possible to plan at this level of detail, in which case there will be no variances to calculate. Second, the more variances that are generated, the more time someone has to spend in investigating them. Investigations take time and distract management away from what they should be doing: securing the future. To overcome this, systems should automatically trawl through the detail and look out for abnormal variances that are being covered up at the summary level. These variances should be brought to management's attention as exceptions to what is being reported.

- *Trends.* Because of their point-in-time nature, variances cannot show whether there is an on-going trend. Trends are not obligated to fall in line with an organisation's planning calendar and may span multiple years before they are noticed. This requires data to be assessed at a detailed level over multiple years and with different spans of time. Retailers are typically good at this, and most plan according to the industry's different seasons, which may or may not fit in with their fiscal calendar.

- *Abnormal events.* The last issue we will cover here is that, by themselves, variances cannot show whether they were caused by a one-off event or are part of an on-going trend. There are many organisations where an abnormal performance in one month (for example, 20 per cent over sales due to an unusual client purchase) generates a target for the following year that has been set by applying an arbitrary growth rate. Assuming for a moment that growth is likely, applying it to a previous abnormal event means we now have a target that is unrealistic.

This also happens with expenses. Many of you will be familiar with the urge to unnecessarily spend your entire budget in the current year, because if you do not you will lose it in the next year. This sort of game-playing is hard to justify unless you look at the detail behind the numbers to highlight what is abnormal and what the real trends are.

The issues covered here apply to both actual results and those being used as forecasts. To tell a more insightful story behind any number requires detail. The level of detail will differ depending on what managers need to know in order to take insightful decisions.

REPORTING PERFORMANCE FROM THE PLANNING FRAMEWORK

Bearing in mind the previous comments, the business planning framework prescribes two logical models whose role is to provide relevance and context and which can be assessed for data issues. These models compliment the operational activity model (OAM) described in chapter 5, 'Operational Activity Model'. The OAM is designed to answer the following questions:

- What did we achieve against the plan in relation to resources, workload, and outcomes for each business process?
- How are each of these looking for the future? Is performance getting better or worse?

Variances will indicate that some things are not going according to plan and will need to be investigated. Similarly, there will be underlying trends that may not surface in the OAM reports, and so these too will need to be identified and researched. That is the aim of the models described in this chapter, which provide backup to the OAM.

There are two types of models that can be used when reviewing actual and forecast results:

- The detailed history model (DHM) supports investigations into past performance. It focuses on what went on internally within the organisation at a detailed level.

- The performance measures model (PMM) takes a higher, external view of performance that is related to what is going on in the business environment and in comparison to competitors or peers.

These models are now described in more detail.

IDENTIFYING DHMS

Given that the focus of the DHM is in analysing actual results reported in the OAM, the starting point in deciding what models to create are the measures held within that model. As explained in chapter 5 'Operational Activity Model', measures are grouped into those that monitor objectives, business process goals, performance measures, activity measures (that can be split into work done and outcomes), risk, assumptions, income, and resources.

Of these, the ones that can be broken into further detail are those that deal with income and resources, as these will be made up of transactions held within the general ledger. Some of the workload and outcome measures may also have further details, which can be used to analyse business process activity.

It is not desirable to create DHMs for every measure, as this could distract management from what is important. Instead, DHMs should be created for those measures whose values play a significant part in either directly resourcing or monitoring a business process.

When defining a DHM, the question should be asked, 'What information do I need in order to understand the actual results being presented in the OAM'? The answer to this question determines the level of detail, the analyses that are required, and the type of history model that will meet those needs.

In chapter 4, 'Business Planning Framework', we outlined three types of DHM, each of which provides a different type of support:

- *Transaction data set.* These are tables of data that can be queried and summarised. An example of this type could contain the general ledger transactions behind each account code. These would be loaded from the General Ledger (GL) on a regular basis and could consist of date, department, account code, supplier, and amount. Capabilities within the DHM would summarise this data by department, month, and account codes that are then fed into the appropriate place within the OAM.

  The way it would be used would be to support a particular expense query. For example, if there was a variance in the travel budget, the user would be able to drill down into the supporting DHM to see the transactions that made up the actual result. The user could then issue another query that extracts transactions for a prior month to see if any expenses had been held over and hence had caused this month's variance.

As with the other types of DHM, the ease of use and capabilities provided to an end user will depend on the technology solution being used. As a minimum, this type of DHM should support the following examples:

- *Filters.* List all transactions making up a particular account code.
- *Summaries.* Total all transactions for a particular account code and over a selected period.
- *Sorting and ranking.* Show the top 10 departments as ranked by travel expenditure.
- *Secure access.* The content held within a DHM should automatically filter out data that the user is not allowed to see.

- *Multi-dimensional model.* This second type of DHM allows users to produce cross-tabular analyses. Data is stored and referred to by its business dimensions. Users then have free access to the way in which data is presented, which can incorporate charts, additional calculations, and colour-coded exceptions. Examples of this type of model include sales analyses that could include types of customers, products sold, discounts provided, returns, and shipping costs.

  Unlike the transaction data set, a multi-dimensional model is able to provide the following:

  - *Multiple views of the data.* For example, show sales revenue by product and customer, customer profitability, returns by product and location.
  - *Trends.* For example, calculate a rolling 12-month average and show this by month for the current year versus last year.
  - *Exceptions.* For example, show all customers whose year-on-year growth has been negative.

- *Unstructured model.* This final type of model is for providing non-numeric support, such as links to news reports, social media discussions, and competitor product videos. By linking these into the OAM, qualitative information can be provided that can make a substantial difference in the way results are perceived.

CASE STUDY—DHMS

In our XYZ, Inc. case study, the following three DHMs have been defined: sales analysis, human resources (HR), and general expenses.

Sales Analysis

This is a multi-dimensional model that is used to review past sales and spot trends in product groups. The dimensions and members of the model were set as follows:

- *Region.* Members are the sales region of the United States, Europe, and Asia.
- *Customer.* Members are customers whose revenue exceeds $50,000 in a year. Customers with smaller revenues are summarised as 'other' for analysis purposes.
- *Product.* Members are the product lines offered.
- *Channel.* Members are 'direct' and 'on-line' to distinguish between how the product was purchased.
- *Year.* Members are the past three years.
- *Period.* This is set at weeks within a year.

- *Measures.* The members include the following:
    - ○ *Volume.* The quantity of each product ordered.
    - ○ *Gross revenue.* The total amount charged for each product.
    - ○ *Discount.* The amount of any discount given on each product.
    - ○ *Net revenue.* The amount invoiced.

From this DHM, users can produce analyses regarding the products being sold, through which channels, in what areas, and the profit margins being achieved. This is calculated from the detailed sales data by product and customer. Figure 7-1 is an example of the kind of report that can be produced.

Figure 7-1A: Sample Sales Analysis Report to Back Up Results Stored in the Operational Activity Model

Region:	Total											
Channel:	Direct			**Product Analysis For The Past Three Months By Week**								
Year:	2014											
		Week 1	**Week 2**	**Week 3**	**Week 4**	**Week 5**	**Week 6**	**Week 7**	**Week 8**	**Week 9**	**Week 10**	**Avg. Price**
Pens	**Volume**	8000	8400	9600	10660	11800	12300	13450	16500	17430	19450	
Net Revenue		$4,560	$4,788	$5,472	$6,042	$6,726	$7,011	$7,667	$9,405	$9,935	$11,087	$0.57
Stationary	**Volume**	34400	32400	33400	31400	36700	35600	3500	37200	35600	32800	
Net Revenue		$11,696	$11,016	$11,356	$10,676	$12,478	$12,104	$11,900	$12,648	$12,104	$11,152	$0.34
Pencils	**Volume**	72240	70102	69120	68720	63450	62140	59860	57890	55640	51240	
Net Revenue		$9,391	$9,116	$8,986	$8,934	$8,249	$8,078	$7,782	$7,526	$7,233	$6,661	$0.13
Desk Stands	**Volume**	1680	2980	3580	4300	6300	8900	11400	14500	17400	18300	
Net Revenue		$2,990	5,304$	$6,372	$7,654	$11,214	$15,842	$20,292	$25,810	$30,972	$32,574	$1.78
Flip Charts	**Volume**	780	925	1300	1415	1690	2340	2630	3200	3820	4230	
Net Revenue		$2,020	$2,396	$3,367	$3,665	$4,377	$6,061	$6,812	$8,288	$9,894	$10,956	$2.59

Figure 7-1B: Sample Sales Analysis Report to Back Up Results Stored in the Operational Activity Model

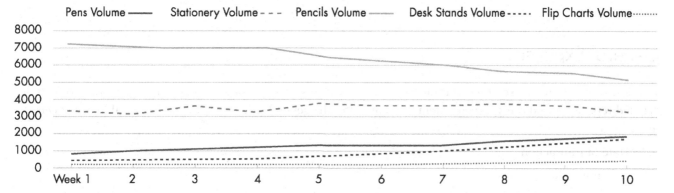

HR

This is a transaction data set used to monitor staff and welfare entitlements. The fields defined for each record are as follows:

- Period (that is, the period to which this record belongs)
- Employee name

- Title
- Salary grade
- Department
- Status (for example, full-time, part-time, no longer working)
- Basic salary paid
- Overtime amount paid
- Pension contribution paid
- Hours worked in period

The table is updated each period with records being appended to build up a history of employee costs. These records can then be selected and summarised via queries to provide a picture of how costs change by grade over time. Table 7-1 depicts a sample table of a history of employee-related costs.

Table 7-1: Sample Employee Table to Back Up Costs Reported in the Operational Activity Model

PERIOD	NAME	TITLE	GRADE	DEPARTMENT	STATUS	BASIC	COMMISSION	PENSION	HOURS
Jun-14	M. Smith	Manager	5	US Sales	Full-time	1560	450	130	48
Jun-14	D. Rodney	Sales Executive	3	US Sales	Full-time	1450	250	90	42
Jun-14	G. Jones	Sales Executive	3	US Sales	Full-time	1320	520	85	45
Jun-14	T. Griffiths	Sales Executive	3	US Sales	Full-time	1210	320	85	43
Jun-14	B. Hanks	Support	2	US Sales	Full-time	870	—	45	43
Jun-14	G. Phillips	Support	2	US Sales	Part-time	540	—	—	24
Jun-14	D. Boake	Support	1	US Sales	Part-time	535	—	—	22

General Expenses

This last transaction data set holds transactions for all expenses except those relating to HR. It is used to provide detailed reports behind every expense item as recorded in the general ledger. The fields in the table have been set as follows:

- Date of transaction
- Account code
- Department
- Supplier
- Invoice number
- Detail
- Amount
- Partial or full payment

Table 7-2 presents a sample expenses table.

Table 7-2: Sample Expenses Table With Detailed Transactions, as Recorded in the General Ledger

DATE	ACCOUNT CODE	DEPARTMENT	SUPPLIER	INVOICE NO.	DETAIL	AMOUNT	PARTIAL FULL PAYMENT
13-Jul-14	GE22010	US Sales	S. Atkins	Inv 12103	Rent for office space	-$123.45	Full
15-Jul-14	GE22020	US Sales	EDF	Inv 12110	Power for office	-$745.62	Full
16-Jul-14	GE22070	US Sales	S Pacific	Inv 12125	Rail fare to Boston	-$25.23	Full
22-Jul-14	GE22080	US Sales	Holiday Inn	Inv 12132	Hotel expenses for G Smith	-$234.61	Full
22-Jul-14	GE22090	US Sales	N Starks	Inv 12133	Hire of projector	-$77.89	Full
29-Jul-14	GE22090	US Sales	G Hind	Inv 12148	Hire of stand	-$345.62	Partial
30-Jul-14	GE22110	US Sales	Postal Service	Inv 12159	Postage for month	-$74.35	Full

DEFINING THE PMM

PMM Content

As mentioned earlier, while the DHM looks at past performance in light of what happened internally, the PMM in contrast takes an outward view that looks at past and future performance in light of what is going on in the market.

In order to do this, the PMM has a number of industry-recognised measures, which require a range of additional data to be collected that may not exist within the OAM. It is not the purpose of this book to recommend what those measures should be, as they are not necessarily applicable to all industries. Some will be dependent on the management methodology being used to manage the company. For example, if the organisation subscribes to total quality management practices, then a range of measures will have already been defined, as would those whose practices support economic value added principles. What is important is that the measures cover a range of business areas that can be related to the organisation's business processes.

Bernard Marr, a leading authority on organisational performance, has produced a book on measures. *Key Performance Indicators: The 75 Measures Every Manager Needs to Know* has a great selection of key performance indicators that has been grouped into the topics typically found in the perspectives of a balanced scorecard.

The book answers key questions on why the measure is useful, how to calculate and interpret the measure (with examples), what its limitations are, and where to find out more information. It also includes measures on the impact of social media and how to calculate an organisation's social networking footprint. If you are challenged with identifying and selecting what you should be measuring, then this book is worth reading.

PMM Business Dimensions

For the XYZ, Inc. case study, the PMM consists of the following dimensions and members:

- Organisational departments.
- Versions that include current year actual, current forecast, target, and benchmark. The latter is used to hold industry standard values where available. This dimension could also be extended to hold comparatives to major competitors.
- Time is held as quarterly totals, as this is seen to be sufficient for management purposes.
- Measures are those that are used to calculate performance as viewed from a market perspective, some of which already exist within the OAM.

Case Study Measures for XYZ, Inc.

The following measures, which monitor performance across a range of business areas, have been defined within the PMM.

Financial Performance

These measures are the familiar ones of the following:

- *Return on equity.* This has been set as one of XYZ's corporate goals. It is measured using the following formula:

$$\left(\frac{Net\ profit}{Shareholder\ equity}\right) \times 100$$

Net profit and shareholder equity come from the OAM and are included within the PMM.

- *Working capital ratio.* This measure helps XYZ to compare the working capital employed with competitors in the same industry. It is calculated by the following formula:

$$\left(\frac{Current\ assets}{Current\ liabilities}\right) \times 100$$

Values for these measures come from the OAM.

Customer Performance

Retaining customers is vital to XYZ's future success. To help them monitor performance in this area, they use the following measures:

- *Customer retention rate.* This is calculated by the following formula:

$$Number\ of\ customers\ at\ start\ of\ year\ /Number\ of\ customers\ at\ end\ of\ year$$

XYZ's management would always want to see this rising. The number of customers is not held in any planning model, so these are loaded directly into the PMM from the internal customer relationship management system.

- *Customer complaints.* This is a straightforward statistic that is collected directly from XYZ's support system.

Marketing Performance

Given the potential growth of online ordering, the performance of Web-based marketing activities is crucial to future success. To grow, XYZ must be able to utilise the power of search engines and social media sites. To monitor performance in this area, two measures are used that only appear within the PMM:

- *Search engine ranking.* This is measured by keyword, and results are provided directly from the relevant search engines. The aim is to see which keywords provide the best value in terms of how XYZ is ranked and the cost involved. To calculate this, the PMM reports 20 selected keywords in terms of rank, click-through rate, and the marketing amount spent on each one.

- *Klout score.* The values for this measure are provided directly by the third-party organisation of the same name. Klout uses around 35 variables on Facebook and Twitter to come up with a score of between 0 and 100. Zero indicates that XYZ's social media activity is having no influence on users, but a score of 100 indicates that XYZ is having total influence on what is being discussed. Klout scores are free and provide an interesting way of monitoring social networks.

Operational Processes

Operational process measures allow management to assess how well its production facility is performing. The measures in this area include the following:

- *Capacity utilisation rate.* This is measured by the following formula:

$$\left(\frac{Actual\ capacity}{Possible\ capacity}\right) \times 100$$

The result indicates whether there are efficiencies to be gained and whether there are any issues with the production process. If these measures were to be set as business process goals, then they would be stored within the OAM. As it is, they are being kept just within the PMM.

- *Quality index.* This measure indicates whether the products being sold are fit for purpose, which directly impacts customer satisfaction and hence any reorder rate. There are many ways in which this can be measured, with most organisations tracking several quality measures. For XYZ, they monitor product returns, which are loaded directly into the PMM from the sales order system.

Employee Performance

This set of performance measures looks at employee relationships. Two measures are deemed important to XYZ:

1. *Revenue per employee.* This measure looks at how much revenue is generated for each person employed. Because employee costs form a significant proportion of overall costs, it is essential that this does not increase as online sales cause prices to drop. Both parts of this measure come from the OAM.

2. *Employee churn rate.* This measure reports staff turnover and is generated from values loaded directly from the internal HR system.

Social Responsibility

This last set of measures are seen by management as crucial to the way XYZ is viewed. Social responsibility is an increasingly important discussion point on social media sites, so XYZ is keen to promote its 'green' credentials. The chosen measures only exist within the PMM and consist of the following:

- *Carbon footprint.* This measure expresses the amount of carbon dioxide emitted as part of the production process. Values are reported as the number of units per ton, with a target level set at 18 tons per year. The industry average is around 20 tons per year.

- *Energy consumption.* This measure is related to the last in that it provides management with a way to promote XYZ as being more socially advanced. The value is calculated as the amount of energy purchased in a quarter, which can then be related back to the energy consumption used to produce each unit of product.

Reporting From the PMM

There are many ways in which measures stored within the PMM can be reported. One of the better ways is as a dashboard that uses dials that compare actuals to targets for the purpose of monitoring how the organisation is performing in each category. These dials can be set to display variances from target, from plan, and from an industry benchmark.

Where performance is lacking, management can develop initiatives within the strategy improvement model to bring the organisation back into line with the targets set.

This completes our description of the models that provide insight into past performance. The next chapter looks at the OAM support models that are used to predict the future.

8

PREDICT AND OPTIMISE PLANNING MODELS

Planning is primarily concerned with future performance, and in particular, managing the difference between what could be achieved and what is likely. This requires organisations to understand the impact of business momentum and to challenge whether the current business processes are adequate to reach desired goals.

PREDICTING THE FUTURE

In most surveys on performance, the ability to accurately forecast the future is nearly always at the top of a manager's wish list. This is because knowing what the future may bring enables them to focus their resources to best effect. For example, if it is known that a product is going to sell 1,000 units a month, then production and raw material purchases can be geared to this level. This in turn reduces working capital requirements by minimising stock levels and eliminates wasted resources that would otherwise go unused. Similarly, if it is known that an investment is not going to deliver the perceived level of return, then a decision can be made earlier to cancel that investment and transfer assigned resources onto projects that are better able to deliver.

However, forecasting is notoriously difficult to do. Not only because of the unknowable and uncontrollable business world that shapes the impact of what we do in the market, but also because the very act of contemplating the future can lead us to do things differently that itself generates a different future from the one we would have obtained.

Believe it or not, organisations do not stop if they do not have a plan or a budget! For most organisations, the momentum of current activities will continue to generate costs and income, irrespective of what is planned. The value of these is fairly easy to forecast in the immediate future but as time goes on, the upper and lower limits of what this could be will diverge, as illustrated in figure 8-1. The reason for the divergence is most likely to be external influences such as competitor actions, market perception about our products, an unexpected change in the cost of raw materials, or a range of other events, most of which are uncontrollable.

Figure 8-1: Impact of Business Momentum and External Events

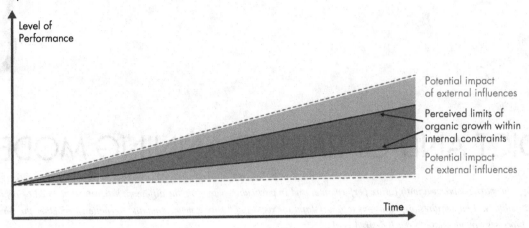

In recognising this, there are four questions relating to the future that need to be answered:

- What could be achieved by the organisation in the anticipated business environment? That is, what is possible and what is not?

- What is likely to be achieved if things continue as planned? As any person approaching an exam knows, there can be a big difference between 'what could' and 'what is likely'.

- How can the gap between what could be achieved and what is likely to be achieved be bridged? In other words, how can resources be optimised within the current plan?

- What fundamental changes are required to make further improvements? For example, are the current business processes the right ones to deliver business goals, or should new ones be introduced?

The answer to each question is included in the following logical planning models, which work in conjunction with the operational activity model (OAM) described in chapter 5, 'Operational Activity Model':

- *Target setting model (TSM)*. This model answers the question of what could be achieved in the long-term. It takes into account assumed market conditions for the future as well as recent trends in past performance. From this model, senior management can form aspirations about the high-level goals that could be achieved, complete with supporting financial statements. Once agreed upon, this is communicated to the rest of the organisation as a top-down plan containing departmental targets.

- *Detailed forecast model (DFM)*. This model looks at the current short-term reality to answer the question of what is likely to happen irrespective of budgets and targets. It takes known facts about revenues and expenses within the current business environment, to build a bottom-up view of the immediate future.

- *Optimise resources model (ORM)*. This third model looks at the most efficient way of aligning current resources with forecast outcomes. It takes a short-term view, but recognises that results should lead to long-term goals. Because of this, any reallocation of resources and effort is bound to be a compromise.

- *Strategy improvement model (SIM)*. This final model allows managers to answer the last question: what can be done about improving future performance? This model references the short-term reality, as provided by the DFM, and the long-term goals, as set by the TSM. Managers can then assess a range of changes to its business processes that could be implemented either singly or in combination.

The first three models—TSM, DFM, and ORM—are the subjects of this chapter, and the SIM will be covered in chapter 9, 'Strategy Improvement Model'.

TARGET SETTING MODEL (TSM)

Driver-Based Modelling

The TSM is a simple, idealistic mathematical model that relates the outcomes of organisational business processes (for example, products made, new customers acquired, and customers supported) to long-term objectives and resources. In many ways, it is similar to the OAM, except for the rules that it uses and the versions being held. Whereas the rules within the OAM are used to report the relationships between workload and outcomes, the TSM uses them to generate targets from a range of base data. This is also known as driver-based modelling. In effect, there are a few independent variables, such as forecasted unit sales volume, and the others are dependent variables (for example, based on unit level consumption rates and prices).

To illustrate how this works, let's consider the simple example shown in figure 8-2. In the model, we want to generate a net profit figure by relating the activities that contribute to its value. As we did in the example in chapter 5, we ask what drives net profit, which in our case is revenue and costs. These are related by the calculation of revenue less costs.

We now ask what drives each of these elements. If we follow the revenue side of the equation, revenue is calculated from units sold multiplied by price per unit. In our example, management sets the price per unit, and as it is not driven by anything else, it is called a driver.

Figure 8-2: Simple Example of a Driver-Based Model

We now ask what drives units sold. In the example, this is calculated from the number of orders multiplied by average order size, which is set by management based on past experience, and so becomes a driver. Finally, the example calculates number of orders by multiplying the number of visits by the sales conversion rate, both of which are entered and are therefore drivers.

We can now do the same exercise for costs, which we will not do here, but hopefully it is obvious from figure 8-2. When this analysis is complete, the relationships identified can be used to build a driver-based model where management can enter values into the drivers (for example, number. of visits, conversion rate, average order size, price per unit, and so on), which then uses formulae to create a summary of profit and loss (P&L).

The example covered here is a simple one. More sophisticated models recognise constraints, such as production volumes, the impact of discounts, late delivery penalties, or that more staff will be needed at certain levels of sales. They also recognise that there is nearly always a time lag between the driver and the result it creates. It should also be noted that these models only work for those measures that can be directly related to drivers, such as costs and revenues. Other data, such as overheads, will still need to be included to produce a full P&L summary. Activity-based costing methods address modelling for indirect and shared expenses using similar driver-based principles.

Because of their simplistic nature, driver-based models are not able to take into account unpredictable external influences, such as the unexpected market growth and changes in government legislation that impact taxes. This is where versions come into play. To see the impact of uncontrollable influences, the TSM is set up to hold a variety of scenarios where management can re-run the calculations with different driver values that simulate changing assumptions. For example, the model can be run with different sales conversion rates or unit costs, each of which will generate a new version of the P&L summary. These can then be displayed side-by-side so management can see the impact of each change. A benefit to this model is sensitivity analysis to identify which drivers most impact outcomes.

The aim in doing this is to allow a range of options to be evaluated concerning the future. These options will revolve around business drivers, which, if based on business process outcomes, will cause management to rethink how these are conducted and what could be improved. The end result of the TSM is a scenario that management believes will give them the best outcomes for the available resources. These values are then used to set top-down targets within the OAM that can be referenced by individual departments during the budget process.

TSM Content for XYZ, Inc.

The starting point in deciding the content for the TSM is the output to be fed into target version of the OAM. For our case study, this consists of a high-level P&L statement and the business process outcomes by department. In our example, the TSM does not go down to an activity level, as senior executives want managers at all levels to rethink what these should be once the high-level goals have been set.

From a business dimension point of view, the TSM consists of the following:

- Major product categories.
- Organisational departments.
- Versions including current year actual and current forecast. This dimension is also used to portray a variety of scenarios on predicted performance.
- Time periods that are defined as annual totals, although there is no reason why this could not be at a lower level, such as quarter or month.
- The P&L measures and business goals that are set up as they exist within the OAM. There are also a number of new measures that represent drivers of future performance.

In general, drivers can be grouped into the following types:

- *Assumptions.* These drivers are those that relate to general changes within the business environment (for example, inflation or market growth).
- *Outcome factors.* These relate activity to outcomes of a business process (for example, sales conversion rate).

- *Industry drivers.* These convey an industry specific best practice (for example, stock turn for consumer goods manufacturers).

These drivers are used by rules assigned to the P&L and business process outcome measures. In our case study, they act on past performance to produce future targets, as we will see in the following examples.

In the TSM case study, the drivers used are shown in table 8-1.

Table 8-1: Sample Drivers for the XYZ, Inc. Case Study

	CURRENT YEAR	YEAR 1 FORECAST	YEAR 1	YEAR 2	YEAR 3	YEAR 4	YEAR 5
Drivers:							
Products							
Market growth - direct	5%	6%	9%	15%	15%	12%	10%
Average direct price	$0.59	$0.58	$0.59	$0.58	$0.55	$0.55	$0.55
Market growth - online	8%	12%	14%	23%	27%	32%	35%
Average online price	$0.49	$0.50	$0.50	$0.49	$0.47	$0.47	$0.47
Raw material cost per unit	$0.15	$0.17	$0.18	$0.17	$0.16	$0.16	$0.16
Manufacture cost per unit	$0.09	$0.10	$0.10	$0.08	$0.08	$0.07	$0.07
Operational Costs							
Commission Rate	7.50%	7.50%	7.0%	7.0%	7.0%	7.0%	7.0%
Marketing activities as % total sales	3.69%	3.80%	4.0%	3.9%	3.8%	3.7%	3.5%
Customer service as & total sales	2.60%	2.80%	2.9%	2.7%	2.5%	2.5%	2.3%
Personnel cost growth	3.30%	2.50%	2.3%	2.3%	2.5%	2.5%	2.5%
Energy inflation rate	9%	8%	8.9%	9.2%	9.2%	8.9%	9.2%
Other inflation rate	2.98%	3.00%	3.2%	3.2%	3.2%	3.2%	3.2%
Corporate Specific							
Interest rate	11%	11%	11%	11%	11%	11%	11%
Social welfare rate	5%	5%	5%	5%	5%	5%	5%
Tax rate	21%	21%	21%	21%	21%	21%	21%
Total no. shares	12450	12450	12450	12450	12450	12450	12450
Dividend per share	$0.08	$0.08	$0.10	$0.12	$0.12	$0.12	$0.12
Share price	$4.50	$4.53	$4.56	$4.72	$4.85	$4.96	$5.25
Market size	$12,345,450	$13,000,000	$13,210,000	$14,100,000	$15,100,000	$16,150,000	$17,280,000

The first set is marked as products and contain assumptions about the growth of the market, the expected price, and some basic costs to produce each unit. The first two columns show what is currently being achieved and the latest forecast. These values came from the OAM and cannot be changed. The remaining columns, Year 1–Year 5, are used to enter driver values for the next five years. In our case study, XYZ has five product categories, so this block is repeated for each one.

The second set of drivers, operational costs, relate to various business processes. To keep the example simple, some are assumptions about inflation in different expense categories, and others are industry-specific in that they define the amount a department can spend as a per cent of total costs. As with product drivers, the value currently being achieved is displayed alongside the latest forecast to help management set levels for the next five years. These drivers operate on costs at a departmental level.

The last set of drivers also includes assumptions about future tax rates, share ownership, and market size. These are required for calculating the value of key objectives.

The model itself is quite detailed in that it uses the preceding drivers at a product and departmental level. Table 8-2 shows a portion of the model that calculates future revenue targets.

Table 8-2: XYZ, Inc. Case Study Revenue Forecast Generated From Product Drivers

	CURRENT YEAR	YEAR 1	YEAR 2	YEAR 3	YEAR 4	YEAR 5	DRIVEN BY
Gross Revenue:							
Pens							
Direct volume	194500	212005	243806	283077	314022	345424	Direct growth rate
Online volume	34500	39330	48376	61437	81097	109481	Online growth rate
Direct sales	$114,755	$125,083	$141,407	$154,207	$172,712	$189,983	Avg price × volume for direct
Online sales	$16,905	$19,724	$23,849	$28,722	$37,913	$51,183	Avg price × volume for online
Total revenue	**$131,660**	**$144,807**	**$165,257**	**$182,929**	**$210,625**	**$241,166**	**Subtotal**
Raw material costs	$34,350	$44,116	$50,416	$55,929	$64,651	$74,434	Avg mat cost × volume for direct
Manufacture costs	$13,433	$16,491	$15,183	$17,252	$17,767	$20,963	Avg manufacture cost× volume for online
Total manufacturing	**$47,783**	**$60,606**	**$65,599**	**$73,181**	**$82,418**	**$95,396**	**Subtotal**
Gross revenue	**$83,877**	**$84,201**	**$99,658**	**$109,748**	**$128,207**	**$145,769**	**Subtotal**
Stationery							
Direct volume	328000	347680	372018	405499	441994	486194	Direct growth rate
Online volume	73480	73480	73480	73480	73480	73480	Online growth rate
Direct sales	$118,080	$118,211	$119,046	$129,760	$137,018	$145,858	Avg price × volume for direct
Online sales	$22,044	$21,236	$19,987	$19,987	$19,362	$18,737	Avg price × volume for online
Total revenue	**$140,124**	**$139,447**	**$139,032**	**$149,746**	**$156,380**	**$164,595**	**Subtotal**
Raw material costs	$20,074	$18,257	$18,176	$19,542	$20,374	$21,408	Avg mat cost × volume for direct
Manufacture costs	$11,494	$11,080	$10,473	$11,056	$11,093	$11,186	Avg manufacture cost× volume for online
Total manufacturing	**$31,568**	**$29,337**	**$28,650**	**$30,599**	**$31,467**	**$32,594**	**Subtotal**
Gross revenue	**$108,556**	**$110,110**	**$110,382**	**$119,148**	**$124,913**	**$132,002**	**Subtotal**

In table 8-2, we have provided a column that explains the driver being used to generate each line. The model accesses data in a prior period and uplifts it according to the value assigned to the driver. For Year 1, the prior year is the current year actual result, which is used to produce the Year 1 target. Year 2 then uses the Year 1 figures and associated drivers to create Year 2, and so on. These calculations are done for revenue and costs at a product level. Subtotal rules then produce summaries that can be used within the P&L statement.

For other costs, the TSM works at a departmental level to produce consolidated costs, as shown in table 8-3.

Table 8-3: XYZ, Inc. Case Study General Costs Forecast Generated From Drivers

		CURRENT YEAR	YEAR 1	YEAR 2	YEAR 3	YEAR 4	YEAR 5	DRIVEN BY
Staffing:								
GS21010	Sales & wages	$258,187	$264,642	$270,728	$276,955	$283,879	$290,976	Personel inflation rate
GS21020	Commissions (direct sales)	$64,745	$62,696	$66,061	$72,008	$77,214	$87,077	Commission rate
GS21030	Overtime	$12,500	$12,850	$13,261	$13,686	$14,123	$14,575	General inflation rate
GS21040	Contract labour	$23,450	$24,107	$24,878	$25,674	$26,496	$27,344	General inflation rate
GS21050	Social welfare	$12,909	$13,232	$13,536	$13,848	$14,194	$14,549	Social welfare rate
Total Salaries		**$371,791**	**$377,526**	**$388,465**	**$402,171**	**$415,906**	**$434,521**	**Subtotal**
General:								
GE22010	Rent	$87,500	$90,300	$93,190	$96,172	$99,249	$102,425	General inflation rate
GE22020	Heat, light, & power	$28,750	$31,309	$34,189	$37,335	$40,657	$44,398	Energy inflation rate
GE22030	Water	$13,240	$13,664	$14,101	$14,552	$15,018	$15,498	General inflation rate
GE22040	Telephone	$12,120	$12,508	$12,908	$13,321	$13,747	$14,187	General inflation rate
GE22050	Insurance	$9,865	$10,181	$10,506	$10,843	$11,190	$11,548	General inflation rate
GE22060	Vehicle	$3,345	$3,452	$3,563	$3,677	$3,794	$3,916	General inflation rate
GE22070	Travel & entertainment	$5,423	$5,597	$5,776	$5,960	$6,151	$6,348	General inflation rate
GE22080	Hotel & living	$4,689	$4,839	$4,994	$5,154	$5,319	$5,489	General inflation rate
GE22090	Equipment hire	$540	$557	$575	$594	$613	$632	General inflation rate
GE22100	Office supplies	$689	$711	$734	$757	$782	$807	General inflation rate
GE22110	Postage	$1,245	$1,285	$1,326	$1,368	$1,412	$1,457	General inflation rate
GE22120	Cleaning, office services	$230	$237	$245	$253	$261	$269	General inflation rate
GE22130	Other expenses	$86	$89	$92	$95	$98	$101	General inflation rate
Total General Expenses		**$167,722**	**$174,728**	**$182,198**	**$190,079**	**$198,290**	**$207,075**	**Subtotal**

It should be emphasised that all of the figures shown in the P&L summary are being driven from the few numbers entered as drivers. Having worked out the details, the TSM then goes on to summarise the business goals and process outcomes that this set of drivers would generate. These are shown in table 8-4.

Table 8-4: XYZ, Inc. Case Study Objectives and Business Process Goals Generated From Drivers

	CURRENT YEAR	YEAR 1	YEAR 2	YEAR 3	YEAR 4	YEAR 5
Summary P&L						
Income						
Direct sales	$863,268	$895,652	$943,730	$1,028,686	$1,103,052	$1,243,958
Online sales	$126,003	$132,063	$138,102	$149,418	$164,095	$189,935
Total revenue	**$989,271**	**$1,027,715**	**$1,081,831**	**$1,178,104**	**$1,267,147**	**$1,433,893**
Raw material costs	$175,762	$188,270	$199,211	$213,808	$238,191	$267,552
Manufacture costs	$84,393	$87,453	$87,806	$93,904	$99,484	$109,625
Total manufacturing	**$260,155**	**$275,724**	**$287,018**	**$307,712**	**$337,674**	**$377,177**
Gross revenue	**$729,116**	**$751,991**	**$794,813**	**$870,392**	**$929,472**	**$1,056,716**
Total operational costs	**$655,667**	**$675,580**	**$697,703**	**$724,581**	**$751,446**	**$785,039**

Continued on p. 120

Continued from p. 119

	CURRENT YEAR	YEAR 1	YEAR 2	YEAR 3	YEAR 4	YEAR 5
Operating profit before tax	**$73,448**	**$76,411**	**$97,111**	**$145,810**	**$178,027**	**$271,677**
Tax for period	$15,424	$16,046	$20,393	$30,620	$37,386	$57,052
Net income	**$58,024**	**$60,365**	**$76,718**	**$115,190**	**$140,641**	**$214,625**
Dividends paid	$996	$1,245	$1,494	$1,494	$1,494	$1,494
Retained profit	**$57,028**	**$59,120**	**$75,224**	**$113,696**	**$139,147**	**$213,131**
Corporate Objectives						
Return on equity	22.59%	19.10%	19.61%	22.81%	21.84%	25.04%
Market share	8.01%	7.78%	7.67%	7.80%	7.85%	8.30%
Business Process Goals						
Sales growth	101.30%	103.89%	105.27%	108.90%	107.56%	113.16%
Production costs as % total revenue	37.20%	36.67%	36.11%	35.35%	36.33%	35.69%
Support costs as % total revenue	4.30%	3.96%	3.68%	3.38%	3.41%	3.12%
Product development costs as % total revenue	5.20%	4.22%	4.13%	3.92%	3.76%	3.43%

In use, the TSM would hold different versions of the drivers, with each version simulating a particular business scenario. However, each scenario would access the same P&L data. Reports can then be produced that contrasts each scenario so management can see the impact of value driver changes.

As mentioned earlier, the aim of the TSM is to put together a series of targets that could be achieved, provided the assumptions prove correct and the relationships work out as planned.

Using the TSM

The TSM is mainly used during the strategic planning process. This is where senior executives want to review the future direction of the organisation and to challenge management on how they can improve performance.

The forecast and actual version of data held within the TSM are populated from the OAM. This data is stored here for reference purposes and where rules make use of that data to create targets. Prior to this, management will have reviewed past performance as reported in the OAM and supporting detailed history models (DHMs). They would also have looked at future trends in the market, as shown in the performance measures model (PMM). From this, they are now ready to create various scenarios within the TSM that set targets to be achieved for key business performance measures.

As each scenario is created, it should be documented as to the assumptions made about the future business environment. For example, the market grows at 5 per cent, bank interest is 4.3 per cent, and so on. Where possible, key assumptions affecting a particular set of drivers should be recorded as a measure that can later be compared with what actually happened. Once a particular scenario has been chosen, its values are passed back into the OAM as the target version. This provides the focus for operational managers during the tactical planning or budget process, where they can review their activities and associated costs and work on how those targets could be achieved.

The TSM will not typically determine the level of workload and outcomes of individual business tasks. This is because, in our example, that level of detail is not held within the model and, in the view of the authors, this is better reserved for tactical planning or the budget process. For these processes, the OAM and SIM are the better models to use. However, users will be able to see the high-level targets as set by the TSM.

At a later date, should the assumptions used on the chosen scenario be incorrect or where the business goals are not being achieved, the TSM can be repopulated with the latest actual and forecast data. The TSM is then used to review previous scenarios and create new ones that may become the revised targets for the OAM.

DETAILED FORECAST MODEL (DFM)

Overview

The DFM is typically used in conjunction with the OAM to collect forecasts. Forecasts within the planning framework are defined as values that junior and middle management believe they will realistically achieve in the short term. This can include a range of measures including workload, outcomes, and resources.

Although the OAM can collect forecasts at a summary level, there are measures that benefit from having this at a detailed level. For example, revenue for a manufacturer can come from a range of customers and products, each of which has their individual profitability profile. As a result, the product mix can have huge implications on total revenue and costs. Therefore, to predict profitability with any degree of accuracy requires detailed knowledge of what is being sold, its volume, and to whom.

Similarly, sales of high value items or those that relate to a project are often dependent on timing. In these cases the sales process may be long and when the business is won, the resultant impact on costs and revenues in a particular time period can be significant. Without knowledge of the detail, it is easy to jump to the conclusion that an over- or underperformance is exceptional rather than expected.

For this reason, collecting information concerning the sales order pipeline and using this to populate the sales forecast not only improves accuracy, but also provides insight should any variances occur.

Because different measures can have a wide range of supporting details, there are likely to be multiple forecast models where each has a focus on a particular measure. In the XYZ case study, DFMs exist for sales revenue and personnel costs. As with the DHMs, not every measure warrants its own forecast model. Ideally, they are created for measures where the underlying mix of detailed transactions can have a large impact on results when compared to plan.

Developing the DFM

As previously mentioned, each DFM will typically be focused on a single measure or a range of closely related measures. For example, the case study DFM on personnel holds basic salary, pension, and taxation information, which is then used to populate a number of staffing measures within the OAM.

DFMs will typically hold just a forecast version of data, as actual results will be held in the performance history model. (Remember, we are using the word *model* in a logical sense; the actual implementation may combine these into one physical model.)

For some measures, data may exist in another system (for example, many companies use SalesForce.com to collect sales information). If this is so, then the DFM may simply be a place where the latest data is stored that is cleared out and repopulated each period. Alternatively, the DFM may be a system in its own right that is used to hold and track forecasts.

In our case study, a DFM was developed as a table to hold sales forecasts with the following fields:

- Date that the sales detail was entered
- Region responsible for the sale and where any revenue will be credited
- Sales executive involved
- Company being sold to
- Type (for example, whether the sale is to an existing customer or a new prospect)
- Product(s) being sold
- Value of the order
- Date contract is due to be signed and revenues recognised in the P&L summary
- Per cent chance of the deal going ahead
- Any notes to describe the current situation

Table 8-5: Sales Detailed Forecast Model for the XYZ, Inc. Case Study

DATE	REGION	SALES EXEC	COMPANY	TYPE	PRODUCT	VALUE	DUE DATE	CHANCE	NOTES
23-Jun-14	US	D. Rodney	Tango Solutions	Prospect	Custom pens	$2,340	Nov-14	90%	In final negotiations on price and delivery
28-Jun-14	Asia	K. Choi	Bethesda Inc	Customer	Flip charts	$1,460	Jan-15	70%	Had 2 visits – looking good
29-Jun-14	Asia	K. Choi	James & Sons	Prospect	Stationery	$1,450	Nov-14	60%	Initial call completed
02-Jul-14	Europe	G. Jones	Smith & Co	Prospect	Pens	$1,320	Oct-14	85%	Final presentation next week
05-Jul-13	US	T. Griffiths	Hanks Industries	Prospect	Stationery	$1,210	Nov-14	70%	Had 2 meetings so far
07-Jul-13	US	D. Rodney	Endis Inc	Customer	Stationery	$870	Dec-14	45%	Initial call completed – stiff competition
09-Jul-13	Europe	G. Jones	Smithfields	Prospect	Flip charts	$540	Jan-15	65%	Follow up meeting due next week
11-Jul-13	US	D. Boake	Challenge Inc	Prospect	Pencils	$535	Dec-14	75%	Proposal to be submitted

Table 8-5 depicts a DFM from our case study. A DFM was also set up for personnel costs that are the same costs as held for the DHM described in the last chapter.

As with the history models, the DFM's data can be used to sort, analyse, and summarise forecasts. For example, the data can be used to display all sales due in the next three months ranked by the per cent chance of them being signed. This enables management to look in detail at the forecasts to form their own opinion as to what could happen and to take remedial action should they fall short of what is expected.

Linking the DFM to the OAM

DFMs contain the breakdown of values for measures held within the OAM. On a regular basis, these details are summarised and the resulting value placed in the forecast version of the respective measures within the OAM.

As an option, the DFM could apply the per cent chance measure to the value of each sales situation to produce a modified forecast value within the OAM, or the OAM could contain two measures—one holding a value that assumes all sales opportunities will materialise as held, and the other using the per cent chance. This provides a range of values that could be used to assess future performance.

It is worth storing prior forecast versions so that over time, a picture can be built up on the reliability of forecasts. For example, which sales people are able to forecast with an accuracy of 5 per cent three months in advance? Which measures produce the most variability when viewed six months in advance? Knowing how trustworthy a forecast is can help determine which measures need regular supervision and provide a more detailed DFM.

Also, if managers are aware that forecasts are being monitored closely, then they are more likely to pay attention to the values they submit, which in turn are more likely to be trusted.

OPTIMISE RESOURCES MODEL (ORM)

Overview

The last type of model to be covered in this chapter is one used to optimise resources. If forecasts about future performance are trustworthy and they differ from what was planned, it may make sense to reallocate some resources to minimise costs or take advantage of them.

Examples of this type of model are those that try to balance production capacity with expected sales volume and mix. Some of these models can be quite sophisticated, particularly for manufacturers that produce in multiple locations and where machines used in manufacture can be configured to produce multiple products.

In this case, the model takes into account where the demand for products exist, what is held in stock at which locations, and the costs involved in transporting finished goods to customers. The model also recognises that to change a machine from producing one product to producing another takes time, and so production will be lost during the changeover period.

Armed with these factors, optimisation models are able to simulate various scenarios to work out what is the best way to minimise production costs and ensure customers receive their orders in the quickest time. This highlights a typical characteristic of these models in that they deal primarily with trade-offs (that is, it is generally not possible to meet all demands of both supplier and customer).

Different industries have different types of trade-offs. Quite often, there are specialised models that can be purchased from vendors to optimise resources, with production scheduling and logistics modelling being good examples. Whatever solution is employed, there should be a link to the OAM or to the appropriate DFM as these will receive the optimised values for subsequent monitoring.

Case Study Example

In the XYZ case study, we have developed a production ORM that seeks to balance what the factory produces with the latest sales forecast in order to minimise stock levels. This model contains stock levels of both raw materials and finished goods as projected by the current production schedule.

The process starts with each sales division entering a forecast of the units of each product to be sold by customer for the next three months. This is stored in the sales DFM. The production ORM takes this data and compares it to the predicted stock levels of finished products. A report is produced (shown in table 8-6) that shows the status of stock levels by week as adjusted by the sales forecast. Negative values indicate a shortfall in production to meet the forecast.

Table 8-6: Sample Optimise Resources Model Report Showing Where Product Stock Falls Short of the Sales Forecast

VERSION FORECAST											
	PRODUCT STOCK FORECAST										
		WK_48 W2012	WK_49 W2012	WK_50 W2012	WK_51 W2012	WK_52 W2012	WK_1 W2013	WK_2 W2013	WK_3 W2013	WK_4 W2013	WK_5 W2013
BALLPOINT PEN	Opening Product Stock	1,200	900	-1,220	430	-1,070	-2,250	-1,350	-2,850	-4,400	-3,400
	Products Units Produed	4,300	2,500	2,500	2,500	2,500	2,500	2,500	2,500	2,500	2,500
	Product Units Sold	4,600	4,620	850	4,000	3,680	1,600	4,000	4,050	1,500	4,000
	Closing Product Stock	**900**	**-1,220**	**430**	**-1,070**	**-2,250**	**-1,350**	**-2,850**	**-4,400**	**-3,400**	**-4,900**
FOUNTAIN PEN	Opening Product Stock	1,300	1,070	-2,380	-2,210	-4,910	-5,440	-5,290	-8,120	-7,720	-6,950
	Products Units Produed	1,800	1,000	1,000	1,000	1,000	1,000	1,000	1,000	1,000	1,000
	Product Units Sold	2,030	4,450	830	3,700	1,530	850	3,830	600	230	3,120
	> **Product Units Sold**	**1,070**	**-2,380**	**-2,210**	**-4,910**	**-5,440**	**-5,290**	**-8,120**	**-7,720**	**-6,950**	**-9,200**
FIBER TIP PEN	Opening Product Stock	1,100	720	640	1,360	780	-1,500	-2,430	-1,710	-2,190	-3,120
	Products Units Produed	2,000	800	800	800	800	800	800	800	800	800
	Product Units Sold	2,380	880	80	1,380	3,080	1,730	80	1,280	1,730	80
	Closing Product Stock	**720**	**640**	**1,360**	**780**	**-1,500**	**-2,430**	**-1,710**	**-2,190**	**-3,120**	**-2,400**

Continued on p. 125

Continued from p. 124

VERSION FORECAST										
PRODUCT STOCK FORECAST										
		WK_48 W2012	WK_49 W2012	WK_50 W2012	WK_51 W2012	WK_52 W2012	WK_1 W2013	WK_2 W2013	WK_3 W2013	WK_4 W2013	WK_5 W2013
ROLLER BALL PEN	Opening Product Stock	800	500	-640	-390	-3,140	-3,780	-2,780	-4,780	-5,470	-5,270
	Products Units Produed	2,000	1,000	1,000	1,000	1,000	1,000	1,000	1,000	1,000	1,000
	Product Units Sold	2,300	2,140	750	3,750	1,640		3,000	1,690	800	3,800
	Closing Product Stock	**500**	**-640**	**-390**	**-3140**	**-3,780**	**-2,780**	**-4,780**	**-5,470**	**-5,270**	**-8,070**
MARKER PEN	Opening Product Stock	300		400	-1600	-1,800	-3,400	-3,000	-5,600	-5,200	-5,100
	Products Units Produed	500	1,200	1,200	1,200	1,200	1,200	1,200	1,200	1,200	1,200
	Product Units Sold	800	800	3,200	1,400	2,800	800	3,800	800	1,100	6,300
	Closing Product Stock		**400**	**-1,600**	**-1,800**	**-3,400**	**-3,000**	**-5,600**	**-5,200**	**-5,100**	**-10,200**

Management can now make adjustments to the current production plan to meet the sales forecast. Within the ORM is a recipe that details what raw materials go into which products. As the production volume is adjusted, the ORM is able to compare the stock requirements for raw materials and display this as a report (table 8-7).

Table 8-7: Report Showing Revised Product Stock Levels to Meet Sales Demand

	WK_48 W2012	WK_49 W2012	WK_50 W2012	WK_51 W2012	WK_52 W2012	WK_1 W2012	WK_2 W2012	WK_3 W2012
Forecasted Material Closing Stock								
Barrel	2,400	-12,600	-12,600	-12,600	-12,600	-12,600	-12,600	-12,600
Spring	1,200	-6,300	-6,300	-6,300	-6,300	-6,300	-6,300	-6,300
Nib	3,600	-18,900	-18,900	-18,900	-18,900	-18,900	-18,900	-18,900
Cartridge	2,600	2,600	2,600	2,600	2,600	2,600	2,600	2,600
Pen clip	5,200	5,200	5,200	5,200	5,200	5,200	5,200	5,200
Cap	4,400	4,400	4,400	4,400	4,400	4,400	4,400	4,400
Nib cover	3,300	3,300	3,300	3,300	3,300	3,300	3,300	3,300
Pennant	3,300	3,300	3,300	3,300	3,300	3,300	3,300	3,300

Raw materials can be ordered from suppliers to meet demand.

The result of the ORM is sent back to the OAM as revisions to the resource budget for purchasing goods and manufacturing costs.

The models described so far in this chapter have been used to set targets and to predict and optimise performance in the immediate future. To align the immediate future with the long-range targets will often require a change to the way business is conducted. That is the role of the SIM, which is the subject of the next chapter.

9

STRATEGY IMPROVEMENT MODEL

The business environment is constantly changing. To survive and grow, organisations must continually adapt their business processes either by improving them or by trying out something new. This requires them to collect, assess, and choose initiatives by modelling how they impact existing structures.

Responding to Change

Strategic and operational planning is primarily concerned with assessing change to an organisation's business processes. This change can include the outputs those processes generate, the workload that is employed, and the resources they consume. If an organisation's business processes do not change, then either there is no competition and they will achieve their purpose, or they are on a path that will ultimately lead to their demise.

Imagine selling the same products and services as 20 years ago, or using the same production techniques, marketing campaigns, sales channels, or technology systems as in the past. Customers would almost certainly have moved to another supplier for more relevant products, and the potential operating efficiency gains by using the latest technologies would have been missed, resulting in higher costs relative to competitors.

The need for change comes from different sources, technology being one of them. Most companies are forced to change even if industry or organisation-specific factors do not naturally lend them to change. It is more about technology challenging strategy than strategy challenging technology. Over a decade ago during the dotcom era, technology companies with poor business models were trading at extremely high multiples compared to more established companies with a proven track record of profitable strategy execution. With the passage of time, the most enduring legacy of the dotcom boom is the impact technology has had on these established companies. This has not just been on the cost and ways of doing business, but in some cases on the very obsolescence of the organisation or industry itself.

But not all change is driven by market needs. Some are mandated through government regulation, such as Sarbanes Oxley, that requires a high degree of detail and justification around the use of resources and forecasting accuracy. Some are driven by public perception, as Nike and Starbucks found out when their business models came under the spotlight of social media sites.

Interestingly, one meaning of the word *strategy* is the adaptation important to evolutionary success. This definition captures the very essence of the planning model we are about to describe. Evolutionary means making small changes on a continuous basis in order to adapt the organisation to the ever-changing business environment. It also means learning from the past—what did not work and why—so that management has a complete picture for any reasons behind failure or success.

127

To properly assess change as opposed to having 'gut-feel' reactions, organisations will need to go through a process that typically reviews market forecasts, that looks at impending government regulation, gathers feedback from customers and staff on future prospects, analyses internal capabilities versus competitors, and makes informative views on social media trends. From this, organisations are in a solid position to gather initiative proposals and set priorities on what could be changed.

In some ways, this is still not enough. Many aspects of change cannot be modelled, which means no strategic initiative can ever be assured of success. The UK supermarket giant Tesco's troubled venture into the US grocery market serves as a reminder of the practical challenges of implementing strategic improvement, as well as the financial and other costs of not succeeding. On the face of things, nobody could be critical of the move. They had the industry expertise, occupied a dominant position in their domestic UK market, and, most of all, had prior experience with overseas ventures. However, they came up against formidable opposition within the US grocery market that was already occupied by dominant competitors. Despite all of the planning and foresight, Tesco had to admit defeat and pull out after losing $1.86 billion in just a few years. The lesson here is that once chosen, all strategic initiatives have to be closely monitored, adjusted, and maybe withdrawn, as they may not work as originally planned.

Model Focus

The strategy improvement model (SIM) is used as part of a larger process that involves analysing market trends and the current business operation as depicted in the operational activity model (OAM) and other models. This analysis should provide an estimate of future performance that can be compared with stated objectives and the goals set by the target setting model (TSM). From this, decisions can be made on the changes required to existing business processes.

This paves the way for operational managers to propose initiatives to implement those changes. These initiatives are captured, assessed, and approved within the SIM. Initiatives could be improvements to current operations, such as replacing old machinery, or they could be something entirely new, such as developing a new range of services or entering new geographic markets. In both cases, initiatives typically represent a particular set of activities that are not part of current processes. The common factors between them are as follows:

- They all require a change of management focus (for example, improving productivity if the initiative is to introduce a new manufacturing process, or on generating sales if the initiative is a new product).
- They will almost certainly consume new resources that need to be found. These can come either from current operations or be provided as new investments.
- Proposed initiatives represent a wish list—things that the organisation could do if it had the resources. However, there are usually far too many options that can be done at any point in time, and so the planning process has to perform the following:
    - Determine which combinations of initiatives are to be implemented
    - Ensure consistency between chosen initiatives
    - Assess the necessary resources required for implementation
    - Define the timeframe for delivery
- Once committed, the performance of individual initiatives need to be monitored to ensure that the resources are being applied as planned, and that they are on track to achieve their intended goal.

- Finally, initiatives exist as a defined set of activities with related sets of measures that must be retained or moved in time as a single set. There is no point in performing part of an initiative, or supplying just some of the resources. It must be done entirely or effort will be wasted that could have been better used elsewhere.

Link to the OAM and CFM

From a logical point of view, the SIM consists of two sets of data linked to the OAM and the cash funding model (CFM). The relationship is shown in figure 9-1.

The first step is where managers can propose initiatives. These are linked to business process goals, departmental structures, and resource measures (hence the dotted line link between the OAM and proposed strategic initiatives). Here initiatives can be reviewed, assessed, and gain approval.

Figure 9-1: Schematic Showing the Relationship Between Operational Activity and Strategy Improvement Models

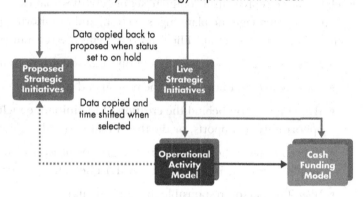

When any approved initiative becomes live, its set of activities and associated data are transferred into the OAM, where it is kept separate from existing operational data. However, the OAM allows the accumulation of resources and other measures to give a total 'business as usual' plus a 'strategy initiatives' position.

This is achieved by defining a new dimension in the OAM for strategy, which is made up of the following members:

- *Total strategy.* This is a consolidation member that accumulates data within the business as usual and total initiatives members.

  - *Business as usual.* This member contains all of the data for current business processes, but without applying any strategic initiatives.
  - *Total initiatives.* This is a consolidation member that contains the accumulation of data from its members; that is, the individual initiatives.

    - *Initiative 1.* This contains the data for a selected initiative as transferred from the SIM.

    - *Initiative 2.* This contains the data for a second selected initiative, and so on.

Keeping initiatives separate allows them to be monitored individually so management can keep a watchful eye on their implementation and resource usage versus expected benefits. Too often, initiatives are assumed to be responsible for an improvement in performance when no attempt has ever been made to actually measure whether this was true or whether the costs involved were worthwhile.

Linking the SIM to the OAM helps organisations to do the following:

- Accurately define the 'business as usual' (or baseline) performance of the current organisational business processes.

- Capture plan versus actual cost of strategy implementation and the benefits being realised.

- Provide a transparent way of assessing priorities in the areas where performance improvement is most needed.
- Avoid vague claims or estimates for initiatives, as the SIM requires clarity.

As time passes, it should be possible to re-plan, suspend, delete, or select new initiatives as required. Should an initiative be suspended, it can be moved back to the proposed initiative data set until required at a later date.

Defining SIM Content

Initiative Content

Each initiative represents a complete set of activities that can be measured in terms of workload, outcomes, and resources. To manage the planning, selection, and monitoring process, a range of data should be collected with each initiative as it is set up. The following items are recommended and will be used in our case study:

- *Initiative name.* This is used to identify individual proposals.
- *Initiative author.* The name of the person and the department making the proposal.
- *Why.* The reason behind the creation of the initiative including what particular issue it addresses, the opportunity it supports, or the threat that it guards against.
- *Business process.* The business process goal or process activity that the initiative impacts the most. (This should already exist within the OAM.) The value to be improved should be clearly defined.
- *Who.* The person responsible for implementation and delivery of results. They may not necessarily be the same person.
- *Departments involved.* This identifies the departments involved in implementation or who are affected. (These should already be in the OAM.)
- *When.* The timescales for which the initiative is to start and end. Also, the minimum duration required to achieve an impact on the target business process.
- *Dependency.* Other initiatives, if any, that are required to be implemented before this one.
- *Resources.* The money, people, and assets required for implementation and how they are split across the departments involved. This also includes resources that are externally sourced.
- *Implementation activity.* The completion milestones through which the status of implementation can be monitored.
- *Risk.* The risks being run and the potential impact on overall performance. For example, what other activities are in jeopardy if this initiative fails? How can risks be measured?
- *Supporting documentation.* Related documents that support the business case and information regarding implementation.
- *Approval process.* The people who are to review and approve the initiative before it can be considered.
- *Initiative status.* This final piece of information informs the status of the initiative. For example, it may require several sessions to complete all of the information defined here, so this should indicate when it has been submitted for approval. Similarly, the status indicates when an initiative has been approved and when selected for implementation. The latter status is the trigger to move the initiative data into the OAM.

Obviously, quite a lot of this data is text and not numeric, so it could prove to be a challenge to many planning systems that are based solely on multi-dimensional technology. Newer software vendor planning products recognise the need for handling text, so the way in which this model is implemented depends on the technology being used.

It is worth commenting that planning technologies exist to support the organisation and not the other way around. If you are looking to invest in a software planning product, then make sure you evaluate the solution's capabilities for handling the set-up, approval, and inclusion of strategic initiatives within a business as usual model. Appendix II has an overview of the capabilities required to implement the planning framework as described in this book.

Linking SIM Content to Management Methodologies

Given the popularity of strategy management methodologies, such as the balanced scorecard derived from a strategy map, it is likely that the terminology and other elements, such as cause and effect, business perspectives, and so on, should be retained. One way of doing this is through the use of attributes that were described in chapter 5, 'Operational Activity Model'. Attributes allow each item that makes up a model to be named as a component part of a methodology. For example, a measure can be identified as a balanced scorecard strategic objective, and initiatives can be identified as belonging to a particular balanced scorecard theme. These attributes can be filtered within a report to produce reports that show cause and effect relationships.

In the case study outlined in chapter 4, 'Business Planning Framework', a schematic can be drawn (figure 9-2) that describes the relationships between initiatives and measures based on the balanced scorecard methodology.

In the diagram in figure 9-2, the hierarchy shown is built into the OAM strategy dimension. Each member has a number of attributes that relates it to the adopted methodology. In supporting the balanced scorecard, these attributes include the following:

- *Object type.* This describes whether the member is a theme or an initiative.
- *Perspective.* This identifies the balanced scorecard perspective that each initiative belongs to.
- *Business process goal.* This identifies the business process goal the initiative supports.

As this structure is built into the OAM, it will need to be updated as new initiatives are selected. Some of the modern planning technologies support this automatically, so maintenance should not be much of an issue.

Figure 9-2: Applying the Balanced Scorecard Methodology to the Operational Activity and Strategy Improvement Models

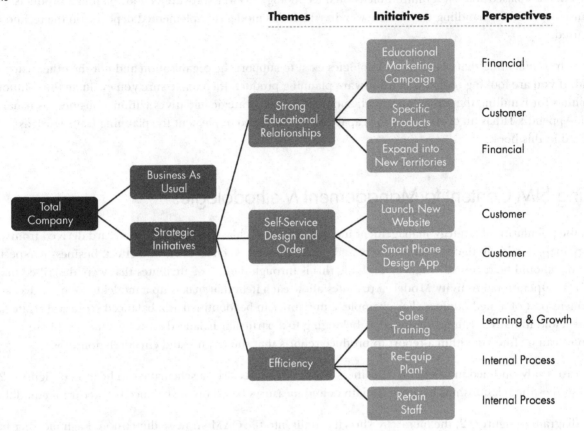

Planning Capabilities

For the SIM model to be of value, it should consist of a number of planning tasks that must occur in a specific sequence, supported by a range of data. At a general level, this includes the following sections.

Communicate Goals

Populating the SIM starts out by communicating the goals of the organisation along with an assessment of the perceived future business environment and the goals that senior managers believe can be achieved. This will include top-down goals that come from the TSM, the high-level strategies to be adopted, and any constraints under which the organisation operates. The aim of this information is to motivate operational managers to propose initiatives that are both relevant to the goals to be achieved and have a realistic chance of being adopted.

Propose and Validate Projects

Initiative proposals are submitted with the level of detail mentioned earlier in this chapter. When the proposer signifies that the proposal is complete, he or she is locked out from making changes, and those whose role is to review initiatives for relevance and completeness are notified. Once they are assured that the proposal is complete and in line with strategy, the initiative status is changed and becomes available to the next stage of the planning process.

Select and Approve Projects

The purpose of this stage is to assess completed initiatives in combinations and with different start and end dates. The aim is to maximise the impact on the organisation with the limited availability of resources.

This is achieved within the SIM either through reports that are able to combine resources across initiatives, or by introducing accumulation hierarchies into the initiative structure. Similarly, it should be possible to vary start dates. The method used for this analysis depends on the planning technology.

Once a particular combination has been approved for implementation, the data within these initiatives is transferred to the OAM where they will be tracked. It should be noted that the original proposed start date may have changed when approved, so any data transferred needs to take this into account.

Monitor and Forecast Projects

Once an initiative has become live, a number of questions will need to be answered by entering actual results and collecting forecasts:

- Did the project start on time?
- What is the status of implementation and is it behind or ahead of schedule?
- What resources have been consumed so far?
- What resources are needed in the future to complete the initiative?
- Will those resources be available at the right time?
- Will the intended impact on overall goals be realised?
- Which departments have missed the planned milestones?
- Have any of the risks involved changed?
- How accurate have previous forecasts been in predicting actual performance?

Assess Alternatives

Depending on the answers received in the preceding section, a number of re-planning activities may take place to answer the following questions:

- What initiatives need to be reconsidered?

- What changes should be made to overall resourcing?

- Is there another initiative we should consider that would make a greater impact on overall results?

This finishes describing the logical models within the planning framework. There is just one more aspect that needs careful consideration, and that is the management processes through which the models are accessed and used. This is the subject of the next chapter.

10

THE PLANNING AND MONITORING PROCESS

So far, we have specified the content of the different framework models to plan and monitor performance. However, it is the management processes that hold them together. In this chapter, we will look at how to define and configure those processes so they act as a single continuous event.

DEFINING PROCESSES

Components of a Process

As mentioned in the Introduction, we live in a complex world. The everyday products we use, even the seemingly simple ones, are complex to the extent that no one person would be able to make them. Take the case of making a watch; this was only possible through the co-ordinated effort of multiple people with different skills all working together to agreed standards and to achieve a common aim.

The only way to manage complexity, be it creating a physical object such as a watch or organising a management challenge such as winning an Olympic medal, is to break the subject down into manageable pieces. Being manageable means that the individual tasks can be carried out in a repeatable and accurate way, and typically by people who only need to be skilled in the part they are required to perform.

The mechanism by which these tasks are organised and conducted is known as a process. For a process to fulfil its function, it needs to have the following:

- *A clearly defined end purpose.* Processes exist for reasons that are often simple to define, although they may be difficult to achieve. The purpose of watch-building is to produce an object that will reliably keep time and allow its users to fulfil their purposes. This may range from being able to schedule business appointments or, in the case of the early watches, navigate around the globe with accuracy. Having an end purpose is vital to defining the individual tasks within the process, some of which may change over time. For example, new production techniques may lead to different ways of fabricating materials and, hence, a change to the task within a process. Despite this, the end purpose rarely changes.

- *Clearly identified actions.* Processes typically rely on a chain of activities that directly relate to the end purpose. There can be no misunderstandings for those involved in carrying out a particular task as to what they are required to do. They must also recognise that their role is to serve something that is greater than their own individual actions. It is only when users work together, performing their designated functions, that the end purpose can be achieved. Allowing people excessive freedom to decide on what actions they are going to do will inevitably lead to chaos and failure of the entire process.

- *Linked inputs and outputs.* Because of the last point, individual tasks in a process will typically take an input that is then transformed or built on to create an output that becomes an input to the next task. Production processes that take raw materials and turn them into finished goods are a great example of the connected nature of tasks within a process. The quality of the end result is dependent on knowing exactly what each task is to receive and exactly what that task needs to deliver. It cannot be up to the individual task manager to decide, as he or she may not necessarily know what is required further down the line. Just imagine the car you would get from a production line if someone during the manufacturing process decided to fit just three wheels with brakes or chose to use different compounds on the braking pads.

- *Co-ordinated timing.* This last point recognises that tasks within a process are often dependent on the completion of other tasks, and that timing is often critical for the overall result. A car has to be built in a specific sequence. Medical operations not only need a correct sequence of activities, but they must also be completed within certain time constraints. You cannot expect a patient having a hip replacement to have the old joint removed one week and the new one inserted the following week.

It is interesting to note that most organisations have clearly defined processes when it comes to the manufacture of a product or the delivery of a service. They know exactly what the purpose is and what has to happen, when, and by whom. It is written down in manuals and constantly reinforced with training, and with validation appraisal on the quality of the end result. It would be unthinkable to depart from the end purpose, to vaguely describe how each task is carried out, not to mandate input and outputs, or to do away with the sequence or timing of activities. Doing so is a recipe for confusion and will guarantee the failure of the organisation.

Yet that is often what happens when it comes to planning. The process required to plan strategy, allocate resources, monitor results, and make subsequent adjustments is rarely written down in documentation or understood by those taking part. Take the budget process, for example. In most organisations, it resembles more of an annual 'guess the numbers' game, as quite often its purpose has not been communicated. All that the budget holders know is that senior managers have a set of numbers they want the rest of the organisation to guess. To help with the guess, spread sheets are distributed to those involved in the game for them to submit their best estimates. These are then consolidated with other managers' guesses and compared with senior management's original set of expected figures.

Not surprisingly, the two do not match, and so everyone is asked to guess again. This is typically called pass two. The problem is that this time, managers are focused on trying to guess the numbers that senior managers are holding. Anything related to strategy has gone, and it is now a competition to see who can discern what the few already know. After a couple of rounds, senior managers inform every one of the values of the numbers they hold and what their guesses should have been. This is known as a top-down budget, which provides managers with a great excuse to miss the numbers. After all, they are not their numbers, so any buy-in is missing.

Those who understand the game know how to play it well. However, the end result will not serve the purpose of the budget, assuming that the organisation had one to begin with. In most organisations, this game lasts around four months and consumes vast quantities of management time that would be better spent elsewhere. No wonder Jack Welch, ex-chief executive of General Electrics, called the annual budgeting process the most ineffectual practice in management.

To turn planning into any kind of valuable exercise, it needs a set of linked planning models that covers all aspects of what can be managed, and it needs a process. That is, it needs a set of tasks that serves an overall purpose, where user interaction is directed to serve that purpose, inputs and outputs of each task are clearly defined, and the tasks provide a logical sequence with timings to enable the organisation to function efficiently as well as respond to unforeseen challenges.

Without a process, planning becomes an academic exercise. However, when embedded within the right process, planning will help managers set realistic targets, make wise choices when allocating resources, accurately assess what actually happened, and steer organisations in the right direction in making changes.

Performance Management Processes and Tasks

Planning should be done within the context of managing organisational performance. The information technology analyst firm Gartner uses the term *corporate performance management* (CPM), which they define as 'the methodologies, metrics, processes and systems used to monitor and manage an enterprise's business performance'. There are other terms in use such as, 'enterprise performance management' and 'business performance management', but for our purpose these are synonymous with CPM. To go with Gartner's definition, they describe the six different processes of strategic planning, tactical planning, financial planning, management reporting, forecasting, and risk management. As mentioned in chapter 4, 'Business Planning Framework', these are often seen as being distinctive processes, when in reality they each consist of a series of linked and integrated planning and monitoring tasks that follow on from each other, none of which can be left out. For example, to collect a budget requires tasks that

- set departmental targets.

- send out budget submission forms with targets, current year actual results, and an area to enter next year's budget.

- collect departmental submissions and send for approval.

- approve or reject budget. If rejected, then the next task is to send the budget back to the originator and ask for resubmission.

- collate departmental budgets to produce a consolidated version.

- analyse results and either approve or reset departmental targets.

To create an effective management process as described by the planning framework requires us to fully define the planning tasks, their sequence, and how they relate to the different planning models. This involves collecting the following information on every task:

- *Department and person involved.* This identifies those responsible for carrying out the task. This could be multiple people in multiple departments. For example, there may be a product manager for each product category, so to review past performance would require each product manager to review their own areas. This could happen in parallel, but each would need to be completed before the start of the next task.

- *Planning model and data view.* This describes for each task the planning model that needs to be accessed and the 'slice' of data to be presented. Because models tend to contain data for multiple departments that span multiple processes, it is important that only the right people can access the right information at the right time. Modern planning solutions are able to do this quite simply, but we still need to focus the user's attention to the data that he or she needs to review in order for the user to create the appropriate output for the next task.

  In some instances, users may need access to multiple models. For example, when reviewing performance, they may need access to the detailed history models in a way that enables them to carry out detailed analyses and to compare those analyses with data in the detailed forecast models before they come to any conclusions.

- *Processing required.* Once access has been granted to data, users need to be directed as to what they can do with it. As mentioned in the last point, we may want to grant access so the users can perform their own analyses. Similarly, we may want them to load their current forecast from an external file. Knowing the kind of processing required by any task helps when choosing a planning solution.

- *Action or output required.* Tasks require an output. This could be a submission of data for approval, as in the case of entering a budget; making a comment, such as following the review of actual results; or approving a submission, as in the case of creating a forecast. In most cases, output will be compulsory and so the expected format needs to be clearly explained. For data submissions, this should include the planning model and data slice that needs to be completed.

- *Completion notification.* This final piece of information indicates when the task has been completed and is no longer available. This could include the following:
  - When a particular action has been performed, such as the approval of a budget.
  - A date or time. For example, forecasts can be entered up until the last day of the month, after which data entry will be blocked.
  - A set condition. For example, budget submissions can be altered up until all submissions have been received.
  - Any combination of this list.

To show how these tasks can be defined in a way that will be familiar to most readers, we are going to use the management processes named by Gartner, as they apply to our case study. It should be noted that the process names and tasks we will be describing are in no way prescriptive, as management teams must agree amongst themselves what those items should be. However, those tasks must be clearly defined, as previously explained.

To avoid boring the reader, we will keep the example at a summary level, but there should be sufficient detail in the description to enable this to be accomplished in full in any organisation.

STRATEGIC PLANNING

Purpose

For XYZ, Inc., strategic planning is defined as a series of senior management tasks whose purpose is to set long-term objectives, and the ways in which they can be accomplished. These tasks involve assessing past performance and the market opportunity from which annual targets are agreed for the next three years.

These targets are set at a company level and include overall objectives, related business process goals, and a high-level of profit and loss (P&L).

Tasks: Inputs, Outputs, and Sequence

The tasks conducted during the strategic planning process have the following sequence, inputs, and outputs:

- *Review current performance.* This is not just a single task, as management needs to assess what products or services are best contributing to objectives and whether the business processes involved are providing good value compared with competitors. They also need to determine the product life cycle and whether these are 'fit-for-purpose' in the forthcoming years. This task requires past actual and forecast data by business process. Output is a projection of likely future performance for the current business model.

- *Analyse market potential.* This set of tasks involves reviewing market forecasts and assessing where the company's own projection of future performance fits. It also involves analysing competitor performance. Some of this has been gathered as part of the sales process (for example, how many times competitors have won against them and what their prices are), and some has been captured from external sources (for example, their profile on social media sites). From this, management can make a judgement on where XYZ could be in three years' time should they make changes to the current business model.

- *Assess risks.* This task involves creating a number of P&L scenarios that assess the value of 'business as usual' for best and worst case assumptions made about the unmanageable aspects of the future. For example, what would the impact be if prices had to drop by 10 per cent due to competitor pressure? What could be done to reduce costs or promote an increase in sales? To go with the P&L output is a description of the scenarios being assessed and suggestions for how the organisation would cope in each one.

- *Set baseline financial plan.* This task takes the scenario from the last task that management believes is the most likely. This is used to create a P&L summary that is split into the following:
    - *Business as usual.* This contains values that would be attained through current organic growth (that is, if the organisation were to continue as it is today with the same business processes and workload).
    - *Strategy impact.* This contains the increase in resources and outcomes that management believes the organisation should strive to achieve by making changes to the current business processes and workload.

  Together, these values form a target P&L for the next three years.

- *Set objectives and strategies.* The final task in this process involves pushing down the high-level P&L to the organisation's departments along with pushing down details concerning the business process areas that need to improve and ways in which that improvement can be accomplished. For example, sales performance will be improved with the development of an online application that allows users to simply create their own personalised stationery. Costs will be reduced with the set-up of a new production facility that is both 'greener' and less expensive to operate.

People and Planning Models

In running each of the preceding tasks, a number of interactions will be required by different people to different areas of the planning models (see a sample model of these interactions in figure 10-1):

- *Analyse current performance.* This requires access to the detailed history models to review past performance and the detailed forecast model to view the current outlook. Users will need the ability to fully analyse data and have an area in the target setting model (TSM) where they can enter a business as usual projection for the next three years. The task ends when the user indicates that the business as usual projection has been completed.

- *Analyse market forecast.* This requires access to the detailed performance measures model that has been suitably updated with external market data and internal data from the operational activity model (OAM). They will then need to be able to enter a strategy impact projection for the next three years into the TSM. The task ends when the user indicates that the strategy impact projection has been completed.

- *Assess risks.* This requires the consolidation of the business as usual and strategy impact data within the TSM. Users are given the ability to create scenarios within this model and to copy the submitted projections. They can then modify data via designated drivers to simulate a particular risk happening.

Figure 10-1: Sample Strategic Planning Tasks and Their Relationship to Existing Planning Models

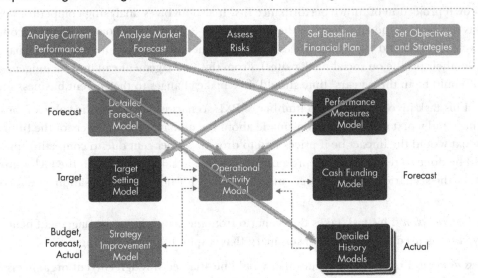

The task ends when the user indicates that sufficient scenarios have been generated for comparison reports that are available for senior management review.

- *Set baseline plan.* This is performed within the TSM and involves choosing the most likely scenario as the target for the next three years.

- *Set objectives and strategies.* This creates individual targets by department in the TSM, which are then transferred to the target version of the OAM. The two parts to the target, business as usual and strategy impact, are retained. Strategies are communicated using the balanced scorecard methodology that requires the strategic themes chosen to be set up as dimension members within the OAM and strategy improvement model.

The cash funding model is now populated to produce a cash flow forecast for management to assess where any cash shortfalls are to be resourced. This may require them to make adjustments to the TSM and repeat some of the preceding tasks. This task and the strategy planning process ends when management approves the targets within the OAM.

TACTICAL PLANNING

Purpose

The purpose of the tactical planning process is to develop a range of strategy initiatives that will help the company achieve the strategy impact targets within the OAM. These targets were set during the strategic planning process and include business process goals and a P&L summary that each department contributes to.

The output required of the tactical planning process is a series of approved strategy initiatives that show how the first year of the long-range strategy targets will be met.

Tasks: Inputs, Outputs, and Sequence

The tactical planning process for XYZ, Inc. includes the following tasks:

- *Develop initiatives.* This task is an on-going task whereby managers can propose new initiatives. These are linked to particular business objectives as outlined in the strategic plan and include a range of data including proposed workload levels, outcomes, and the resources to be consumed. To do this, departmental managers are able to view the strategy impact targets in the OAM and can enter data into the strategy improvement model (SIM). These are sent to a divisional manager who reviews entries for completeness and ensures that they fit within the culture of the organisation.

- *Assess initiative combinations.* This next task assesses combinations of approved initiatives. The aim is to meet the strategy impact targets with minimum cost. To do this the user is able to see the targets in the OAM and can create multiple scenarios within the SIM. They can copy different combinations of initiatives into each scenario and compare their cumulative impact against the set target. The more promising scenarios are then presented to senior management to make a decision on which combinations are to go live.

- *Agree on the plan.* The chosen combination of initiatives from the last task now have their status changed to 'live' within the SIM. This causes the data associated with them to be copied from the SIM into the OAM. During this copy process, the cause and effect structure in the strategy dimension of the OAM is modified so that strategy maps can be produced, and that initiative resources and outcomes are accumulated with business as usual.

People and Planning Models

Tasks from the tactical planning process interact with the following planning models in figure 10-2:

Figure 10-2: Sample Tactical Planning Tasks and Their Relationship to Existing Planning Models

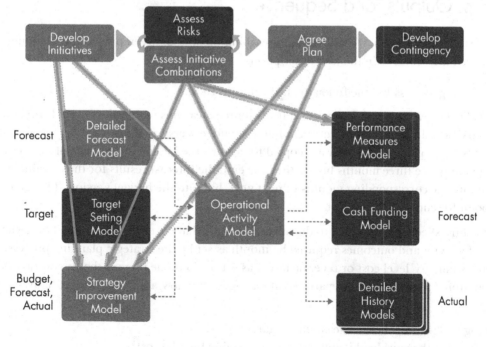

- *Develop initiatives.* Managers only have access to their individual targets in the OAM, and they can only see initiatives that they have created. They have the option to create new initiatives in the SIM and the ability to amend existing initiatives, provided they are not 'live' or have been approved for 'live' use. This task has no end date, so initiatives can be submitted for approval at any time.

- *Assess initiative combinations.* This takes place within the SIM and is completed by those responsible for assessing initiatives. They can view all approved initiatives and can create as many scenarios as they wish that represent different combinations of approved initiatives. The impact of these combinations can be viewed within the OAM.

- *Agree on the plan.* The task requires access to the SIM and OAM. When transferring data to the OAM, the individual initiatives are set up as members within the strategy dimension of the OAM. Results can be viewed in both the OAM and the performance measures model.

FINANCIAL PLANNING

Purpose

The purpose of the financial planning process is to allocate resources to departments in order for the business processes to deliver the targets set for business as usual. These are added to the strategy initiatives chosen to give the total resources required by the company. Funding plans are then developed for any shortfall in predicted cash requirements.

The output of the financial planning process is a budget that is linked to the delivery of defined activities and the outcomes they should generate. This is accompanied by a report that shows the sources of funds.

Tasks: Inputs, Outputs, and Sequence

For the remainder of the processes, we will not be describing the link between people and planning models, as this should now be fairly obvious in the task descriptions.

The financial planning process has the following tasks (figure 10-3):

- *Develop baseline budget.* This task operates on the resource measures within the OAM. It first takes the current years' actual results and places them into the budget version, transposed by one year (that is, actual results for January of this year are copied to become the budget for January of next year). Because budgeting takes place three months before the year end, the forecast results for the remainder of the year are copied into the corresponding months of next year, but into the budget version. This gives users the starting point for entering the budget.

  Next, data entry sheets are provided to departmental users that cover the next year. These sheets show the levels of activity and outcomes required by month as set by the strategic planning process. They are also given a summary level cost or revenue target as set by the same process that is contrasted with the values now stored as the budget. Departmental managers can now adjust the budget figures with the aims of

  - keeping budget costs below the summary target level.
  - ensuring that the workload identified can be sustained by the costs.

Figure 10-3: Sample Financial Planning Tasks and Their Relationship to Existing Planning Models

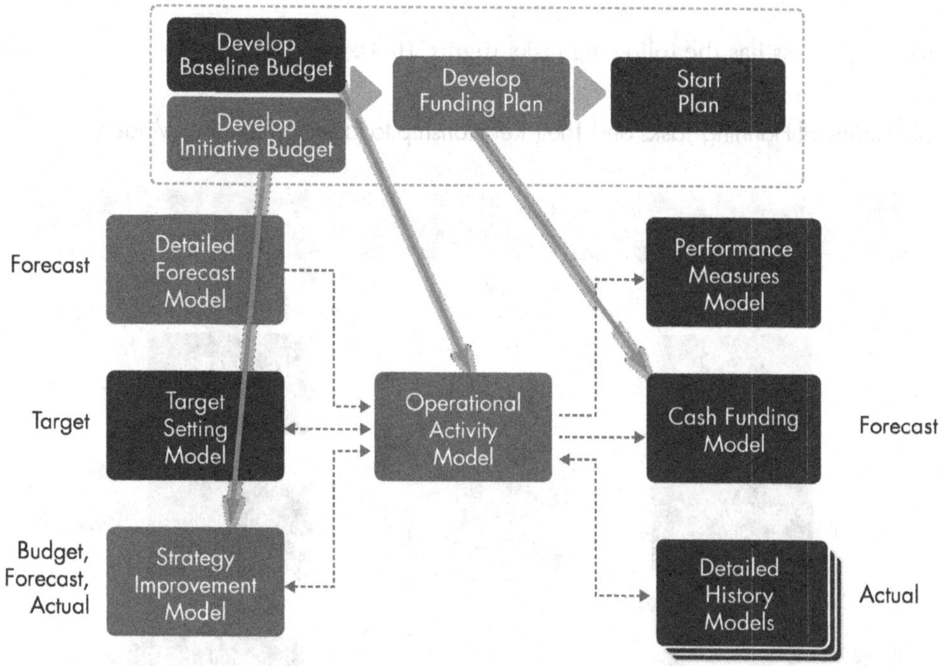

- ○ confirming that the level of outcomes can be generated by the planned workload.
- ○ ensuring revenue targets are met or exceeded for the given target costs.

- *Develop initiative budget.* Strategy initiatives were selected as part of the tactical planning process and are now stored within the OAM. This task allows users to confirm that the original budget that was agreed upon when the initiative was approved still stands.

- *Develop funding plan.* This task takes cash supply and demand as defined by the budget held within the OAM for both baseline and strategy initiatives. The cash impact is transferred into the cash funding model, where it can highlight any additional funding that may be required.

FORECASTING

Purpose

The purpose of the forecasting process is to predict the most likely outcome if things continue as envisaged within the anticipated business environment, and to provide management with choices as to how performance can be optimised.

The output of this process is a report that shows budget versus forecast and selected optimised scenarios.

Tasks: Inputs, Outputs, and Sequence

The financial planning process has the following tasks (figure 10-4):

Figure 10-4: Sample Financial Planning Tasks and Their Relationship to Existing Planning Models

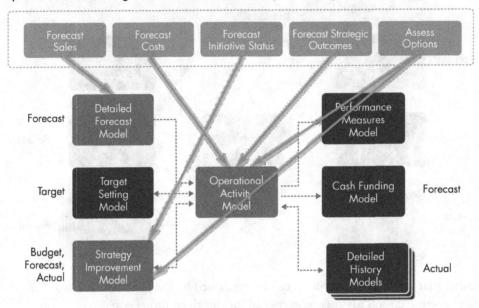

- *Forecast sales.* This is an on-going task that never stops. The sales staff enters sales prospects into the detailed forecast model (DFM). They can only see previous details that they have entered and their own targets. As situations are updated, sales values are summarised and transferred into the forecast version of the OAM.

- *Forecast costs.* This is an on-going task for collecting the latest information regarding costs. These are either entered into a DFM if one exists for the expense item being updated (for example, personnel costs), or directly into the OAM. Users can only see the costs they are responsible for.

- *Forecast initiative status.* This collects data for strategy initiatives that are live. Data is entered into the forecast version of the SIM, where it is summarised and transferred into the OAM. Users can only see the initiatives where they have responsibility.

- *Forecast strategy outcomes.* This collects data regarding business process outcomes. Data is entered directly into the forecast version of the OAM. Users can only see the initiatives where they have responsibility.

- *Assess options.* Results from the prior four tasks are now used to produce a forecast report from the OAM. Depending on the results, management may wish to consider optimising some of the resources (for example, matching production with sales forecasts so that products are produced at an optimal cost and that avoids increasing stock levels).

MANAGEMENT REPORTING

Purpose

The management reporting process brings together current results with budget, forecast, and original strategy targets in a suitable format for assessing results. The purpose for doing this is to allow management to review past activities along with the outlook for the future so that adjustments can be made to initiatives or allocated resources in order to achieve or improve long-term goals.

Tasks: Inputs, Outputs, and Sequence

The management reporting process includes the tasks shown in figure 10-5.

Figure 10-5: Sample Management Reporting Tasks and Their Relationship to Existing Planning Models

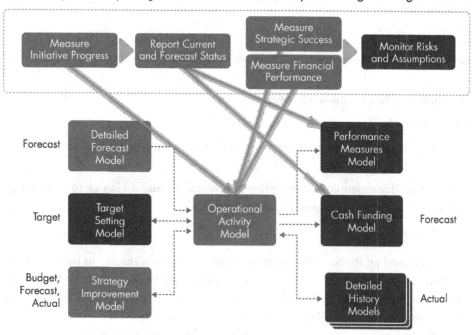

These collect and load actual data, which are then contrasted with budgets, forecasts, and actual data. From this, decisions can be made on whether the performance is acceptable, whether the assumptions were correct about the uncontrollable environment, and what needs to change.

MOVING TOWARD CONTINUOUS PLANNING

Management processes are key to making plans realistic and ensuring that everyone acts in a co-ordinated way to achieve common objectives. There is no other way that this can be accomplished. However, the traditional view of management processes is that they are run at particular times of the year. Strategic and tactical planning are typically annual events, as is budgeting that looks at setting expenditure levels over the next 12 months. Forecasting is either monthly or quarterly, and management reporting is typically monthly.

The key point here is that unknowable and unmanageable challenges rarely occur in line with the management calendar. Competitors can take action at any time, as can government legislation and other events that impact revenue and costs. There is also the ever-increasing presence of social networks and a whole range of other influences that all conspire to invalidate activities and the way in which resources have been planned.

Variances that have no real impact on the bottom line can often be ignored, but others may require an immediate change of direction if future losses are to be avoided. Given that most organisations spend nearly four months creating a budget, doing this on a monthly basis is impractical, but so is ignoring a plan that is not tied to current reality.

Because of the volatile nature of today's business environment, organisations must find a way to continually plan. A mechanism is needed with which they can react to unexpected events and exceptions, as well as a date on the calendar. This is where the task definition covered in this chapter becomes extremely useful. With some of the newer planning solutions on the market, it is now possible to set up management processes as a network of tasks that are controlled by the solutions workflow capability. The popular term for periodic refreshing of the budget is *rolling financial forecasts*.

The way these forecasts work is that in addition to what has already defined, each task has information about how they are triggered (in other words, under what conditions each task is initiated). This can include the following:

- A date (for example, the last business day of the month)
- An event (for example, the completion of another task)
- An exception (for example, the expense forecast being 10 per cent greater than budget by the end of the year)
- A manual intervention (for example, a competitor announcing a major change to its pricing, which management wants to assess by changing their own pricing)
- A combination of all of these points

The initiation logic is now used by the workflow engine to decide which tasks are to be run, at what times, and who should be involved. As they are triggered, 'To-do' lists are automatically distributed to the appropriate people with links to the right areas of the affected models. As the tasks are completed, new ones are automatically triggered or old ones re-invoked, depending on the logic embedded within the tasks. To avoid bottlenecks, tasks can have automatic escalation capabilities should a user not comply with or complete the task in a timely manner. Administrators are able to view the status of any process from a moving timeline that shows what tasks have been distributed, those that have been completed as required, and those that are behind schedule. From this process control panel, administrators can invoke new tasks and cancel or reset those that are on-going.

In short, these workflow-based systems are able to transform planning into a continuous, intelligent, and efficient activity. If things are working well, the system lets people continue as normal, but if the outlook seems to be moving away from set targets, they allow management to respond and re-plan the parts that are affected.

We have now completed the description of the business planning framework. In the last section of the book, we will look at the role of technology and some suggestions about how it can be implemented.

Section 3

IMPLEMENTING A PLANNING FRAMEWORK

LATEST DEVELOPMENTS IN PLANNING AND ANALYTICS TECHNOLOGIES

CORPORATE PERFORMANCE MANAGEMENT (CPM) APPLICATIONS

Specialised software planning systems have been available since the late 1960s. Back then, computer power and the applications that ran on them were expensive and were not widely used. However, as computer technology advanced, computer time-sharing bureaus appeared that were able to offer sophisticated solutions (at the time) that were relatively inexpensive to rent and fairly simple to set up. The software was maintained and hosted by a service bureau, with the companies accessing and using the programs from a computer terminal via a dial-up telephone link—nothing else was needed. (Today's cloud-based solutions are nothing new. It is just that the technology has become faster, more reliable, more powerful, and cheaper.)

During the 1970s and 1980s, the cost of computing continued to drop, which allowed organisations to develop their own internal information technology (IT) capabilities that were often cheaper than the cost of using a bureau. As a consequence, organisations started to purchase software and hardware in order to bring those bureau-based applications in-house. To meet this new demand, many of the existing planning and reporting products were converted to run on-premise, first on mainframes, then mini computers, and then onto networked micros. The continued fall in price of hardware and software along with the awareness of the new planning technologies greatly increased demand with the result that more software vendors entered the market.

In response to increased competition, software vendors had to find ways of differentiating themselves. One route was to move away from applications that focused on one aspect of management, such as budgeting or financial reporting, and instead expand functionality with features to cover more areas. The rationale behind this was twofold:

- First, it meant customers would get two or more systems for the price of one, which gave the vendor a price advantage, while at the same time allow them to charge slightly more for their suite.

- Second, through conversation with customers, it was recognised that a process such as budgeting was also linked to forecasting and management reporting. However, to support these processes data had to be moved between applications, and duplicate effort was required to maintain business structures in the different systems. Combining these capabilities would eliminate this source of pain.

As functionality grew and the idea of software that supported more than one process made sense, the IT analyst firm Gartner launched their paper on corporate performance management (CPM), which, as previously mentioned, they defined as 'the methodologies, metrics, processes and systems used to monitor and manage an enterprise's business performance'.[1] It was not intended to be a description for a software product, but that did not stop vendors from claiming that they had a CPM solution. The trouble was that many of them still offered discreet products with the only level of integration being the label on the software packaging.

To clarify the capabilities of a CPM system, Gartner put forward the following application areas that they felt constitute performance management:[2]

- Financial and management reporting and disclosure
- Budgeting
- Planning, forecasting, and strategy management
- Profitability modelling and optimisation

Throughout the turn of the 21st century, the market for CPM applications exploded. Surveys by Gartner reported that CPM was the highest priority in business intelligence (BI) tools for organisations. This was the catalyst for the big Enterprise Resource Planning (ERP) and database vendors, in particular SAP, Oracle, IBM, SAS, and Infor, to enter the market. As they typically did not have any products of their own, they either acquired many of the smaller CPM vendors or quickly developed their own. Because of their large installed base of clients, they were able to easily cross-sell the acquired solutions and soon captured a large market share. Some of the database vendors sought to integrate the acquired applications into their own existing database technologies and reporting functionality.

That is where we are today. It is a mature market that is made up of a few mega-vendors offering a broad range of solutions, with a handful of smaller vendors whose opportunity lies in supplying niche applications. However, in the opinion of the authors, the market for CPM is about to change. In recent years, new developments in both hardware and software technologies are starting to bring major changes to the way in which applications are conceived, written, and delivered. In the remainder of this chapter we will look at a few of them.

THE RISE OF BUSINESS ANALYTICS

The Next Competitive Edge

Business analytics refers to the ability to investigate past performance through the use of statistical methods that can then be used to drive business planning. Once thought of as being nice to have, applying analytics, especially predictive business analytics, is now becoming mission-critical and a competitive edge for organisations.

The use of analytics that include statistics is a skill that is gaining mainstream value due to the increasingly thinner margin for decision error. There is a requirement to gain insights, foresight, and inferences from the treasure chest of raw transactional data (both internal and external) that many organisations now store (and will continue to store) in a digital format.

An experienced analyst is like a caddy for a professional golfer. The best ones do not limit their advice to the professional for factors such as distance, slope, and the weather, but also strongly suggest which club to use.

BI Versus Analytics Versus Decisions

Here is a useful way to differentiate BI from analytics and decisions. Analytics simplify data to amplify its value. The power of analytics is to turn huge volumes of data into a much smaller amount of information and insight. BI mainly summarises historical data, typically in table reports and graphs, as a means for queries and drill downs. However, reports do not simplify data nor amplify its value; they simply package up the data so it can be consumed.

In contrast to BI, decisions provide context for what to analyse. Work backward with the end decision in mind. Identify the decisions that matter most to your organisation and model what leads to making those decisions. By understanding the type of decision needed, the type of analysis and its required source data can be defined.

Many believe that the use of BI software and the creation of cool graphs are the ultimate destination. BI is the shiny new toy of information technology. The reality is that much of what BI software tools provide, as just described, has more to do with query and reporting often by reformatting data. A common observation is, 'There is no intelligence in business intelligence'. It is only when data mining and analytics are applied to BI within an organisation that has the skills, competencies, and capabilities that deep insights and foresight is created. This can then be used to create better planning models that assess actions for improving business operations and opportunities.

Data mining that uses statistical methods is the foundation and precursor for predictive business analytics. For example, data mining can identify similar groups and segments (for example, customers) through cluster or correlation analysis. This allows an analyst to frame their analytics to predict how their object of interest (such as customers, new medicines, new smartphones, and so on) is likely to behave in the future, with or without interventions. This allows predictive analytics to move from being descriptive to prescriptive, and as such become the foundation for planning.

To clarify, BI consumes stored information. Analytics produces new information. Predictive business analytics leverages data within an organisational function focused on analytics that possesses the mandate, skills, and competencies to drive better, faster decisions and achieve targeted performance.

Queries using BI tools simply answer basic questions. Business analytics creates questions. Further, analytics stimulate more questions, more complex questions, and more interesting questions. More importantly, business analytics also have the power to answer the questions. Finally, predictive business analytics that are bound up in a business model can display the probability of outcomes based on the assumptions of variables.

The application of analytics was once the domain of 'quants' and statistical geeks developing models in their cubicles. However, today it is becoming mainstream for organisations, with the conviction that senior executives will realise and utilise its potential value.

Business Analytics, Big Data, and Decision Management

Much is being written today about big data. Big data has been defined as a collection of data sets so large and complex that it becomes difficult to process using on-hand database management tools or traditional data processing applications. The challenges include capture, validate, storage, search, share, analyse, and visualisation. What is needed is to shift the discussion from big data to big value. Business analytics and its amplifier, predictive business analytics, serve as a means to an end, and that end is faster, smarter decisions.

Many may assume that this implies executive decisions, but the relatively higher value for and benefit from applying analytics is arguably for daily operational decisions. Here is why.

Decisions can be segmented in three layers:

- Strategic decisions are few in number but can have large impacts. For example, should we acquire a company or exit a market?
- Tactical decisions involve controlling with moderate impacts. For example, should we modify our supply chain?
- Operational decisions are daily, even hourly, and often affect a single transaction or customer. For example, what deal should I offer to this customer? Should I accept making this bank loan?

There are several reasons that operational decisions are arguably most important for embracing analytics. First, executing the executive team's strategy is not solely accomplished with strategy maps and their resulting key performance indicators (KPIs) in a performance scorecard and dashboards. The daily decisions are what actually move the dials. Next, although much is now written about enterprise risk management (ERM), the reality is that an organisation's exposure to risk does not come in big chunks. ERM deals more with reporting. Risk is incurred one event or transaction at a time. Finally, in the sales and marketing functions operational decisions maximise customer value much more than policies. For example, what should a front-line customer-facing worker do or say to a customer to gain profit lift?

Operational decisions scale from the bottom up, and in the aggregate they can collectively exceed the impact of a few strategic decisions.

Predictive Business Analytics: The Next New Wave

Today many business people do not really know what predictive modelling, forecasting, design of experiments, or mathematical optimisation mean or do. However, over the next ten years, if businesses want to thrive in a highly competitive and regulated marketplace, use of these powerful techniques will become mainstream within planning, just as financial analysis is today. Executives, managers, and employee teams who do not understand, interpret, and leverage these assets will be hard-pressed to survive.

When we look at what kids are learning in school, then that is certainly true. We were all taught mean, mode, range, and probability theory in our first-year university statistical analytics course. Today, children have already learned these in the third grade! They are taught these methods in a very practical way. If you had x dimes, y quarters, and z nickels in your pocket, what is the chance of you pulling a dime from your pocket? Learning about range, mode, median, interpolation, and extrapolation follow in short succession. We are already seeing the impact of this with Gen Y and Echo Boomers who are getting ready to enter the work force; they are used to having easy access to information and are highly self-sufficient in understanding its utility. The next generation after that will not have any fear of analytics or look toward an expert to do the math.

There is always risk when decisions are made based on intuition, gut feel, flawed and misleading data, or politics. One can make the case that the primary source of attaining a competitive advantage will increasingly be an organisation's competence in mastering all flavours of analytics. If your management team is analytics impaired, then your organisation is at risk. Predictive business analytics is arguably the next wave for organisations to successfully compete and not only to predict outcomes, but reach higher to optimise the use of their resources, assets, and trading partners, among other things.

It may be that the ultimate sustainable business strategy is to foster analytical competency and eventual mastery among an organisation's work force. Today managers and employee teams do not need a doctorates degree in statistics to investigate data and gain insights. Commercial software tools are designed for the casual user.

Game-Changer Wave: Automated Decision-Based Management

What is the next big wave that will follow after analytics? Automated decision-based management. As organisations achieve competency and mastery with analytics, the next step will be automated rules based on the outcomes from applying analytics. The islands of analytics that emerge in an organisation's various departments and processes will be unified in closed-loop ways. Communications will be in real-time.

This does not mean that an organisation's workforce will be reduced in size by robot-like decision making. However, it does mean that algorithms, equations, and business rules derived from superior analysis will become essential to managing towards optimisation. Decision-based managerial software will eventually emerge that is independent of, but is integrated with, an organisation's multitude of data storage platforms and data management 'stacks' between the data and decisions. These future software generated decisions will be aligned with the executive team's strategy and its KPIs. When that day comes, it will be a game-changer and the basis for a book to be written in the future.

Substantial benefits are realised from applying a systematic exploration of quantitative relationships among performance management factors. When the primary factors that drive an organisation's success are measured, closely monitored, and predicted within an overall plan, that organisation is in a much better situation to adjust, advance, and mitigate risks. That is, if a company is able to know, not just guess, which non-financial performance variables directly influence financial results, then it has a leg-up on its competitors and delivers real value to its shareholders, employees, and other stakeholders.

For a more detailed explanation on how business analytics can change the way business is perceived and managed, we would recommend the book *Predictive Business Analytics: Forward Looking Capabilities to Improve Business Performance* by Lawrence Maisel and Gary Cokins.

APPLICATION INTEGRATION

For the past 30 years or more, software aimed at planning has basically been about adding up numbers. However, as technologies such as business analytics become main-stream, there will be significant changes to what those solutions will be able to do in the future.

Most planning and reporting systems are at the stage where transaction systems were 15 or more years ago. Back then, the systems used to record the business were split into sales and purchase ledgers, stock control, sales order books, and so on.

The advent of ERP saw the integration of these solutions into a single system where user interaction was controlled by an encompassing workflow capability. This gave benefits in that it helped automate the reordering of stock and provided warnings should production be out of line with forecasts. End-users, line managers, and senior executives all use the same system to look at the current and future status of production, so clear decisions can be made about production priorities. However, for ERP to be successful, it required organisations to rethink the management processes involved in order to take advantage of the software.

The same will be true of planning and reporting systems in the future. Today, most software vendor solutions are a series of discreet applications that focus on different aspects of performance. However, there is a new category of application emerging that totally integrates the six disciplines of strategic and operational planning with budgeting, forecasting, management reporting, and risk management. These systems will eventually encompass business analytics with traditional BI reporting tools to the extent that, to the end user, they are one application.

With this type of system, users throughout the organisation will be controlled by an encompassing workflow capability that allows them to view the status of strategy, its execution, and their involvement in making it happen. They will be able to gain insight about the immediate past from which decisions can be made concerning what works and what does not work. However, like ERP systems, they will require a re-think of the management processes involved so that they can operate on a continual basis.

CLOUD-BASED APPLICATIONS

Another recent trend that is gaining traction is cloud-based solutions. In a nutshell, a cloud-based solution is one where the software and hardware is not owned or hosted by the client. Instead, customers rent the application from a third-party who then supplies the application's capabilities as a service (more commonly known as software as a service, or SaaS for short). An early example of such an application is SalesForce.com, which is used by thousands of companies to collect and manage sales forecasts.

In the early days of cloud-based solutions, there was much scaremongering concerning access to the data. Can you trust the vendor not to lose the data or allow unauthorised access? If they go out of business, what happens to the data? How would an organisation continue to operate? For sales forecasts there may not be too much of a concern, but with an organisation's strategic plans, operating results, and the mechanism by which plans are set, these concerns are very real.

In recent years, much has been done to alleviate these fears. Organisations are now used to handling their financial transactions over the Internet, and most cloud-based vendors have extremely secure installations. Any hint of malpractice regarding data or access would finish them, so they have a vested interest to be as secure as possible. In terms of companies going out of business, most applications are built on standard technologies and, due to fierce competition, most cloud solutions can be replaced quickly.

The biggest catalyst for adopting a cloud-based solution is economic. Cloud solutions are extremely cost effective. In summary, these costs savings include the following:

- *The elimination of hardware to run the application.* The cloud vendor provides this. This means that as the application grows, there is no requirement to upgrade the hardware, maintain it, place it in a secure facility, or have engineers on standby. Savings here alone can be considerable.

- *The elimination of software at the client site.* All the customer needs is an Internet browser, which comes free with almost any device. As most traditional on-premise applications store data in some form of database, often the software vendor will require the customer to have operating system licenses and database licenses, all of which are extra costs and are not included with the solution software. Cloud-based solutions totally eradicate these hidden costs.

- *The elimination of software installation and upgrades.* With a cloud-based application, users are always on the latest version. As operating systems change and mobile devices gain more power, it is the interest of the application vendor to sort out how to take advantage of new developments. This way, customers do not have to spend time and effort on this.

- *Anytime, anywhere access.* It does not matter what device you use or where you are; provided you have Internet access, you will be able to use a cloud-based application anytime and anywhere.

All of these points result in a substantial lower cost of ownership. This ownership typically comes without any upfront capital costs and annual maintenance payments. Instead, these costs are replaced with a much lower rental cost that can be turned off at any time. It also means that customers do not need to be concerned about hardware capability and the subsequent impact on costs that come from increasing CPU power.

Cloud-based planning solutions are still in their infancy, with some organisations still worried about whether the service may disappear overnight without warning. However, the costs involved, or rather, the lack of them, are so persuasive that for many applications it just may be worth the risk.

IN-MEMORY CHIP TECHNOLOGY

The speed and capacity at which microchips can store and process data is rapidly advancing. In the past, data that was being analysed had to be stored on a device that was physically separate from the processor. This was because the processor was limited in its ability to hold data, and even then this type of memory was very expensive. The separate area was often a magnetic disc (or hard drive) that could hold very large amounts of data and was relatively inexpensive. The disadvantage of this design is that it requires data to be constantly written to and from memory, which incurs a time penalty. The more data to be analysed, the more time is required to swap data between the two types of memory. This resulted in analyses that took hours to run.

The new in-memory chip technology replaces the need for a separate physical disc, which in turn eliminates the time taken to read and write data. The result is vastly increased response times and systems that are able to support real-time processing of massive amounts of information.

The implications are significant. Aspects of so many items mentioned in this book, including drill-down queries and refreshing of models, become nearly instantaneous. For analysts, investigations and explorations of multiple 'what if' scenarios can be processed at the speed of thought.

Just one final word is needed about trying to predict the future of software: You can be sure that no matter what we see today, something else is bound to appear and disrupt what is regarded as normal. Regardless of the future developments that may arise, it is always important to keep in mind that technology is an enabler, and it needs to be evaluated in line with how the organisation is to be managed.

In the final chapter, we will look at ways in which the planning framework can be introduced into an organisation.

Endnotes

1 www.gartner.com/it-glossary/cpm-corporate-performance-management

2 Magic Quadrant for Corporate Performance Management Suites, Christopher Lervolino, John E. Van Decker, Neil Chandler, Gartner 14 February 2013

IMPLEMENTING THE PLANNING FRAMEWORK

In this final chapter, we will look at the challenges of implementing the planning framework and make suggestions on how this should be approached.

PLANNING AND THE ROLE OF THE CHIEF EXECUTIVE

Chief executives are typically appointed with one role in mind: to lead the organisation in achieving its purpose. They are expected to do this ethically, within designated constraints (for example, costs incurred and investment required), and by operating in a manner that demonstrates desired beliefs, values, and attitudes.

It is a role the chief executive cannot do alone, and so he or she must look to key people for ideas, guidance, and support. The chief executive's role, along with his or her executive team, is to answer the question, 'Where do we want to go?' That involves strategy formulation. However, what this book is about is how to answer a second question: How are we going to get there? Strategy execution requires plans, initiatives, process improvements, resources, and the many other factors described in this book. A strategy is never static, but rather, dynamic, as it must be adjusted in response to external factors and new ideas. Hence, flexible and integrated planning is needed.

Those who work in finance have the potential to be amongst the strongest allies of the chief executive, as they are the custodians of the organisation's financial resources. Ensuring that these are allocated in ways that support the mission and then tracking the resulting performance must surely be one of the most valuable services to the chief executive.

The challenge for all chief executives, particularly those who have just been appointed at a new company, is to make a difference that counts. It is all well and good to have big ideas and to talk about how the organisation should adapt to changing business conditions, but to do this in a manner that is acceptable and within reasonable timescales can often prove impossible. This is often due to a number of real and imaginary barriers that work against change, as discussed in the following sections.

Entrenched Beliefs Concerning Performance

To begin with, established organisations already have a way of doing business. They will have existing business processes that consume resources to produce outcomes that are aimed at achieving the stated mission. To go with these processes will be assumptions on what can be accomplished that are often not based on fact or on what the true potential could be if things were to change. Against this background, change is seen as unnecessary. These organisations believe that all that is required is patience and things will work out in the end. Either that, or management must lower their expectations concerning future goals.

Organisational Culture

Closely connected with the last point is the prevailing culture that exists within any organisation. Culture exhibits itself as the standards that people work to and, ultimately, that govern their behaviour. These are built up over time and are not easily changed. It affects the way they treat customers, line managers, partners, and senior executives, and affects the diligence and quality of their work. In short, culture can bring an organisation down.

Those at the top of the organisation set culture and thus its impact on the performance of the business. For example, if there is no clear link between strategy and everyday departmental actions, then strategy will be seen as the preserve of senior management who do not really understand what is going on at the ground level. No matter what kind of change a new chief executive may make, the belief will be that it is unlikely to have any effect, and so the actions necessary to make it happen will be done half-heatedly.

When strategy and change is seen as a wish list that is divorced from day-to-day reality, no one is committed to putting it into action. To make matters worse, no one is held accountable, and so failure is inevitable, which reinforces the belief that management does not understand the business.

The Unwritten Rules of Budgeting

Budgeting plays a vital role in ensuring that resources are allocated to the right programmes. Well, that is the intention, but so often the budgeting process is broken. Part of the problem is what Dean Sorensen calls the 'unwritten rules of budgeting' (that is, the way people believe they must behave in order for budgeting to be successful). These rules are usually the result of previous experiences and include the following:

- *Never submit your real budget the first time and always inflate costs and suppress revenues.* The underlying belief is that budget allocation is not fair. Budgets will always be cut irrespective of whether it is reasonable or accurate.
- *Always under promise and over deliver.* The underlying belief is that organisations value individual heroes and not team players.
- *Always make your budget.* People are rewarded for optimising financial performance and not enterprise performance.
- *Protect your budget.* Power and reference is based on the number of people or the amount of resources commanded. Losing these means a loss of power and influence.
- *Always spend your budget.* Resource allocation is not fair. Managers are unlikely to get the budget back if it is not spent.
- *Only accept responsibility for measures that can be influenced in your department.* People are not rewarded for driving cross-functional performance improvement.

Of course, these rules are crazy, yet we still see them at work as they conspire to circumvent change.

Rewarding Bad Behaviour

It has been said that organisations get the behaviour they pay for. When bonuses are tied to the budget, the budget process focus is turned away from organisational performance and toward personal rewards. This leads to game playing during the budget process. For example, those with revenue responsibility will try to suppress revenue goals, and those with cost responsibility will try to inflate their budgets. Both activities work directly against what the organisation is trying to achieve, which calls for the efficient deployment of resources based on what is happening in the business environment.

Failure to Execute

If planning is one half of managing performance, execution is the other. In fact, it could be argued it is more important than planning. After all, planning is about guiding the organisation through the business landscape, avoiding pitfalls, and making the most of its limited resources in order to achieve the mission. If the plan cannot be executed, then what is the point in developing one in the first place? Without a plan, organisations are at the mercy of both customers and competitors that will lead it away from achieving corporate objectives.

Organisations find it hard to execute. *Forbes* magazine reported that less than 10% of all organisations successfully execute their strategies.[1] The Conference Board, a global, independent business membership and research association, reports that "Many CEOs rate consistent execution of their firms' strategic objectives as a major concern".[2]

For most organisations, setting strategy is the preserve of senior managers in conjunction with middle management that provide feedback on what is going on in the marketplace and where they think it is heading. However, execution is typically delegated down to junior management and the front-line workforce who interact daily with customers and suppliers. Their alignment of activities with strategy is essential, as is the feedback on whether the strategy is working and any adjustments that need to be made as a result of actual and forecast results.

The key to overcoming these barriers to change is to confront them. This can be accomplished first by admitting that they exist. Second, by using the planning framework described in this book as a discussion on what really drives value and the role that planning should play in enhancing organisational value.

IMPLEMENTING CHANGE

The business planning framework is the culmination of many years of working with multiple organisations, both big and small. It is highly unlikely that it can be implemented in one go. Instead, an incremental approach is recommended that gradually moves an organisation from its current methods to one that is more relevant for today's business environment.

The following sections include suggestions on how this can be done that will also help overcome the barriers to change.

Agree on the Role of Planning

As mentioned in chapter 1, 'Planning Fundamentals', every organisation has a purpose and a set of business processes through which it hopes to achieve its aims. For the organisation to be successful, management at all levels should understand a number of key aspects of the business. This is because they will be required to work together, and without that shared common knowledge they will end up working against each other. In our experience, quite often, the knowledge that should be common is anything but common or understood.

The following are a number of key questions that all managers should know how to answer:

- What is the aim of the organisation? How is it quantified, over what period, and for what business environment? This knowledge sets the aspirations of the organisation on which management need to focus.
- Are the business processes the right ones for now and for the future? Do managers really understand how the organisation adds value for its intended customers and the role their area plays? Knowing how their responsibilities contribute to overall goals gives meaning to actions they perform and the resources their department consumes.

Having established answers to these questions, managers will then need to agree on the planning processes required, for what purpose, and the supporting planning models they need. This is where the planning framework can help by suggesting what these, from which discussions can be had and an agreement reached.

Model Existing Processes

There should be an acknowledgement that the only things that can be truly managed are the business processes that deliver outcomes for customers, the workload that departments should carry out for each task within a business process, and the resources that the workload consumes. To establish the current state of the business, an operational activity model (OAM), as discussed in chapter 5, 'Operational Activity Model', should be developed that associates resources with activity workload and outcomes. This need not be at a detailed level to begin with. What we are trying to do is to get an idea of where resources are being consumed today and the outcomes that are being generated.

Once this has been done, get senior managers together to review the reports produced by the OAM, to discuss questions such as the following:

- Are the short-term business goals in line with our long-term aims?
- Are the business process outcomes sufficient to deliver the business goals?
- Is the workload reasonable in producing the outcomes for each business process?
- Is the cost worth the workload effort?
- How does current and projected performance compare to peer organisations, competitors, and market expectations?

In reviewing these results, it is not a question of establishing which departments are doing a good job and which managers are failing. The focus should be on what the management team believes it needs to do to achieve organisational aims. By knowing the current state of performance, it is easier to target where performance can be improved.

Establish Improvement Themes

It is rarely possible to make sweeping changes, as this often proves disruptive to the day-to-day running of the organisation, resulting in even worse performance. The McKinsey article 'Managing CEO transitions'[3] emphasises the need to concentrate on just a few things, otherwise managers will become confused and focus will be lost. Organisations that have successfully managed change articulate those changes with a few simple themes (for example, quality and throughput or superior customer relations). These themes set what is important and provide the context for any changes that are made.

The article also goes on to stress the importance of balance between short- and long-term objectives. Too often, organisations focus on immediate emergencies, with the result that the long-term (and hence strategic) goals are nothing but dreams. One crisis leads to another, and direction is set by short-term needs rather than serving the long-term purpose. In this landscape, management will assume that strategy does not really matter and that the promise of a better life ahead is false.

To this end, change programmes must look at providing for short- and long-term goals. By expressing short-term pain in regard to a better future, managers are more likely to take on change with more enthusiasm.

Plan- and Resource-Specific Change Programmes

Managers are those people who have reached a level of maturity concerning the purpose of the organisation and the way in which it can reach its goals. As such, they are given responsibility over its resources and activities. Their rewards and future success depend on how well they support the organisation in its mission, and over time, they will acquire detailed knowledge about what works and what does not within a given business environment.

To get managers on board with change, one way would be to ask them for suggestions on particular programmes that are linked to the improvement themes previously set. Better yet, accept their ideas and the related measures that indicate progress to provide them ownership as well as to hold them accountable to.

This could be supported by a strategy improvement model (SIM) to collect details of proposed programmes, which can be assessed with others to see the combinations that have the best overall effect. As the SIM is connected to the OAM, changes can be seen in the context of current operations and budgets can be apportioned accordingly to what makes the most sense.

Monitor Implementation

There is nothing worse than not monitoring change. After all the effort of analysing the need for change and making convincing arguments, to then not monitor its impact gives the impression that no one was serious at the start. The areas that need monitoring include answering the following questions:

- Are the implementation milestones being met?
- Are the resources being consumed in line with what was planned?
- Is the workload and outcomes at the planned level?
- Is the change having a measurable impact on business process performance?

The last point may be difficult to gauge, as any increase (or decrease) in performance may be down to the change, the current operations excluding the change, the impact of previous actions whose affect was delayed, other factors, or just luck. However, knowing that many factors may be involved, it is still useful for management to discuss the level of performance being achieved and to come to a shared view of the reasons.

As well as looking at what happened, it is vital to forecast answers to the same questions, only as viewed in the future (for example, will the future milestones be achieved? Will the planned resources be sufficient?). The reason for doing this is to determine whether the change can continue to run as present or whether it needs to be adjusted, cancelled, or replaced.

Use Technology to Support Change

Planning technology is there to support the organisation. That means it should enable plans to be created and adjusted in the way you want to work and not the other way around. To set up this framework in anything other than a simple company will require enterprise-planning technology. As mentioned in chapter 11, 'Latest Developments in Planning and Analytics Technologies', enterprise systems are undergoing rapid change as they seek to support planning in an unpredictable business environment. They need to support continuous planning and allow organisations to manage business processes, which for many of them is very different from their original design.

If you need to look for a new software solution, make sure the capabilities outlined in Appendix II can be managed easily within the solution being considered.

Continually Develop the Planning Models Within the Framework

The last point is that the development of the OAM and its supporting models never stops. Managers should continually challenge not only their business processes, but also the way in which business processes are measured and resourced. There is no simple answer to managing performance—if there were, then someone would have thought of it before now. The reality is that the business world is far more complex than any model can cope with, and even if one model did, its impact would be to change the business world, and it would no longer work.

For this reason, it is important not to make the models too complex. Their purpose is to provide a basis for a shared discussion on what drives performance and ways in which that performance can be optimised. They are a management tool to help communicate knowledge and intuition about the future, but are useless if that knowledge is absent.

In these last few points, we have described a few initial steps for using the framework. Once the OAM and SIM have been developed, the next logical steps for management reporting are to add the detailed history model for selected accounts and the performance measures model. If your initial purpose is to support budgeting, then maybe the target setting model followed by the detailed forecast models are next.

Rather than give you the order, it would be best for the management team to agree on the priorities of what models need to be developed. Initially, these can be at a summary level, with more detail being added once they are operational.

Well, that is it. Hopefully, you have found the book interesting and we have given you some useful ideas on how to improve the planning process where you work. Common issues with any book are that some of the text can quickly become out of date and that it is not always possible to illustrate examples in detail. For these reasons, we have set up a website where you can get updates and share experiences with other planners. To access this website, visit www.BusinessPlanningFramework.com.

Endnotes

1 www.forbes.com/sites/larrymyler/2012/10/16/strategy-101-its-all-about-alignment/

2 www.conference-board.org/publications/publicationdetail.cfm?publicationid=1888

3 'Managing CEO transitions', Tsun-Yan Hsieh, Stephen Bear, McKinsey, May 1994.

APPENDIX I

CGMA BUDGET AND PLANNING SURVEY RESULTS

This appendix contains summaries from the planning survey conducted specifically for this book by the American Institute of CPAs in the United States and Chartered Institute of Management Accountants in the United Kingdom.

EXECUTIVE SUMMARY

This report contains a detailed statistical analysis of the results to the survey titled *CGMA Budget and Planning Survey*. The results analysis includes answers from all respondents who took the survey in the 49 day period from Wednesday, June 26, 2013 to Wednesday, August 14, 2013. 497 completed responses were received to the survey during this time.

SURVEY RESULTS & ANALYSIS

Survey: CGMA Budget and Planning Survey

Author

Filter

Responses Received: 497

1) How would you characterize the finance function's level of involvement in the following planning processes?

	VERY LIMITED	LIMITED	MODERATE	HIGH	VERY HIGH
Strategic Planning	2.6% (13)	9.4% (46)	18.7% (92)	42.0% (206)	27.3% (134)
Tactical Planning	1.6% (8)	9.0% (44)	26.1% (127)	41.1% (200)	22.2% (108)
Financial Planning / Budgeting	0.8% (4)	1.0% (5)	6.8% (33)	16.7% (81)	74.6% (362)
Cash Planning	1.8% (9)	2.4% (12)	8.6% (42)	19.6% (96)	67.6% (331)
Capital Planning	2.7% (13)	3.3% (16)	14.8% (72)	36.2% (176)	43.0% (209)
Forecasting	0.8% (4)	3.5% (17)	9.8% (48)	27.8% (136)	58.2% (285)
Risk Management	3.5% (17)	10.4% (51)	25.1% (123)	38.3% (188)	22.8% (112)

1.1) Strategic Planning: (How would you characterize the finance function's level of involvement in the following planning processes?)

RESPONSE	COUNT	PERCENT
Very Limited	13	2.6%
Limited	46	9.4%
Moderate	92	18.7%
High	206	42.0%
Very High	134	27.3%

1.2) Tactical Planning: (How would you characterize the finance function's level of involvement in the following planning processes?)

RESPONSE	COUNT	PERCENT
Very Limited	8	1.6%
Limited	44	9.0%
Moderate	127	26.1%
High	200	41.1%
Very High	108	22.2%

1.3) Financial Planning / Budgeting: (How would you characterize the finance function's level of involvement in the following planning processes?)

RESPONSE	COUNT	PERCENT
Very Limited	4	0.8%
Limited	5	1.0%
Moderate	33	6.8%
High	81	16.7%
Very High	362	74.6%

1.4) Cash Planning: (How would you characterize the finance function's level of involvement in the following planning processes?)

RESPONSE	COUNT	PERCENT
Very Limited	9	1.8%
Limited	12	2.4%
Moderate	42	8.6%
High	96	19.6%
Very High	331	67.6%

1.5) Capital Planning: (How would you characterize the finance function's level of involvement in the following planning processes?)

RESPONSE	COUNT	PERCENT
Very Limited	13	2.7%
Limited	16	3.3%
Moderate	72	14.8%
High	176	36.2%
Very High	209	43.0%

1.6) Forecasting: (How would you characterize the finance function's level of involvement in the following planning processes?)

RESPONSE	COUNT	PERCENT
Very Limited	4	0.8%
Limited	17	3.5%
Moderate	48	9.8%
High	136	27.8%
Very High	285	58.2%

1.7) Risk Management: (How would you characterize the finance function's level of involvement in the following planning processes?)

RESPONSE	COUNT	PERCENT
Very Limited	17	3.5%
Limited	51	10.4%
Moderate	123	25.1%
High	188	38.3%
Very High	112	22.8%

2) To what extent does management information and analysis inform resource allocation or planning choices in each of the following processes?

	VERY LIMITED	LIMITED	MODERATE	GREAT	VERY GREAT
Strategic Planning	1.9% (9)	9.5% (46)	29.2% (141)	37.7% (182)	21.7% (105)
Tactical Planning	1.9% (9)	9.2% (44)	28.8% (138)	39.7% (190)	20.5% (98)
Financial Planning / Budgeting	0.8% (4)	2.7% (13)	15.8% (75)	34.8% (165)	45.8% (217)
Cash Planning	2.1% (10)	8.1% (39)	19.5% (94)	35.1% (169)	35.3% (170)
Capital Planning	1.3% (6)	7.9% (38)	23.2% (111)	39.5% (189)	28.0% (134)
Forecasting	0.6% (3)	5.6% (27)	19.8% (95)	36.4% (175)	37.6% (181)
Risk Management	3.7% (18)	14.8% (71)	31.2% (150)	33.3% (160)	17.0% (82)

2.1) Strategic Planning: (To what extent does management information and analysis inform resource allocation or planning choices in each of the following processes?)

RESPONSE	COUNT	PERCENT
Very Limited	9	1.9%
Limited	46	9.5%
Moderate	141	29.2%
Great	182	37.7%
Very Great	105	21.7%

2.2) Tactical Planning: (To what extent does management information and analysis inform resource allocation or planning choices in each of the following processes?)

RESPONSE	COUNT	PERCENT
Very Limited	9	1.9%
Limited	44	9.2%
Moderate	138	28.8%
Great	190	39.7%
Very Great	98	20.5%

2.3) Financial Planning / Budgeting: (To what extent does management information and analysis inform resource allocation or planning choices in each of the following processes?)

RESPONSE	COUNT	PERCENT
Very Limited	4	0.8%
Limited	13	2.7%
Moderate	75	15.8%
Great	165	34.8%
Very Great	217	45.8%

2.4) Cash Planning: (To what extent does management information and analysis inform resource allocation or planning choices in each of the following processes?)

RESPONSE	COUNT	PERCENT
Very Limited	10	2.1%
Limited	39	8.1%
Moderate	94	19.5%
Great	169	35.1%
Very Great	170	35.3%

2.5) Capital Planning: (To what extent does management information and analysis inform resource allocation or planning choices in each of the following processes?)

RESPONSE	COUNT	PERCENT
Very Limited	6	1.3%
Limited	38	7.9%
Moderate	111	23.2%
Great	189	39.5%
Very Great	134	28.0%

2.6) Forecasting: (To what extent does management information and analysis inform resource allocation or planning choices in each of the following processes?)

RESPONSE	COUNT	PERCENT
Very Limited	3	0.6%
Limited	27	5.6%
Moderate	95	19.8%
Great	175	36.4%
Very Great	181	37.6%

2.7) Risk Management: (To what extent does management information and analysis inform resource allocation or planning choices in each of the following processes?)

RESPONSE	COUNT	PERCENT
Very Limited	18	3.7%
Limited	71	14.8%
Moderate	150	31.2%
Great	160	33.3%
Very Great	82	17.0%

3) How would you characterize the degree of influence and impact of the finance function in the following planning processes?

	VERY LIMITED	LIMITED	MODERATE	HIGH	VERY HIGH
Strategic Planning	3.7% (18)	8.2% (40)	25.5% (124)	40.7% (198)	22.0% (107)
Tactical Planning	3.3% (16)	9.7% (47)	27.5% (133)	40.1% (194)	19.4% (94)
Financial Planning / Budgeting	1.4% (7)	1.4% (7)	7.4% (36)	24.2% (117)	65.5% (317)
Cash Planning	1.7% (8)	3.5% (17)	9.3% (45)	25.3% (122)	60.2% (291)
Capital Planning	2.3% (11)	5.6% (27)	21.1% (102)	32.9% (159)	38.1% (184)
Forecasting	1.0% (5)	4.4% (21)	10.8% (52)	31.1% (150)	52.7% (254)
Risk Management	3.3% (16)	12.0% (58)	32.0% (155)	32.4% (157)	20.2% (98)

3.1) Strategic Planning: (How would you characterize the degree of influence and impact of the finance function in the following planning processes?)

RESPONSE	COUNT	PERCENT
Very Limited	18	3.7%
Limited	40	8.2%
Moderate	124	25.5%
High	198	40.7%
Very High	107	22.0%

3.2) Tactical Planning: (How would you characterize the degree of influence and impact of the finance function in the following planning processes?)

RESPONSE	COUNT	PERCENT
Very Limited	16	3.3%
Limited	47	9.7%
Moderate	133	27.5%
High	194	40.1%
Very High	94	19.4%

3.3) Financial Planning / Budgeting: (How would you characterize the degree of influence and impact of the finance function in the following planning processes?)

RESPONSE	COUNT	PERCENT
Very Limited	7	1.4%
Limited	7	1.4%
Moderate	36	7.4%
High	117	24.2%
Very High	317	65.5%

3.4) Cash Planning: (How would you characterize the degree of influence and impact of the finance function in the following planning processes?)

RESPONSE	COUNT	PERCENT
Very Limited	8	1.7%
Limited	17	3.5%
Moderate	45	9.3%
High	122	25.3%
Very High	291	60.2%

3.5) Capital Planning: (How would you characterize the degree of influence and impact of the finance function in the following planning processes?)

RESPONSE	COUNT	PERCENT
Very Limited	11	2.3%
Limited	27	5.6%
Moderate	102	21.1%
High	159	32.9%
Very High	184	38.1%

3.6) Forecasting: (How would you characterize the degree of influence and impact of the finance function in the following planning processes?)

RESPONSE	COUNT	PERCENT
Very Limited	5	1.0%
Limited	21	4.4%
Moderate	52	10.8%
High	150	31.1%
Very High	254	52.7%

3.7) Risk Management: (How would you characterize the degree of influence and impact of the finance function in the following planning processes?)

RESPONSE	COUNT	PERCENT
Very Limited	16	3.3%
Limited	58	12.0%
Moderate	155	32.0%
High	157	32.4%
Very High	98	20.2%

4) How would you characterize the amount of time your organization spends in the following planning processes?

	FAR TOO LITTLE	SOMEWHAT TOO LITTLE	ABOUT RIGHT	SOMEWHAT TOO MUCH	FAR TOO MUCH
Strategic Planning	11.3% (55)	32.2% (156)	49.5% (240)	4.9% (24)	2.1% (10)
Tactical Planning	9.4% (45)	35.1% (168)	47.6% (228)	6.9% (33)	1.0% (5)
Financial Planning / Budgeting	2.7% (13)	13.7% (66)	59.0% (284)	19.5% (94)	5.0% (24)
Cash Planning	3.9% (19)	17.8% (86)	68.5% (331)	8.1% (39)	1.7% (8)
Capital Planning	4.0% (19)	30.2% (144)	58.7% (280)	5.5% (26)	1.7% (8)
Forecasting	6.0% (29)	24.6% (119)	51.9% (251)	13.6% (66)	3.9% (19)
Risk Management	9.9% (48)	37.3% (180)	48.4% (234)	3.7% (18)	0.6% (3)

4.1) Strategic Planning: (How would you characterize the amount of time your organization spends in the following planning processes?)

RESPONSE	COUNT	PERCENT
Far too little	55	11.3%
Somewhat too little	156	32.2%
About right	240	49.5%
Somewhat too much	24	4.9%
Far too much	10	2.1%

4.2) Tactical Planning: (How would you characterize the amount of time your organization spends in the following planning processes?)

RESPONSE	COUNT	PERCENT
Far too little	45	9.4%
Somewhat too little	168	35.1%
About right	228	47.6%
Somewhat too much	33	6.9%
Far too much	5	1.0%

4.3) Financial Planning / Budgeting: (How would you characterize the amount of time your organization spends in the following planning processes?)

RESPONSE	COUNT	PERCENT
Far too little	13	2.7%
Somewhat too little	66	13.7%
About right	284	59.0%
Somewhat too much	94	19.5%
Far too much	24	5.0%

4.4) Cash Planning: (How would you characterize the amount of time your organization spends in the following planning processes?)

RESPONSE	COUNT	PERCENT
Far too little	19	3.9%
Somewhat too little	86	17.8%
About right	331	68.5%
Somewhat too much	39	8.1%
Far too much	8	1.7%

4.5) Capital Planning: (How would you characterize the amount of time your organization spends in the following planning processes?)

RESPONSE	COUNT	PERCENT
Far too little	19	4.0%
Somewhat too little	144	30.2%
About right	280	58.7%
Somewhat too much	26	5.5%
Far too much	8	1.7%

4.6) Forecasting: (How would you characterize the amount of time your organization spends in the following planning processes?)

RESPONSE	COUNT	PERCENT
Far too little	29	6.0%
Somewhat too little	119	24.6%
About right	251	51.9%
Somewhat too much	66	13.6%
Far too much	19	3.9%

4.7) Risk Management: (How would you characterize the amount of time your organization spends in the following planning processes?)

RESPONSE	COUNT	PERCENT
Far too little	48	9.9%
Somewhat too little	180	37.3%
About right	234	48.4%
Somewhat too much	18	3.7%
Far too much	3	0.6%

5) How satisfied are you that the following planning processes are achieving their purpose in your organisation?

	VERY DISSATISFIED	SOMEWHAT DISSATISFIED	NEITHER SATISFIED NOR DISSATISFIED	SOMEWHAT SATISFIED	VERY SATISFIED
Strategic Planning	9.8% (48)	22.3% (109)	21.3% (104)	34.8% (170)	11.9% (58)
Tactical Planning	5.9% (29)	23.8% (116)	26.2% (128)	34.4% (168)	9.6% (47)
Financial Planning / Budgeting	3.5% (17)	13.3% (64)	21.0% (101)	38.6% (186)	23.7% (114)
Cash Planning	2.5% (12)	10.5% (51)	27.2% (132)	35.0% (170)	24.9% (121)
Capital Planning	3.3% (16)	14.3% (69)	29.8% (144)	37.5% (181)	15.1% (73)
Forecasting	3.9% (19)	18.3% (89)	22.4% (109)	38.5% (187)	16.9% (82)
Risk Management	5.0% (24)	19.6% (95)	37.6% (182)	28.5% (138)	9.3% (45)

5.1) Strategic Planning: (How satisfied are you that the following planning processes are achieving their purpose in your organisation?)

RESPONSE	COUNT	PERCENT
Very dissatisfied	48	9.8%
Somewhat dissatisfied	109	22.3%
Neither satisfied nor dissatisfied	104	21.3%
Somewhat satisfied	170	34.8%
Very satisfied	58	11.9%

5.2) Tactical Planning: (How satisfied are you that the following planning processes are achieving their purpose in your organisation?)

RESPONSE	COUNT	PERCENT
Very dissatisfied	29	5.9%
Somewhat dissatisfied	116	23.8%
Neither satisfied nor dissatisfied	128	26.2%
Somewhat satisfied	168	34.4%
Very satisfied	47	9.6%

5.3) Financial Planning / Budgeting: (How satisfied are you that the following planning processes are achieving their purpose in your organisation?)

RESPONSE	COUNT	PERCENT
Very dissatisfied	17	3.5%
Somewhat dissatisfied	64	13.3%
Neither satisfied nor dissatisfied	101	21.0%
Somewhat satisfied	186	38.6%
Very satisfied	114	23.7%

5.4) Cash Planning: (How satisfied are you that the following planning processes are achieving their purpose in your organisation?)

RESPONSE	COUNT	PERCENT
Very dissatisfied	12	2.5%
Somewhat dissatisfied	51	10.5%
Neither satisfied nor dissatisfied	132	27.2%
Somewhat satisfied	170	35.0%
Very satisfied	121	24.9%

5.5) Capital Planning: (How satisfied are you that the following planning processes are achieving their purpose in your organisation?)

RESPONSE	COUNT	PERCENT
Very dissatisfied	16	3.3%
Somewhat dissatisfied	69	14.3%
Neither satisfied nor dissatisfied	144	29.8%
Somewhat satisfied	181	37.5%
Very satisfied	73	15.1%

5.6) Forecasting: (How satisfied are you that the following planning processes are achieving their purpose in your organisation?)

RESPONSE	COUNT	PERCENT
Very dissatisfied	19	3.9%
Somewhat dissatisfied	89	18.3%
Neither satisfied nor dissatisfied	109	22.4%
Somewhat satisfied	187	38.5%
Very satisfied	82	16.9%

5.7) Risk Management: (How satisfied are you that the following planning processes are achieving their purpose in your organisation?)

RESPONSE	COUNT	PERCENT
Very dissatisfied	24	5.0%
Somewhat dissatisfied	95	19.6%
Neither satisfied nor dissatisfied	182	37.6%
Somewhat satisfied	138	28.5%
Very satisfied	45	9.3%

6) What type of technology solution do you use for the following planning processes?

	ENTERPRISE PLATFORM MODULE	SPECIAL PURPOSE (THIRD PARTY) APPLICATION	CUSTOM/ PROPRIETARY SOLUTION	SPREADSHEET/ PERSONAL PRODUCTIVITY TOOL	NONE	OTHER
Strategic Planning	4.3% (21)	5.8% (28)	8.8% (43)	53.3% (259)	22.8% (111)	4.9% (24)
Tactical Planning	5.0% (24)	5.2% (25)	10.4% (50)	50.6% (244)	22.8% (110)	6.0% (29)
Financial Planning / Budgeting	15.7% (76)	16.8% (81)	9.7% (47)	55.9% (270)	1.0% (5)	0.8% (4)
Cash Planning	7.2% (35)	7.0% (34)	9.7% (47)	70.9% (343)	3.9% (19)	1.2% (6)
Capital Planning	5.6% (27)	5.8% (28)	8.5% (41)	67.2% (323)	11.6% (56)	1.2% (6)
Forecasting	10.1% (49)	12.0% (58)	9.1% (44)	64.3% (312)	3.1% (15)	1.4% (7)
Risk Management	1.4% (7)	7.6% (37)	8.0% (39)	38.6% (187)	37.7% (183)	6.6% (32)

6.1)   Strategic Planning: (What type of technology solution do you use for the following planning processes?)

RESPONSE	COUNT	PERCENT
Enterprise Platform Module	21	4.3%
Special Purpose (Third Party) Application	28	5.8%
Custom/ Proprietary Solution	43	8.8%
Spreadsheet / Personal Productivity Tool	259	53.3%
None	111	22.8%
Other	24	4.9%

6.2)   Tactical Planning: (What type of technology solution do you use for the following planning processes?)

RESPONSE	COUNT	PERCENT
Enterprise Platform Module	24	5.0%
Special Purpose (Third Party) Application	25	5.2%
Custom/ Proprietary Solution	50	10.4%
Spreadsheet / Personal Productivity Tool	244	50.6%
None	110	22.8%
Other	29	6.0%

6.3)   Financial Planning / Budgeting: (What type of technology solution do you use for the following planning processes?)

RESPONSE	COUNT	PERCENT
Enterprise Platform Module	76	15.7%
Special Purpose (Third Party) Application	81	16.8%
Custom/ Proprietary Solution	47	9.7%
Spreadsheet / Personal Productivity Tool	270	55.9%
None	5	1.0%
Other	4	0.8%

6.4)　Cash Planning: (What type of technology solution do you use for the following planning processes?)

RESPONSE	COUNT	PERCENT
Enterprise Platform Module	35	7.2%
Special Purpose (Third Party) Application	34	7.0%
Custom/ Proprietary Solution	47	9.7%
Spreadsheet / Personal Productivity Tool	343	70.9%
None	19	3.9%
Other	6	1.2%

6.5)　Capital Planning: (What type of technology solution do you use for the following planning processes?)

RESPONSE	COUNT	PERCENT
Enterprise Platform Module	27	5.6%
Special Purpose (Third Party) Application	28	5.8%
Custom/ Proprietary Solution	41	8.5%
Spreadsheet / Personal Productivity Tool	323	67.2%
None	56	11.6%
Other	6	1.2%

6.6)　Forecasting: (What type of technology solution do you use for the following planning processes?)

RESPONSE	COUNT	PERCENT
Enterprise Platform Module	49	10.1%
Special Purpose (Third Party) Application	58	12.0%
Custom/ Proprietary Solution	44	9.1%
Spreadsheet / Personal Productivity Tool	312	64.3%
None	15	3.1%
Other	7	1.4%

6.7) Risk Management: (What type of technology solution do you use for the following planning processes?)

RESPONSE	COUNT	PERCENT
Enterprise Platform Module	7	1.4%
Special Purpose (Third Party) Application	37	7.6%
Custom/ Proprietary Solution	39	8.0%
Spreadsheet / Personal Productivity Tool	187	38.6%
None	183	37.7%
Other	32	6.6%

7) How satisfied are you with the alignment of the following planning processes with the strategic plan in your organization?

	VERY DISSATISFIED	SOMEWHAT DISSATISFIED	NEITHER SATISFIED/ DISSATISFIED	SOMEWHAT SATISFIED	VERY SATISFIED
Tactical Planning	5.7% (28)	20.5% (100)	31.4% (153)	33.1% (161)	9.2% (45)
Financial Planning / Budgeting	2.9% (14)	17.2% (84)	19.3% (94)	42.8% (209)	17.8% (87)
Cash Planning	2.7% (13)	15.0% (73)	29.8% (145)	36.0% (175)	16.5% (80)
Capital Planning	3.7% (18)	18.6% (91)	30.7% (150)	34.8% (170)	12.1% (59)
Forecasting	4.8% (23)	18.7% (90)	26.1% (126)	36.7% (177)	13.7% (66)
Risk Management	6.6% (32)	17.6% (85)	41.8% (202)	26.7% (129)	7.2% (35)

7.1) Tactical Planning: (How satisfied are you with the alignment of the following planning processes with the strategic plan in your organization?)

RESPONSE	COUNT	PERCENT
Very dissatisfied	28	5.7%
Somewhat dissatisfied	100	20.5%
Neither satisfied/dissatisfied	153	31.4%
Somewhat satisfied	161	33.1%
Very satisfied	45	9.2%

7.2) Financial Planning / Budgeting: (How satisfied are you with the alignment of the following planning processes with the strategic plan in your organization?)

RESPONSE	COUNT	PERCENT
Very dissatisfied	14	2.9%
Somewhat dissatisfied	84	17.2%
Neither satisfied/dissatisfied	94	19.3%
Somewhat satisfied	209	42.8%
Very satisfied	87	17.8%

7.3) Cash Planning: (How satisfied are you with the alignment of the following planning processes with the strategic plan in your organization?)

RESPONSE	COUNT	PERCENT
Very dissatisfied	13	2.7%
Somewhat dissatisfied	73	15.0%
Neither satisfied/dissatisfied	145	29.8%
Somewhat satisfied	175	36.0%
Very satisfied	80	16.5%

7.4) Capital Planning:(How satisfied are you with the alignment of the following planning processes with the strategic plan in your organization?)

RESPONSE	COUNT	PERCENT
Very dissatisfied	18	3.7%
Somewhat dissatisfied	91	18.6%
Neither satisfied/dissatisfied	150	30.7%
Somewhat satisfied	170	34.8%
Very satisfied	59	12.1%

7.5) Forecasting:(How satisfied are you with the alignment of the following planning processes with the strategic plan in your organization?)

RESPONSE	COUNT	PERCENT
Very dissatisfied	23	4.8%
Somewhat dissatisfied	90	18.7%
Neither satisfied/dissatisfied	126	26.1%
Somewhat satisfied	177	36.7%
Very satisfied	66	13.7%

7.6) Risk Management: (How satisfied are you with the alignment of the following planning processes with the strategic plan in your organization?)

RESPONSE	COUNT	PERCENT
Very dissatisfied	32	6.6%
Somewhat dissatisfied	85	17.6%
Neither satisfied/dissatisfied	202	41.8%
Somewhat satisfied	129	26.7%
Very satisfied	35	7.2%

8) Which of the following strategic planning methodologies does your organization use?

RESPONSE	COUNT	PERCENT
Balanced Scorecard	128	26.7%
Performance Prism	29	6.1%
Other	322	67.2%

9) Does the methodology drive links between the planning processes in which you are involved?

RESPONSE	COUNT	PERCENT
Yes	162	33.6%
No	125	25.9%
Sometimes	195	40.5%

10) To what extent is incentive compensation in your organization linked to strategic goals?

RESPONSE	COUNT	PERCENT
Very Limited	174	35.5%
Limited	87	17.8%
Moderate	119	24.3%
Great	79	16.1%
Very Great	31	6.3%

11) To what extent is incentive compensation in your organization linked to your annual budget?

RESPONSE	COUNT	PERCENT
Very Limited	148	30.2%
Limited	65	13.3%
Moderate	97	19.8%
Great	108	22.0%
Very Great	72	14.7%

12) To what extent is "gaming" an issue in the planning process?

RESPONSE	COUNT	PERCENT
Very Limited	169	34.8%
Limited	122	25.1%
Moderate	135	27.8%
Great	44	9.1%
Very Great	16	3.3%

13) Does your organization do rolling forecasts?

RESPONSE	COUNT	PERCENT
Yes	270	54.9%
No	222	45.1%

14) How long is your forecast horizon?

RESPONSE	COUNT	PERCENT
12 months	127	47.6%
15 months	10	3.7%
18 months	38	14.2%
24 months	48	18.0%
Other (please specify)	44	16.5%

OTHER RESPONSES
60 months
less than one year
VARIES 12MOS TO 5 YEARS
5 yrs
120 months
quarterly
5 years
36 months
36 months
12 mos for budget, 5 years for Strategic Plan
6 months and 12 months
6 months
5 years
6–9 months
13 weeks
3 Years
through end of fiscal year

Continued on p. 187

Continued from p. 186

OTHER RESPONSES
60 months
To year end, 12 month and 5 year forecasts
Detailed 12-mo; Macro 5-year
6 years
120 months
60 months
36 months
4 months
Not sure. I am not invoived in a lot of these que
36 months
3 months
As far out as there is a payment/receipt
5-year cash flow forcast
60 months
36 months
36 mo
6 months
60 months
5 years
5 years
36
10 years
36 months

Continued on p. 188

Continued from p. 187

OTHER RESPONSES
three years
5 years
36 months
5 years

15) How often do you update your forecast?

RESPONSE	COUNT	PERCENT
Monthly	120	44.6%
Quarterly	123	45.7%
Other (please specify)	26	9.7%

OTHER RESPONSES
as needed, usually ~2X per quarter
Annually
weekly
Semi annual
continuously
weekly
Every 4 months
semi annually
as needed
Annually
As needed
Annual
semi-annual

Continued on p. 189

Continued from p. 188

OTHER RESPONSES
weekly
Bi-Annualy
daily rolling forecasts
Haly-yearly
every 6 mo
Quarterly, but only after the 1st 6 months of year
When things change significantly
As needed
annually
weekly
every 6 months
Annually
Annual
Annually and auarerly

16) Is scenario planning part of your organization's planning processes?

RESPONSE	COUNT	PERCENT
Yes	225	46.4%
No	260	53.6%

17) Why not?

RESPONSE	COUNT	PERCENT
Not considered necessary for our business	116	23.3%
Do not have the necessary skillets	44	8.9%
Do not have sufficient "band-width" to develop/sustain	91	18.3%
Other (please specify)	27	5.4%
OTHER RESPONSES		
only for cash and as required		
Done ad hoc, not through formalized process		
Unwillingness of owner to engage in planning type activities		
In time as we evolve into a larger, more complex organization we will need to.		
need software		
Industry specific issues		
Not enough time		
don't know		
We have a 3rd party strategic planer and he is not interested in our scenarios		
It's never been discussed.		
no senior mgmt interest		
owner-management do not support		
do not have the necessary resources		
New software implemented, not working yet		
done infrequently		
No time or adequate resources		
Do not know why not.		
just learning about the process of senerio planning		

Continued on p. 191

Continued from p. 190

OTHER RESPONSES
Operational management does not have time to formulate alternative scenarios
Basic scenarios are done if necessary—but limited to simple models
This quest in not applicable to a retiree
Leadership budget focused
Not attempted yet; rolling out new tool.
Owners do not understand the importance
Lack of resources to go into that depth
not a high priority

18) Which of the following represent significant barriers to improving the planning processes in your organization? Select all that apply

RESPONSE	COUNT	PERCENT
Leadership and corporate culture that supports the status quo	244	49.1%
Inadequate systems and technology	204	41.0%
Inadequate staffing of finance function	147	29.6%
Limited skills of finance function	85	17.1%
Limited skills of people outside of the finance funcition	186	37.4%
Other (please specify)	44	8.9%

OTHER RESPONSES
time
changing business processes
Little desire for a formal strategic planning process
none
NONE
leadership resists change

Continued on p. 192

Continued from p. 191

OTHER RESPONSES
short-term focus
Organization bureaucracy
None
Financial plan is pre-set at the top and departmental budgets must fit into that top-level plan
There are no significant barriers
size of the organization and age of the owner
time
Volunteer board members who assume that our industry is substantially identical to their industries.
None of the above
Federal/state funding issues
Not enough time
Limited finance staff
Rapid changes in our target market
None, we improve our processes each year after planning.
No real barriers. Changes made as necessary.
Culture, but we aren't a corporation, so it's not "corporate culture".
Time and schedules
Reality vs. Corporate "wishful thinking"
very small company
Limited available time
lack of alignment on a better way.
Leadership struggles between board and management
timing of shipments, customer requirements, etc. since we are an agricultural company

Continued on p. 193

Continued from p. 192

OTHER RESPONSES
Do not know.
Gettng Board Members together & committed to a date
time
Limited time—very good people maxed out
N/A
NA—Adequate resources for what we do and the assets we employ.
Not applicable to a retiree
Not enough time
None
No major barriers
Ownership influence
Available time
Egos within the leadership team
Board members thinking they know more than they do
Limited attention given to longterm capital planning
Commitment level of non-financial executives.
small organization

19) If you could change one thing in the planning processes in which you are involved, what would it be?

hire dedicated position with big picture capabilities
more frequent and better focused
more time to spend on development
VALUE THE FINANCE FUNCTION NOT JUST SALES
Hire a CFO that has an appreciation and skillset for planning
less detail

Continued on p. 194

Continued from p. 193

More management participation
Do it in less time with more time for analysis.
Implement longer-term strategic planning with regular updates and linkage to the tactical (i.e., annual) planning process
more review of results against projections and budget
integrate financial systems
ownership
earlier involvement by senior management
Be more involved in the decision making instead of just providing information.
Better performance measures that tie to critical organizational success factors. Too often performance measure that are available are tengential to key initiatives.
Secure the foundation and fund the future
Budgeting
More rolling forecasts and less annual and fuure planning and budgeting for 3–5 years out.
More ownership of inputs into the budget process and the affects it has on the organization budget/cashflow
nothing
Commitment of ownership to fully undertake planning and budgeting activities and stick to that plan.
rolling forecasts
More planning based on real numbers not what they want them to be
More Involvement of Senior Mgt.
Better capital improvements forecasting.
Increase the buy-in among operational managers to be more than a just an annual process. Make it something they use to help with tactical decisions.
staff outside of finance takew the process seriously
More overall picture-less line item driven

Continued on p. 195

Continued from p. 194

?
Better structure
Finance has a far too limited role and voice in strategic and tactical planning. Finance influence doesn't become strong until the budget phase.
for me to actually be involved would be a great start
More forward thinking beyond one year.
Replace the head of the organization with someone who isn't an idiot.
Actual follow thru.
throw much of the forecasting onto the department managers
More analysis involved in the various planning processes to provide even stronger support for forecasts, budgets, etc.
gather information from one source our ERP system
Commitment by senior management to place accountability on goals and objectives of the plan and the budget.
More automation to allow for time to what if and analyze.
More bottom up planning
More cross-functional participation.
Create committees to research the particular process
Start earlier
True bottom-up budgets
More intergregration between Spreadsheet, Databases, and Computer SW.
More time to develop the topics for the tactical plen.
More staff
n/a
Executive management
Less versions of the annual plan.

Continued on p. 196

Continued from p. 195

Better tools & processes.
Make it less time-consuming
Drive it deeper into working capital and balance sheet planning
better info from department heads
12 month rolling forecasts with annual budget and better linkage of strategic plan to action plans and budgets
Better information management. a lot of USA firms seem to lack compared to uk and Asia
More participation in the decisions to cut budgets and where the budgets are cut.
Coordination of various areas and enhanced communication and accountability
Focus on strategic goals to set the stage for the future.
I am satisfied with the planning process
Get rid of the gaming in the budget process.
proceed with a bottom up approach instead of a top down approach when taking decisions
Change the goals to be achieved
To have the proper amount of time to do thorough analysis. But finances (i.e. income) is not enough to take time from billable time.
None
skills of people outside finance function!
Synchronization between planning and resource allocation
Number of iterations
Involvement from more people
Advance warning before new projects begin.
A better look at the big picture and some realism and non emotional decisions with regard to cutting costs, in particular the "chiefs" salaries continue to go while the small salaries are laid off
Have a true planning process with goals, objectives and accountability

Continued on p. 197

Continued from p. 196

To many initiatives which are "revolutionary" are planned when more time and funds for "evolutionary" changes are needed.
Greater comfort with change and risk.
The length of the year dedicated to planning.
Improve accountability of sales relative to performance metrics.
Strategic direction
Frequency is not helping in accuracy.
More robust accountability, assessing past performance to inform future planning.
Get more involvement from the operational team
Continue to move toward an environment where the planning process is a part of our regular activities, not a periodic exercise
Directly link executive performance to thier discrete understanding of the P&L's they allegedly manage.
Reaction time from plan to implemenation.
staff have realistic and organization wide goals, not individual goals
communication at all levels
Stakeholder from all business areas need to commit to the same organization goals.
Better and more timely communication from leadership
Finance would be part of the final decision makers of the plan and incentive would be included for finance.
Better information on the front end of the process
More time allocated to planning. Better control over accountability
Get rid of arbitrary cuts by upper management
modernize technology and review the selected key indicators on a monthly basis to assess the continuing value of the indicators in light of desired outcomes
Incorporate budgets/forecasts into our planning
A stronger focus on growth over prior year's actual. It would yield more control over expense control. Now, it's growth vs. prior year's budget.

Continued on p. 198

Continued from p. 197

Would like to extend forecasting out to 18 months
None
Purchase a tool/software that would ease the data compilation and use assumption input to adjust varaibles
Not sure
buy in from management that planning is needed
None
Longer range goals
To be more involved in the process.
Improve skills of people outside of the finance function
Amount of time for management review.
Hire another employee to expand compliance and planning work
More flexible budgeting
have regional management take process more intelligently and strategically.
more involvement at corporate level versus departmental levels
A better awareness of how functions interact with each other and inform each other's budgets and plans
Improve my own skillset.
Need more help
Change the culture with more emphasis on the strategic planning and links to the other planning processes.
Add additional staff
More structure to the process
More long term thinking by the City Council
Streamline and make process simpler
I would have it be driven by our Asset Liability/Budgeting Model. Right now, our 3rd party strategic planner doesn't use any forecasting data we can provide.

Continued on p. 199

Continued from p. 198

don't major in the minors and focus on the "kill shots" to the business and greater opportunities
Sales forecasting
Include more people at the ground level
leadership in having various functional areas totally committed and highlighting the interrelationships required to meet overall corporate goals
Better technology
More involved employees.
Tie the financial budget to the strategic plan.
interest in strategic thinking
More realistic goals and corresponding expense budgets.
More time for recreation
Less micromanaging of the process
What's the character limit for this field???
Better Tools
The most significant barrier to an effective planning process in our situation is a lack of buy-in which leads to poor or no implementation and a reduced desire to properly plan.
Less suppossive certainty
N/A
We are upgrading our financial system for cost allocation and grant budgeting and management.
Reduce use of spreadsheets. Implement robust planning software.
shorten time period for process
fewer unilateral decisions
Follow through on the plan rather than changing the plan.
Needs to be started earlier relative to decision-making time. Accept reality and strategize how to improve vs. setting goals that Execs "expect"

Continued on p. 200

Continued from p. 199

spend more time
change in the leadership, to make everything else happen.
have technology that can actually DO a functional cashflow forecasts and compile related cashflow trending.
Other people meeting their deadline .
Bayism
More cross-functional input.
Better forecasting and business intelligence support
Stop focusing on current month (short term goals) and focus on long term health of company (big picture)
to enhance the accuracy of forecasting
Finance should have a greater role in the planning process
More emphasis placed by the board.
Make it simple
Use of a more team approach.
Actually have a formal, simple process
More data analyze
None
Implement a technology driven solution to effect decentralised maintenance of the plan.
Convince leadership of importance
Additional staff.
Out sourcing process
Better communication
More involvement from other departments
mandatory tied to compensation
Shorten it

Continued on p. 201

Continued from p. 200

Upgrade skills of most people involved with planning.
Leadership and corporate culture
not now
shorten the time span for developing annual budget; allow easier adjustment of budget throughout the year
Change Management
eliminate the annual plan and use rolling forecasts.
Develop clearly designed roles and responsibilities in the planning process
To actually have a time bound process.
More effort at developing a strategic plan process for the corporation, rather than just at the product line level.
involve finance function more
Eliminate mandated targets.
Implement a robust enterprise planning system.
BETTER FOLLOW-UP AND EXECUTION AFTER PLANNING MEETINGS
Increased leadership support
Principals/Ownership of the company would get better educated regarding all of the above
Rolling forecast and budgeting processes.
More resources and time allocated to it
Begin & approve a budget timelier
Skill set of people outside of the finance function—specifically those in sales/development
We do not review or hold each other accountable
Improve cycle time of information availability needed for planning and analysis.
Simplify the overall process.
Improved more functional technology

Continued on p. 202

Continued from p. 201

Better systems and technology, although not necessary to perform planning, would offer opportunities for better analysis and improved skill set.
Shorten the length of time spent on annual budget and add mid-year or quarterly forecasting to the mix
more training in stratagic planning techniques to non financial personnel
Obtain buy-in from the Founder/Owner for a formal strategic planning process
Better follow-up on execution.
The process works well for us.
more risk reward analysis of goals
change the make-up of the Board of Directors
focus President more
Provide more funding for it.
More dedicated time to think it through
Get more people to understand the art of planning not the science.
Leadership mindset outside of the finance function.
More imput from managers—more disclosure from executives. Each seem to hold relevent matter back and each are slow in delivering current information.
Implement a formal integrated planning process
time spent
Increase time spent on strategic discussions with senior management
Executive attention/direction
Add more robust technology capacity.
Rolling forecast
do it
We are a government—budget for more than one year and forecast cash.
Simplify capture of plans and links

Continued on p. 203

Continued from p. 202

N/A
Improved business knowledge and leadership skills at the highest levels of the organization would make a significant difference.
Greater involvement by lower levels of management
More emphaisis on the financial function
Realize that most third party applications have significant limitations when used by complex organizations.
Corporate defined metrics developed and used across different divisions
Extend it out more than one year/calander year.
Replace annual budgets with rolling forecasts
nothing
Discount the political influence of certain leaders.
regualer reviews of forecast
None
implement budgeting/forecasting software
No
Stop having bonuses determined solely on making EBITDA budget
reduce the frequency of budget updates
If the volunteer organization that I do some work with ever selects another business simulation program, I would like to be on the committee that selects it.
I would simply allow for more strategic meetings that involve all members of management.
Financial forecasting cycle from 12 months to 3 years
Lengthen the planning timeline.
Better utilization of technology
More frequent meetings communicating issues, planning variables.
Having more awareness and active management of budgets by all department budget managers.

Continued on p. 204

Continued from p. 203

Leadership
I am no longer employed. Answers are based on the prior involvement in the planning process.
Deeper involvement from non financial personnel
Benchmarking against goals established
Getting the right BI Tools
Greater integration with third party benchmarking metrics and regionalized data
More innovation, better collaboration among functional dept.
people in charge
Allow divisons to participate more in the strategic planning process.
The "buy in" of the rest of the management team as to the importance of the planning process.
better understanding at C level of information
Add a professional to FPA
Greater collaboration between operational functions
Better tools and more frequent review. Annually is not productive
Top down support to hold managers accountable
Excessive (in my opinion) focus on pre-incentive compensation, pre-tax profit rather than what ultimately trickles down to the equity shareholders who provide the risk capital to the company.
get other top management involved
n/a
Implement performance measurement to allow us to move beyond budgeting
more structure
Better forecasting of capital project needs as usually over forecast what can be achieved. Leads to borrowing more funds or needing more revenue than was actually required.
Better alignment with ownership requirements

Continued on p. 205

Continued from p. 204

TIME
The systems/technology... WAY TOO manual, and more prone to mistakes.
More individual accountability and participation in the implementation.
Not deeply involved in this area.
Follow-through
Our organization is currently under-going a strategic re-evaluation. The biggest outcome I would like to see if a strategy driven by a defined business identify (who the firm is in its market) with tactical goals cascading from the stragety. This level of planning has been missing in the recent past.
Eliminating the annual budget process and rely solely on the rolling forecast.
Make information available to more people in the organization
shorten the window for planning during a cycle.
To incorporate one that is actually utilized by the owners
Build more structure and timeline into the process.
have started making changes and expect barriers to dissolve in future
Better technology
Better division between Board and staff
start earlier
Greater participation by involved non-accounting persons
Use of forecasting tools which provide more sophistication than our spreadsheet based process.
Better process and systems
Change from static budget process to rolling forecasts...which will be implemented in the coming fiscal year
Place more emphasis on the Strategy—not the financial projection/numbers.
execution and accoutability
do no further than 36 months out.

Continued on p. 206

Continued from p. 205

More involvement of Finance Function
Make it more inclusive of senior management.
more system integration for easier analysis
A greater number of open meetings & discussions to include representatives of multiple departments—as opposed to a "speech" with limited to no discussion
Earlier involvement
Some sort of software application that could help streamline the process
More priority and manpower devoted to it
development of priorities before budgeting and planninb
Adequate staff to prepare and maintain.
Getting better input and setting reasonable goals for planning and budgeting purposes
More long range planning process
We need more realism in our growth projections
Additional staffing and training
If I had more time to invest in it.
Speed up the process
Work towards rolling forecasts rather than annual budgets.
Integrate "Daily Management" with "Management Accounting"
Have our engineering department devote more time to long term capital planning, this would then facilitate better financing planning, capital maintenance and long term capital investment requirements.
Revenue and G&A cost
Reduce heavy reliance on budget
What can you accomplish realistically in one year.
Have people take more time preparing prior to starting their planning activities
Focus on significant projects and not the details.

Continued on p. 207

Continued from p. 206

Linking planning with budgets with cash plans and capital plans
tie longer-term financial information to the planning process rather than the short-term budget solution
Formailze process and commitment with Executive Team.
More time for analysis
Better incorporation of consideration of strategic risks.
Management commitment to processes and the strategic plan.
Create better links between planning processes.
Emphasis placed on change, it seems to be difficult to implement improvements.
Use of more technology
Flow of Communication
Enforce adherence to goal dates and deadlines
need adequate resources for higher level planning
Greater company involvement
I would like to see better integration between all the various/disparate planning processes (strategic, tactical, financial, enterprise risk, etc).
Getting individuals to have a broader business perspective and associated skills (and using them)
Select the individuals involved in the process who have an open mind to changing the status quo and not undermind the process.
need more staff accountants to make sure recent historical data is posted timely

20)   To what extent would you agree with the following statements?

	VERY LIMITED	LIMITED	MODERATE	GREAT	VERY GREAT
The results of our organization's key financial and non-financial outcomes (e.g. profits, margins, volumes, market share, etc.) show an improving trend.	6.5% (31)	20.6% (98)	42.0% (200)	25.6% (122)	5.3% (25)
These key financial and non-financial outcomes have results that are comparable with/ better than direct competitors or equivalent organizations	5.8% (28)	17.4% (84)	43.2% (208)	27.2% (131)	6.4% (31)

20.1)   The results of our organization's key financial and non-financial outcomes (e.g. profits, margins, volumes, market share, etc.) show an improving trend. (To what extent would you agree with the following statements?)

RESPONSE	COUNT	PERCENT
Very Limited	31	6.5%
Limited	98	20.6%
Moderate	200	42.0%
Great	122	25.6%
Very Great	25	5.3%

20.2)   These key financial and non-financial outcomes have results that are comparable with/better than direct competitors or equivalent organizations (To what extent would you agree with the following statements?)

RESPONSE	COUNT	PERCENT
Very Limited	28	5.8%
Limited	84	17.4%
Moderate	208	43.2%
Great	131	27.2%
Very Great	31	6.4%

21) What level of organization are you assessing?

RESPONSE	COUNT	PERCENT
Entire corporate entity	374	76.6%
Business unit, division, or corporate headquarters group	114	23.4%

22) (AICPA MEMBERS ONLY) Please indicate the number of employees for the organization you are assessing

RESPONSE	COUNT	PERCENT
1–49	114	24.0%
50–99	38	8.0%
100–249	78	16.4%
250–499	57	12.0%
500–999	45	9.5%
1,000–4,999	74	15.6%
5,000–9,999	21	4.4%
10,000–24,999	18	3.8%
25,000–49,999	11	2.3%
50,000 or more	18	3.8%
Does not apply	1	0.2%

23) (CIMA MEMBERS ONLY) Please indicate the number of employees for the organization you are assessing

RESPONSE	COUNT	PERCENT
1–50	13	12.1%
51–250	19	17.8%
251–1000	9	8.4%
1001–10,000	7	6.5%
10,000+	5	4.7%
Does not apply	54	50.5%

24) Please indicate the annual revenues/turnover for the business unit you are assessing

RESPONSE	COUNT	PERCENT
Under $10 Million	106	21.7%
Over $10 Million–$100 Million	172	35.2%
Over $100 Million–$500 Million	96	19.7%
Over $500 Million–$1 Billion	32	6.6%
Over $1 Billion–$5 Billion	43	8.8%
Over $5 Billion–$10 Billion	10	2.0%
Over $10 Billion	29	5.9%

25) Which of the following best describes your title or position. (Please choose one).

RESPONSE	COUNT	PERCENT
CEO	7	5.1%
COO	3	2.2%
President	2	1.4%
CFO	42	30.4%
CAO	2	1.4%
VP	3	2.2%
Director	22	15.9%
Controller	23	16.7%
Accounting/Audit Manager	15	10.9%
Tax Manager	0	0.0%
Technology Manager	0	0.0%

Continued on p. 211

Continued from p. 210

RESPONSE	COUNT	PERCENT
Staff	9	6.5%
Other (please specify)	10	7.2%

OTHER RESPONSES
Manag
I am retired only do pro bono work
Not currently employed
Country CFO
Finance Manager
Internal Audit
PARTNER
AVP Business Unit Controller
senior analyst
Principal
Production Systems / Quality Engineer
Manager of FP&A

APPENDIX II

REQUIREMENTS OF A PLANNING SYSTEM

From a technology point of view, enterprise planning requires a set of integrated capabilities. Integration in this respect means that each function described is available for any data set within the same business model and can be used without limitation in order to support the goal of the system. In the authors' experience, the following product capabilities are essential.

FLEXIBLE BUSINESS MODEL

A business model is used to describe any data to be collected, modelled, transformed, and reported for the purposes of planning and monitoring performance. The model will hold relationships between departments, products, services, and activities. Data will typically be held in a multi-dimensional form that is also able to support the following:

- *Holding a range of data with differing dimensionality.* For example, sales may need to be modelled at a customer and product level by region, and a strategic initiative may need to be modelled by activity and date. At some point, all of these different kinds of data with their different levels of granularity will need to be combined to give the full picture.

- *Driver-based planning.* Planning where entering a few variables, such as sales volume or staff numbers, can generate a range of related data, such as production and staffing costs.

- *Time intelligence.* As the planning horizon contracts, the ability to model some data at a weekly or even daily level becomes more important.

- *The development of initiatives that are targeted at certain areas of the business.*

- *Storing initiatives separately from the main plan.* As initiatives are selected, their data should be combined with the 'business as usual' plan to give the overall situation.

- *Coping with changing business structures.* Over time, structures such as the organisation's departments or strategy map will change. As a learning exercise, it is important to know what structures have existed for what time and how long, and to use this information to compare how things have changed over time.

- *Electronically load or manually collect actual results and forecasts for comparative purposes.*

AUTOMATED WORKFLOW

Planning is a continuous series of activities that involves different people at different times. This cannot be easily controlled through menu systems because the order and content of those menus will be determined by exceptions and events that may not be known in advance. To support continuous planning, the technology solution must be able to

- model the processes involved in planning and monitoring as a single continuous process.
- trigger any part of the performance management process based on exceptions or events.
- prompt users as to what they are responsible for and when they need to respond. This should be automatically generated from the modelled process and when activities are triggered through exceptions.
- send notifications of deadlines that have been violated and automatically escalate any items not completed within a predefined time.
- provide administrators with an interactive process timeline where they can look out for bottlenecks and re-assign or re-start tasks as appropriate.

TIME AND DATE INTELLIGENCE

Planning is primarily concerned with dates, whether that be starting an initiative, making resources available, asking someone to respond to a request, or the setting of a deadline to complete a particular action.

Time is not just a silo for containing data; it should be a true calendar that not only understands the normal spans of time such as days, weeks, months, and quarters, but can also be configured to understand weekends, holidays, seasons, and any other kind of time grouping that may exist within an organisation.

To go with this calendar, all data should be assigned a date (this is, a true date and not just a storage cell), irrespective of whether it belongs to a normal business function or a strategic initiative. The ability to assign true dates has some powerful management capabilities:

- First, it means data can be aggregated into multiple time spans as dictated by the chosen calendar(s). This allows the same results to be used in local management reports using the local calendar while at the same time reporting the base data according to the group adopted calendar.
- Second, because all data is date-based, the planning system is able to work out how to combine data with different periodicities (for example, combining data entered on a monthly basis with that entered on a weekly or seasonal basis). When using a true calendar, the system can intelligently work out the implications of holidays, and even when a week starts, to produce a consistent, accurate reflection of results in any defined time period.
- Lastly, the system should be able to warn users and management alike when agreed actions have not started or are failing to achieve the goals set. This early warning can be used to automatically trigger remedial action rather than relying on someone to notice the variance in a report that may then be ignored.

In addition to data, business structures, such as the way in which sales departments are organised, should also be date based. When reporting results in covering a particular time span, the system should allow the use of actual, current, proposed, or previous historical structure—or all of them. This allows users to see the impact of change without having to duplicate data or effort.

MEMBER ATTRIBUTES

Most enterprise systems in use for business planning are defined through the set-up of dimensions (for example, organisation, measure, time, version, and so on) and dimension members that are sometimes (for example, in the case of a department structure) organised by hierarchy. Although this is still essential, a planning system should also allow dimension members to be associated with one or more attributes.

Attributes define the characteristics of a member, as we discussed when defining the operational activity model. Attributes can include a range of textual types, including dates (very useful for when defining strategic initiatives), responsibility, and logical operators.

The system should allow these groupings to be used to analyse data irrespective of their hierarchical position (for example, show all initiatives that support the corporate goal of increasing sales, show initiatives whose actual start date is after the planned start date, and so on).

INTEGRATED REPORTING AND ANALYSIS

A planning system needs to combine information from both the normal operation of the business and strategic initiatives. It needs to have access to operational and financial data as well as to actual and planned dates, assigned responsibilities, and much more. This is more than numbers-based reporting; it needs to combine date, text, and structures that are then presented in a way that supports decision making. This is typically far more than can be achieved with a third-party add-on tool, and where reliance is placed on a single data store.

For this reason, a CPM system should allow the following:

- Data to be combined from the different data sets as required (for example, to combine key performance indicators [KPIs] with expenditure and external market data in such a way that could lead management to assess whether a plan is being executed)

- Data to be reported with different structures (for example, using member attributes or different versions of a structure)

- The inclusion of charts, grids, gauges with narratives, and number grids

- The set-up of complex reports that relate KPI data to resources and the achievement of results

- Reports that can sort and filter information based on dates, attributes, structure versions, and the person viewing them

- Reports that can be combined into packs that represent a specific topic (for example, all reports associated with monitoring execution)

AUDIT TRAIL

All data held by a planning system should be tracked in terms of how it was entered and modified throughout the different processes. This information should be available within selected reports so that managers can see the story behind each and every number.

INTELLIGENT ENTERPRISE-WIDE ACCESS

Finally, because a planning system is going to be accessed by many people across the organisation, the application should provide a simple way to manage and control them. This should include the set-up of a user passport that defines the following:

- Their role in a particular process
- The data they can view or modify
- The functionality they have access to, such as building reports or creating processes
- General settings, such as their language, credentials, and contact information

The planning system should also support approval processes (for example, when setting the start date or resources for a strategic initiative, and escalation paths should an activity be behind schedule).

Printed in the United States
By Bookmasters